Nikki Grahame was born in North_____ in 1982. Her parents separated when she was a child and she cites both _his and the death of her beloved grandfather as catalysts __ _he start of her severe eating disorder. Between eight _ _nineteen years old, Nikki was in and out of hospitals _a _nstitutions as she battled with anorexia nervosa. At _n_ _oint, her weight was so dangerously low that she we_ _nto a coma; one of the doctors treating her said that h_ _ _as the worst case of anorexia he had seen in 32 y_ _r. Although she will never be 'cured' of the illness, N_k_ made the decision that she wanted to live her life _ _ and has not looked back since. Her time as a _ _ant in *Big Brother 7* made her a household name _ _ince leaving the house, Nikki has established a c_ _ in the media. She has written columns for *OK!*, *The S_ _d More* magazine and has been a presenter on *Big B_ _er* spin-off *BBLB*. She has also won a National T_ _sion award. Nikki devotes a lot of her spare time to i_ _sing awareness of eating disorders and hopes that by s_ _g her life story, she will help others who fall victim to _rexia.

Fragile

The true
story of my
lifelong
battle with
anorexia

Nikki Grahame

British Library Cataloguing-in-Publication Data:

...alogue record for this book is available from the British Lib...

Design by www.envydesign.co.uk

...ted and bound by CPI Group (UK) Ltd, Croydon, CR0 4Y...

JOHN BLAKE

Published by John Blake Publishing Ltd,
3 Bramber Court, 2 Bramber Road,
London W14 9PB, England

www.johnblakepublishing.co.uk

www.facebook.com/Johnblakepub facebook
twitter.com/johnblakepub twitter

First published in hardback in 2009 and paperback in 2010 as
Dying to be Thin. This edition published in paperback in 2012

ISBN: 978-1-85782-661-6

A cata _____ rary.

Pri _____ Y

13 5 7 9 10 8 6 4 2

Papers used by John Blake Publishing are natural, recyclable products made
from wood grown in sustainable forests. The manufacturing processes
conform to the environmental regulations of the country of origin.

Every attempt has been made to contact the relevant copyright-holders,
but some were unobtainable. We would be grateful if the
appropriate people could contact us.

I would like to dedicate this book to my mum, dad and sister, for dragging them to hell and back.

I would also like to thank all of the doctors and carers who looked after me: Brian Lask, Dee Dawson, Paul Byrne and Sam Swinglehurst.

CONTENTS

In order to protect their identities, many names
of patients in the hospitals and institutions
have been changed.

FOREWORD

This new edition of Nikki Grahame's book is an update on what's been happening following the release of *Dying to be Thin* in 2009. Nikki has achieved unimaginable success since her last hospital admission at the age of 19; she has proved to herself that life can be wonderful and there is good to be found in this world. After so many years of misery and battles with herself and every single person who tried to help her, countless doctors and health professionals, her family and school friends, finally she has made a place for herself and glimpsed happiness. She has also become an aunty to my lovely little boy, Sunny Wren.

And for a while Nikki seemed to overcome the illness that has owned her and monopolised our family life for so long but something I have learnt – in the seemingly endless years that she has battled anorexia – is that it never really goes away. Not completely. Especially not when the illness takes over a person, as it did my sister. It is always with her, like her shadow, a closest friend and at the same time, a most hated enemy. And time again that shadow has cast its darkness over her. Once again, with an outpatient's admission to an eating disorders unit, she must find the strength to fight, literally for her life. And whilst it is no doubt hardest of all for Nikki herself, it is utterly heartbreaking for us, her family.

Nikki is the strongest person I have ever known, so brave and determined, but she is still my little baby sister and fragile in my eyes. My instinct to protect her is as strong as ever. I know that my nagging her to put on weight, cut down on exercise and take better care of herself must be tedious and I'm frequently told exactly what to do with that advice. Anorexics often need to feel a sense of control, with their desire for control being projected onto their relationship with food. Through my family's experience with Nikki's illness we have seen that our best intentions to help her have sometimes had the opposite effect: leading to her fighting us harder, and the anorexia becoming stronger. Trying to give Nikki the space and understanding she needs whilst attempting to manage our own fears for her has proved to be a challenging balancing act!

The years of illness have taken their toll on our relationship. At too young an age, sisterly mischief and fun was pushed aside for envy and resentment. Nikki was jealous of my freedom; that I was at home, at school, out with friends, amongst the living and not the dying. In turn I resented her for taking my parents away from me (I would spend days on end alone in the house whilst Mum was at the hospital tending to Nik). With the development of her illness, it felt as if the world forgot about me. Of course, I felt guilty for being free and healthy and whilst frantically worried about her, I was also envious of the attention she was getting. I was desperately concerned about my mum, who was helpless in the face of Nikki's determination to starve to death, too. These confusing and negative feelings made me so angry with my sister.

Our relationship is still troubled; perhaps it always will be. I hope that in time my son will bring us closer together – Nikki is a wonderful aunty. Due to the damage caused by her illness she is unable to conceive naturally, a consequence not often considered by anorexics whilst caught up in the condition. Being Sunny's aunty may well be the closest she ever comes to motherhood. Sometimes I am overwhelmed with sadness at the harm and suffering this illness has caused my sister and our family.

There were many contributing factors to Nikki's recent struggles. The experience of writing the first edition of this book was extremely painful for her and during that process she was reacquainted with various bad habits and unhealthy rituals that have always been so hard for her to let go of. Life in the public eye has also proved to be quite stressful – whilst she thrives in front of a camera, the uncertainty of a career in show business can be very unsettling. Combined with the fickle and loud voice of the media in this country, it's really no surprise that someone as vulnerable as Nikki has succumbed to such a serious relapse.

For a long time I believed she was finally OK, although I would still have the occasional nightmare about crumbling bones and feeding tubes, which after 20 years of trauma seems fairly natural! But over the last couple of years she has slipped further and further from us and the sad reality is that we could lose her. I hope there has been some catharsis for Nikki in the writing of this second edition. We have always known that before she can begin to receive help, she must first admit to herself that there is a problem, which she has done in the following pages. I am so proud of her for this and for everything else she has achieved in life.

Nikki is a patron of the National Osteoporosis Society and an ambassador for Body Gossip, and hopes to raise awareness of anorexia and other eating disorders through this book.

Natalie Grahame, May 2012

PROLOGUE

I was clutching the gleaming metal award so tightly in my hands that my knuckles had turned white.

In front of me, around each of the six golden tiers of the Royal Albert Hall, were more than five thousand people, clapping, cheering and even screaming my name.

Through the bright lights I could see Simon Cowell, David Walliams and Billie Piper, all applauding ... me!

It was the most amazing moment of my life.

I'd just been presented with the award for Most Popular TV Contender 2006 at the National Television Awards for my time in the *Big Brother* house earlier that year.

My mum and I had spent hours searching for the perfect dress for that night and here I was in a £275 Betsey Johnson bluey-green silk gown and a pair of £375 Gina shoes. It was the most I'd ever spent on an outfit and I had never, ever felt so special.

I'd been dropped off at the Royal Albert Hall in a limousine and as I walked down the red carpet, hundreds of people stood 20 deep at either side, calling my name and elbowing one another out of the way to ask me to sign autographs. Beyond them was a bank of paparazzi photographers taking my photograph from every angle.

For anyone, that night would have been special. But for me it was miraculous. Because for so long no one had even imagined I would still be alive then, let alone receiving a coveted television award.

I had been just eight years old when I began a determined and resolute campaign to starve myself to the brink of death. Or beyond that if need be, as I wasn't much bothered if I lived or died.

At that time, the late 1980s, I was one of the youngest people in Britain to have ever been diagnosed with anorexia nervosa – a psychiatric illness which makes people, usually teenagers, desperate to become as thin as possible and develop an obsessive fear of gaining any weight at all.

For the best part of the next decade I stumbled around a miserable circuit of hospitals, specialist units, my own home and foster care, as doctor after doctor tried and failed to make me eat.

My childhood was shattered and I grew up in institutions surrounded by kids with the most horrific mental problems. At night there was no one to kiss my head as I curled up in my hospital bed. In the morning there was no one to cuddle me when I woke up sleepy and scared.

I became brutalised, like a wild child who had lost touch with normal behaviour. I'd scream and scratch and yell and fight when people tried to make me eat.

A perfectionist from the start, I was determined not just to be anorexic. I wanted to be the best anorexic Britain had ever known. Many of my doctors think I achieved that. They stuck tubes up my nose, stitched tubes into my stomach and pumped me so full of drugs to control me that I became like a zombie. But still I wouldn't willingly give in to their demands that I should eat.

Once I lay in a hospital bed just 15 minutes from death as my mum begged me to cling on to life. Twice I took overdoses in a bid to end my misery. The first time I was just 13 years old.

But gradually, miraculously, I discovered that there could be a special life for me outside of hospitals and institutions if I chose to live it.

This is the story of that choice, and it is the choice I hope and pray other kids with anorexia will one day find the strength to take.

CHAPTER 1

FUN, FOOD AND FAMILY

Looking back to the house at 37 Stanley Road before everything went wrong, it always seems to have been summer. Back then everything was good, better than good. I had one of those childhoods you normally only see in cereal adverts.

We didn't have bags of money or live in a huge mansion, but we had fun. There were summer holidays to Greece, Mum and Dad would cuddle up on the sofa to watch a video on a Saturday night, I had a grandad I adored who had an endless supply of corny jokes, and sometimes my older sister/occasional friend/usually arch enemy Natalie even let me play with her collection of scented erasers!

There was Mum and Dad and Natalie and me (and Rex, our dog). And it worked. My mum, Sue, was tall and slim. She was shy compared with other kids' mums but she doted on me and Nat. She worked as a dinner lady but was always home in time to cook our tea – and she was an amazing cook. Nothing fancy, but proper home cooking

1

that we all sat around the table to eat. Every night it was something different – spaghetti Bolognese, lasagne or a macaroni cheese that was worth running the full length of Stanley Road for.

Then there was my dad, Dave. And while of course I loved Mum, with Dad it was something more – I adored him.

Mum always laughs that the love affair between me – Nicola Rachel-Beth – and Dad started within minutes of my arrival at Northwood Park Hospital on 28 April 1982. After Natalie, Dad had been hoping for a boy but when I burst into the world screaming my lungs out he was, for some reason, totally smitten. From that point onwards I was the apple of his eye.

After the birth, the nurses wheeled Mum away to stitch her up. She left Dad sitting in a corner of the room by a window, holding this little bundle with jet-black, sticky-up hair and chubby cheeks.

When Mum was brought back an hour later, the sun had gone down and the room was pitch-black but Dad hadn't even got up to switch the light on. He was still sitting in exactly the same position, transfixed by the new arrival – me.

As I got older the bond only grew stronger. But it was kind of OK because there was an unspoken agreement in our house – Mum had Natalie and Dad had me.

I couldn't leave Dad alone. And for him little 'Nikmala' was pure delight.

By the time I was four or five, every time Dad left the house to go to work or pop down the pub I'd go belting down the road after him, begging to be allowed to stay with him.

I'd spend hours standing outside the betting shop at the corner of our street after Dad disappeared inside, rolled-up racing pages clenched in his hand as if armed ready for battle. Kids weren't allowed in and the windows were all covered over, but whenever the door was pushed ajar I'd sneak a glimpse of that mysterious male world of jittery TV screens, unfathomable numbers and solitary gamblers, all engulfed in thick cigarette smoke.

It became a standing joke in our family that whenever Dad emerged from the bookies' with a brisk, 'Right, off home now, Nikmala,' I'd reply, 'Can't you take me to another betting shop, Dad? Please?'

By the age of five I'd started going running with Dad. He loved keeping fit and so did I.

Dad worked shifts at a big bank in London, looking after its computer system. It meant he wasn't around a lot of the time but the moment he stepped inside the door I was all over him.

Everyone wanted to be around Dad, to laugh at his jokes and hear his stories. Well, at the time I thought it was everyone, but looking back I think it was probably just women. In fact even at seven I knew that Dad was a bit of a ladies' man. He couldn't take us for a plate of chips at the Wimpy without chatting up the girl behind the counter.

You name her, Dad would try to turn on the charm for her – my nursery school teacher, the lifeguards when he took me swimming on a Sunday morning, holiday reps; pretty much anyone really. But at that point it just seemed harmless, a bit of a fun. I had no idea what was really going on in my parents' marriage and how it would soon tear our family apart.

3

We also spent a lot of time with my Grandad, my mum's dad. He always had a pipe sticking out of the corner of his mouth and Natalie and I called him 'Popeye'. He had just one tooth in his bottom gum which he'd wiggle at me, ignoring my squeals, as I sat on his lap, cosy in the folds of his woolly cardigan.

Up until I was seven everything was fun. With just two years separating us, Natalie and I were constant playmates. Then, as now, our relationship veered between soul mates one day and sworn enemies the next, but hey, at least things were never boring.

We were always very competitive with each other. Natalie was a jealous toddler the day I first appeared home from hospital in the back of the family Morris Minor. And we still fight over Mum's attention now. Mum always went out of her way to treat us fairly and make sure we both felt included in everything. But it was never enough to stop the bickering. If I even thought about touching one of Natalie's favourite Barbie dolls, she'd go mad. But I was just as protective over my toys.

When I was five or six I would pore over the family photo albums and jealously interrogate Mum about any pictures I didn't appear in.

'Why are you cuddling Natalie in this picture and I'm not there?' I'd demand. 'You weren't born then, Nikki,' Mum would explain.

In another picture from that old album Dad is pushing me in the buggy while Mum holds Nat's hand. 'But why weren't you pushing me that day, Mum?' I said. Even though I had Dad's total devotion, I wanted Mum's too. And if that meant trampling all over Natalie to get it, so be it.

My competitive nature and quick temper had probably been bubbling under since birth. I cried pretty much continuously for the first fortnight after I was born, which should have given Mum a bit of a clue what she was in for.

And as a toddler I was pretty tough. Certainly any three-year-old who ever went for a spin in my favourite bubble car at the Early Learning Centre in Watford never made that mistake twice. Mum found me pulling one kid out of the car by his jumper before leaping in and driving off round the shop myself.

At play school I had to stand in the toilet on my own one morning for putting a wooden brick on one of the other kids' heads. Another time I was hauled up for kicking one of the boys.

At infant and then junior school I was always up to something, getting into scrapes. Dad called me his 'little bruiser' but I knew he was proud of me for sticking up for myself. But I was popular in class too – I had a big group of friends and I was always the leader.

I was in the Brownies, went to the church's holiday club, loved swimming at weekends and was always out playing on my bike after school with kids from our street. My friends Zanep and Julidah from down the road were always round our house and we'd play for hours in the twin room I shared with Natalie.

Our house was a fairly typical chalet bungalow in the north-western suburbs of London, with two bedrooms overlooking the street at the front and above these a big attic which we used as a playroom. Our garden was magical. Back then it seemed huge to me, with its long slope of grass stretching from a wooden-boarded summerhouse all the way down to the living room window.

To one side of the garden was a 'secret' passageway which got narrower and narrower until it reached the special spot Natalie and I used for burying treasure – well, Mum's old jewellery from the 1970s. In another corner there were swings, a slide and a climbing tree.

On the patio at the top of the garden, we would help Dad light bonfires in the winter and in summer we would stage our theatrical productions there, prancing and dancing up and down.

Sometimes I think that house in Stanley Road will haunt me for the rest of my life – I was so happy there and I was a kid there. Because what I didn't know then was that the time spent living in that house up until I was seven *was* my childhood – all of it.

The only thing that made it OK to be called inside from that magical garden was the thought of one of Mum's dinners. Up until the age of seven I would eat pretty much anything she put in front of me. I was never one of those 'just three chips and half an organic sausage' type of kids.

I'd fed well as a baby and as soon as I went on to solids, anything Mum served up, I'd eat. On Sunday it would be a big roast and then midweek we would have home-made burgers, meatballs or liver and veg. And that would be followed by a proper dessert – a steamed pudding or fruit with custard. I loved Mum's food. We all did.

And going out to restaurants was a real treat too. I was only two when we all went on holiday to Crete and I ordered a huge plate of mussels in a restaurant. 'You might not like those, Nikki darling,' Mum warned, but I wasn't going to be dissuaded.

When my meal arrived everyone in the restaurant was

staring at this tiny little toddler tucking into a huge plate of shellfish – but I loved it.

Back then food was fun and a big part of our family life. But within a few short years there was no fun left in either food or our family.

CHAPTER 2

THINGS FALL APART

'Will you please stand on your feet and not on your head?' Mum yelled at me one Saturday morning. 'You spend more time upside down than the right way up,' she grumbled.

It was about the millionth time she'd had a go at me about it, half jokingly, half worried I might do myself some permanent damage by spending so much time performing handstands. I'd even watch TV upside down. And when I wasn't doing that I would be cartwheeling and backflipping my way up and down the wooden floor of our hall.

'OK,' Mum finally said, 'if you love all this acrobatics so much we might as well put it to some use.' The following week she'd signed me up for the Northwood Gymnastics Club. I was beyond excited. I was still only six years old but getting dressed up in a royal-blue leotard, my long, dark-brown hair pulled back in a pony tail, I felt so important – like a proper gymnast.

All those hours spent on my head had obviously been worth it, because I quickly showed a real ability at gymnastics. And I loved it all – the training, the competitions and just messing around with the other girls afterwards. Cartwheels, somersaults and flips on the mats, vaulting and the asymmetric bars – I couldn't get enough of it.

Within a couple of weeks the coach must have decided I had some natural talent because I was selected to become part of the gym's squad.

I was so proud of myself. It was amazing. But being part of the squad instantly meant a lot more pressure. I was representing the London Borough of Hillingdon and there was a gala every six months and a new grade to work for every couple of months. And that meant a lot more training. Within a couple of months this had shot up from gymnastics once a week to sessions three evenings a week and for three hours on a Saturday morning. We'd often do a full hour of tumbling followed by an hour of vaulting. It was exhausting and any sense of enjoyment quickly seeped away.

Being the way I was, I couldn't be happy unless I was the best in the squad and unfortunately there were girls there who were clearly better than me. One Saturday morning we were in the changing rooms, messing around in our leotards at the end of a tough, three-hour session. One of the other girls was standing behind me, staring at me, when she suddenly said, 'Haven't you got a big bum, Nikki?'

I could feel myself going bright red but I just laughed and pulled my shell suit on quickly. How embarrassing.

That evening I crept into Mum's bedroom when she and

Dad were watching telly downstairs. I opened their wardrobe door and stood in front of the full length mirror bolted to its inside.

I analysed my bum carefully. Then I stared at the slight curve of my tummy and then my fleshy upper arms.

Maybe that girl at gymnastics was right – maybe my bum was a bit on the lardy side. Maybe that was why I still couldn't get those flips right.

After all, that other girl's arms were much thinner than mine. And she had a tiny bum and virtually no tummy at all and she was brilliant at flips. In fact she was better than me at almost all the routines. Plus, she was really popular with the other girls too.

And I guess that is how it all began. Somewhere in my seven-year-old brain I started to think that to be better at gymnastics and to be more popular, I had to be skinny. And because I didn't just want to be better than I was at gymnastics, but to be the best, then I couldn't just be skinny. Oh no, I would have to be *the* skinniest.

'I'll keep my tracksuit bottoms on today, Mum,' I said as I went into the gym the following week. She didn't think anything of it then, but I'd decided I didn't want anyone laughing at my fat bum ever again.

Yet it would be too easy to say that one girl's catty comments sparked off the illness which was to blight the next ten years of my life and which will inevitably be with me in some way until the day I die.

No, I think that was just what brought things to a head. Looking back, I think I was already vulnerable to any kind of comment that may have been made about my size. Because already a whole truckload of misery was slowly building up behind the front door at Stanley Road.

Dad was having a really rough time at work. Things had always been rocky for him there, but it was getting worse. He kept clashing with his bosses and felt everyone was out to get him. After he joined the union and became heavily involved with it, he felt his bosses were out to get him for being an activist.

'They're destroying me,' I'd hear him rant at Mum.

'Just keep your head down and stop causing trouble, Dave,' she would tell him. 'We need the money.'

But that would just drive Dad into a fury. 'You don't understand what it's like working there,' he'd rage.

For 18 months he was involved in disciplinary action and subject to reports. It sent him – and all of us – crazy.

Because Dad was convinced he was about to be sacked, he started working part-time at a stamp shop he set up in part of his dad's jewellery shop off the Edgware Road. So, on top of all the stress at work, he was also working really long hours in his second job, desperate to keep paying the mortgage so we could stay in our perfect home.

He was angry all the time. Looking back, he was probably suffering from depression or stress, perhaps both, but at seven all I could see was that the dad I adored had turned overnight into some kind of raging monster.

In many ways I feel sorry for my dad because he'd had a really tough childhood. He was born in America but at six his father moved to London with a new wife while his mother, Magda, stayed in New York with her new husband. Magda had custody of Dad but, according to the family story, his dad went over there and brought him back to Britain. Having got him back, though, his dad and his new wife realised they didn't really want him. They didn't take care of him and he ended up stuck in a children's home.

Magda still lives in Manhattan in some plush apartment but my dad doesn't have much contact with her and he doesn't speak to his father at all. So Dad has had it hard himself in life – he says that's why he can't show emotion in front of his kids. But I tell you, he could certainly show anger back then.

And although I can see the reasons for his behaviour now, at that time I was just a little girl who desperately wanted her daddy. And Dad had changed so much – he didn't want me following him to the betting shop any more and there were no more runs around the streets.

One day I entered a gymnastics competition and won second place. I was so proud of myself and sprinted straight from the gym to Dad's stamp shop, my silver medal bouncing around my neck as I ran down the road.

I walked into the shop and said, 'Hi,' waiting for Dad to notice the shining medal on my chest and to throw his arms around me and tell me how proud he was of his favourite daughter. I waited as he looked up and gave me half a smile over a book of stamps. Then I waited some more. And some more. He didn't notice, and it was soon obvious he was never going to notice. He hadn't seen my medal and, worse still, he hadn't registered the sheer joy on my face. In the end I said, 'Look, Dad, I came second.' I can't even remember how he reacted. Whatever he did or said, that isn't the bit I remember about that day.

Dad began missing my and Natalie's birthday parties. And if we had friends round after school and were being noisy he'd go mad. One evening I had my friend Vicky Fiddler round to play. We were busily brushing each other's hair at the kitchen table when Dad burst into the room in a fury. 'Who's this?' he yelled, glaring at us both.

I was devastated he could act so mad in front of one of my friends.

He was always so angry. For as long as I can remember he had called me 'Fatso' and 'Lump' but it had always seemed like a joke. Now the things he was saying seemed more cruel. He said to Natalie that at night sawdust would fall out of her head on to the pillow because she was so stupid.

At that time Dad was working a lot of night shifts too, which meant Natalie and I had to creep around the house all day, terrified we would wake him up. And when he was on normal day shifts we would skulk around when he was due home, waiting for the sound of his key in the lock, at which point we would run upstairs and hide.

One afternoon we accidentally scratched his back-gammon board with my shoe buckle and were so terrified of how he'd react that we spent the entire afternoon hiding in Mum's wardrobe.

Dad wasn't violent towards us – although I can remember the odd whack if we were playing up – but just really, really angry. Most of his anger he was taking out on Mum and they were rowing all the time. A lot of their fights happened first thing in the morning when Dad came in tired and grumpy from a night shift and got into bed with Mum. Natalie and I didn't need to eavesdrop at their door to hear what was going on. We'd wake up and look at each other as we heard every word being hurled across their bedroom. Often it was about stuff I just didn't understand, other times it was Dad's problems at work or how we'd keep our house if he didn't have a job.

As the months went by it felt like they were rowing about everything, right down to what dress Mum was wearing. One time I remember her coming downstairs all dressed up for an evening out. 'Why are you wearing that?' Dad said. Mum's face crumpled and she looked totally lost. 'You've never had any class,' he sneered at her as she turned around and slowly went back upstairs to change.

I understand now how complicated marriages can be and that there are two sides to every story. And there were probably times when Mum was nasty to Dad or wound him up, but I don't remember them. I just remember Mum becoming less and less sparkly, less and less pretty and more and more ground down. She stopped having friends round to the house and looked exhausted all the time.

One day I heard Dad tell her she was hopeless and had no vision.

'You and your family have never thought I was good enough,' Mum shouted back at him. Mum had been brought up a Catholic and Dad's family hadn't liked it, although by this point the two of them couldn't even agree what channel to watch on the telly, let alone on big things like religion. They never went out the way they had once done and there was no more cuddling up in front of a video.

I was seven and all I wanted was for my daddy to play with me and Natalie and to talk to us, but all we saw of him was him arguing on the telephone with this massive firm, being horrible to our Mum and shouting at us.

Things took a turn for the worse around about the time I turned eight, in the spring of 1990. Mum sat me and Nat down one day and told us Grandad was ill – really ill. People kept talking about the 'C-word' and although I didn't really have a clue what it really meant, it was clearly bad.

Mum took me out of school to visit Grandad one afternoon at the Central Middlesex Hospital, where he was being treated. She'd popped into the baker's on the way to collect me and she gave me a gingerbread man to eat on the train on the way there. It all started out feeling like a real treat.

But as soon as I saw Grandad in the hospital I knew something was badly wrong. I think it was the first time I'd ever seen him without his woolly cardigan on and that was enough of a shock. Instead, he was wearing a white hospital smock which seemed to smother him, he was so thin and pale. There was no pipe sticking out of his mouth any more and any Popeye strength had clearly been sapped away.

I sat on Grandad's bed and chattered about gymnastics and Brownies and the latest dramas at Hillside Infant School while Mum squeezed into an adjoining toilet with a doctor 'for a word in private'. It was the only place they could find to tell her that her father was dying.

When Mum walked back into the room her whole body was shaking except for her face, which was totally rigid.

The doctor had just told her the results of surgery on a blockage in Grandad's bowel. 'We opened him up but saw immediately there was no point in operating – it was too far gone, so we just sewed him up again. Mrs Grahame, I'm terribly sorry, but there is nothing further we can do for your father.'

Mum nearly passed out from shock but pulled herself together to come back into the room, where I was still talking Grandad through my flip routines.

We chatted for a bit longer, then Mum and I walked back to the station. When we got home she told me run out and play in the garden while it was still sunny. It was years later that she admitted to me that, while I cartwheeled up and down the lawn, she slid down our living room wall and sobbed and sobbed and sobbed.

Mum had always adored her father and it was obvious there was something special between them. I think that is why she had always understood and accepted the closeness of the bond between me and Dad.

Mum's childhood had been pretty tough. Her family were hard-up and Grandad had a fierce temper, but no matter how violent or angry he had been, she always idolised him and never blamed him for any of the troubles between her parents.

When Grandma died of cancer when she was 51 and Mum was 18, Mum had been upset, but not devastated. But, faced with the prospect of losing Grandad, she just went into freefall – she couldn't cope at all.

Grown-ups don't use the word 'terminal' to kids and even if she had done, I don't suppose I would have known what it meant. But I could see myself that every time we went to visit Grandad he was thinner, paler and more ill-looking. He didn't have the energy for corny jokes any more and seemed to find it exhausting enough just breathing in and out. He was fading away in front of us.

And as Grandad slipped away, it seemed Mum was going the same way. 'But he's never been ill in his life and he's not even 70,' she would repeat again and again. She would get choked up at the slightest thing and tears were never far away.

So there we were that summer of 1990. Mum sad all the time, Dad mad all the time. Mum and Dad fighting, me and Natalie fighting. Grandad dying.

Then Rex fell ill and was taken back and forth to the vet. He was diagnosed with a tumour on his back leg and the vet said there was nothing more they could do. He'd have to be put down. Dad adored Rex, so when I saw him crying as he stroked his head one morning, I knew what it meant.

Rex was 18 and he'd been there all my life. The house felt so quiet without him. No mad mongrel racing up and down the hall every time the doorbell went. Just silence.

It was tough going back to school at the start of that new term. I'd never been academic but I'd always had fun at Hillside and been popular with the other girls. But even teachers noticed I had lost my energy and enthusiasm. Now there were so many more things to think about in my life than there had been a year ago.

And rather than just playing French skipping in the playground with all the other girls, I would spend more and more time staring at my friends, asking myself the same old questions: 'Is my bum bigger than theirs?', 'Are my legs chubbier?', 'Is my tummy fatter?'

Nicola Carter was one of my best friends even though her bum was smaller than mine, her tummy flatter and her legs thinner. She had long, brown hair like mine and freckles scattered across her nose but oh, she was so skinny. She looked amazing.

All the kids in our class called us 'Big Nikki' and 'Small Nikki'. Well, you can imagine how that made me feel. I was clearly just too big.

With so much bad stuff going on at home I threw myself into gymnastics more and more. And the more gymnastics I did, the more competitive I became about it. I may only have been seven but I was incredibly determined and driven. I only ever wanted to be the best. I knew I wasn't as good as the other girls, not as pretty as them and not as thin as them. But rather than just think, Oh well, that's the way it goes, I was determined to become the best, the prettiest and the skinniest.

Gymnastics had become a constant round of grades and competitions and although there wasn't much enjoyment left in it for me, I was still desperate to excel.

One evening I was standing in the gym with the other nine girls as we waited for the results of our grade five to be read out. Finally the coach got to me. 'Pass,' she said. 'Not distinction this time, Nikki. That's a bit useless for you, isn't it?' She probably didn't mean anything by it and if she did she was probably just trying to gee me up a bit, but all I heard was the word 'useless'. It stuck in my brain like a rock and I just couldn't shift it.

Shortly afterwards Mum was watching me line up to collect my badge at a county trials competition. She remembers that as I waited my turn she looked at my face and all she could see was torment and misery. I was only seven and I'd reached a pretty good standard as a gymnast but I felt useless.

I had to improve, I had to get better. And for that, I had to get thinner. I also deserved to be punished for not being as good as I should have been. Well, that's what I thought. So I started denying myself treats.

Every week Mum would buy me a Milky Bar and Natalie a Galaxy to keep in our sock drawer. It was up to us when we ate them but we were both ultra-sensible and limited ourselves to one cube a day as that way they lasted longer. I'd also treat myself to a cube before training on a Saturday morning.

But when I started feeling more and more useless at gymnastics and more and more unhappy finding myself in the crossfire between Mum and Dad at home, I thought, I'm not going to have my cube of Milky Bar today. I don't need it.

That very first time I denied myself, it felt good. Like I'd finally achieved something myself. And I liked the feeling so much that I did it again.

The other treats I had loved as a little kid were Kinder Eggs. I'd always been an early riser, which drove my parents mad, so years earlier Mum had made a deal with me that if I stayed in bed until seven o'clock I got a chocolate egg.

For ages it was just brilliant. Early in the morning I'd be wide awake but as soon as seven o'clock came round on my panda bear alarm clock, I'd go rushing into Mum and Dad's room, climb into bed between them and claim my Kinder Egg.

But when I started wanting to be skinnier I started opening my reward, throwing away the chocolate and just keeping the toy inside.

And if anyone else, like my auntie, offered me a bag of sweets I'd just say I was full up or I didn't like them. When I deprived myself it felt good. But even then I knew this had to remain a secret – I couldn't tell anyone.

During that long, miserable summer the rows between Mum and Dad just grew more vicious. Mum was usually teary and weak, Dad raging or sullen. And Grandad was fading away. Everyone was pulling in different directions, caught up in their own personal tragedy.

For me, how to avoid eating became something to think about instead of what was going on at home.

By the end of the summer Grandad was really ill. One evening all four of us went to visit him. After a while Dad, Natalie and I went and sat in the corridor so that Mum and Grandad could have a bit of time alone together. We'd been sitting there about 20 minutes when she came out of his room shaking. She didn't need to say anything. Grandad had gone. He was 69.

All the way home in the car I wailed until we got back indoors and Dad tipped me into bed exhausted.

Mum was utterly distraught and lost the plot entirely. She was 36 but felt her life was over too. It was like she was drowning but had no idea how to save herself.

'Pull yourself together,' Dad would shout at her when he found her crying yet again. It was his idea of tough love but Mum couldn't pull herself together. Dad couldn't understand why not, so they drifted even further apart.

Mum went to the doctor and said she was in a mess, she couldn't cope any more with her grief, Dad's anger and their fighting. The doctor said she would talk to Dad about things if he'd make an appointment to see her.

'Please go to the GP, Dave,' Mum begged one evening as she washed the dishes. 'You need support for all the stress at work otherwise we're not going to survive this. I haven't got any energy left to fight you any more. We need proper help.'

But Dad just refused. 'I'm not going,' he said. And I think at that moment, with Mum leaning against the kitchen sink and Dad standing in the conservatory, my parents' marriage ended.

A couple of days later – about a fortnight after Grandad died – Mum woke up and thought, Right, this is it. Life really is too short for all the rowing and fighting. I want a divorce. Just like that, after 15 years of marriage, she decided she'd had enough. Natalie and I would have had to be blind, deaf and very stupid not to realise that this time things were really bad. But, because divorce is such a big thing for a kid to get their head around, I don't think either of us had really thought it would happen.

One morning, soon after Natalie had left for her school and I was waiting for Mum to walk me to mine, she came into my room, knelt down in front of me and just hugged me and burst into tears. I said, 'Mum, why are you crying?' And she just wouldn't tell me. I kept asking her why, but she couldn't say.

It was a Saturday morning a couple of weeks later when Dad and Mum told us what was really happening. They had been rowing for hours, shouting and screaming at each other. Nat and I just wanted them to hurry up because Dad always took us swimming on a Saturday morning.

Then they came out of the kitchen and took us into the living room. 'Right,' said Mum, 'Your dad and I are going to separate.'

I felt numb. Mum was crying, then Dad started sobbing like a baby. Every time she went to speak, he would shout over her. Then Mum was screaming, 'Let me speak, let me speak,' but when she began he stormed out of the room. It was like something out of *EastEnders* – I didn't think this could happen in real life.

My whole childhood had been blown apart.

Half an hour later, Dad took me and Natalie swimming and we had a really cool competition to see who could stay underwater the longest. Weird, isn't it?

CHAPTER 3

A BIG,
FAT LUMP

I pulled my Benetton stripy top over my head and slid my jeans with the Minnie Mouse patches down over my ankles, then just stood and stared.

I was standing, again, in front of the floor-length mirror inside the door of the wardrobe in Mum and Dad's bedroom, wearing just my knickers. In reality I was probably a tiny bit chubby at the time, but all I could see was someone mega fat compared with everyone else at gymnastics *and* everyone else in my class at school, if not the rest of the world.

By now I was spending more and more time analysing my body and staring at the bodies of other girls around me to see how I compared. At that time cycling shorts were really in fashion and everyone was wearing them. I'd look at anyone wearing them and if their thighs touched when their feet were together they were fat. If their thighs didn't touch they were skinny and I wanted to look like them. Mine touched.

School swimming lessons were a total nightmare – all those girls in their swimming costumes looking slim and gorgeous and athletic, and then there was me. I was just a big lump. I felt fat compared with all my friends and virtually everyone else.

I spent ages working out which girls in my class had bigger thighs than me, which had rounder tummies and which had chubbier arms.

And just when I thought I couldn't look any worse plodding from the changing rooms to the swimming pool, the unthinkable happened – Nicola Carter got a green swimming costume with ruffles on it. Exactly the same as mine! Now it would be obvious to everyone that my bum was totally massive next to hers. I'd never ever live down the 'Big Nikki' label.

I hated the way I looked. Giving up chocolate had made me feel good but it hadn't really done anything to make me lose weight, so I had to take more drastic action. At eight years old I was too young to understand about calories, but I knew – like all kids do – that some things are 'bad' for you. For goodness sake, adults never stop going on about it: 'Don't eat all those crisps, they're bad for you' or 'Eat your cabbage, it's good for you.'

So really it was quite easy to know what to do – just follow the grown-ups' rules. I started denying myself all the 'bad' things that Mum, Dad, my friends' parents and teachers had ever talked about – chips, pastry, custard, puddings, chocolate and crisps. If Mum was going to cook 'bad' foods I'd suggest something else instead, saying I'd gone off chips or wasn't in the mood for custard. And at first, preoccupied with her own losses and sadness, Mum didn't have a clue what I was up to.

I took any opportunity I could find to deprive myself of 'bad foods'. One Saturday afternoon it was Joanna Price's birthday party. Her parents had arranged for a swimming party but while everyone else was chucking each other in the pool and screaming crazily, I stood quietly at the shallow end, checking out their thighs and tummies. Afterwards, back at Joanna's house, I carefully picked all the fruit out of a trifle, leaving the jelly and custard at the bottom of my bowl. I was determined I would be the skinniest girl in a swimming costume for the next party.

Then I started giving away my food at lunchtime. Every morning Mum would send me off to school with my yellow teddy-bear lunchbox filled with sandwiches, a bag of Hula Hoops, a Blue Riband chocolate bar and a satsuma. And every night I returned with the box empty except for a few crumbs stuck to the bottom.

What Mum didn't know was that I'd hardly touched the food she had put inside. It was easy to offload the crisps and chocolate to any of the greedy-guts who sat near me at dinner break. After a couple of months I started depriving myself of the sandwiches too. They were more difficult to give away, so I'd stick them straight in a bin instead.

With a couple of hundred kids all sitting eating their lunch in the school hall, there was no way a teacher could notice what I was doing. One day my friend Joanna asked why I kept giving my food away but I just laughed and changed the subject. I didn't really have an answer for that question myself.

As I never, ever felt hungry, I didn't care about going without lunch. I just felt good inside when I denied myself.

I felt kind of victorious, as if I had won a battle that only I was aware was taking place.

By the autumn of 1990 my thinking had moved determinedly into a place where I was going to eat as little as possible and become as skinny as possible. Then I started skipping breakfast. Before, Mum had always made me and Natalie sit down for a bowl of Frosties or Ricicles. But it was so frantic in our house in the morning that it was dead easy to chuck them in the bin or ram them down the plug hole of the sink without Mum or even Natalie noticing.

Mum would be dashing in and out of the shower to get dressed and make her own breakfast and I quickly learned how to get rid of any evidence very fast indeed. Other mornings I'd say to her, 'Don't bother sorting any breakfast for me. I've already made myself a couple of slices of toast.' Even then I was like a master criminal – I'd crumble a few crumbs of bread on a plate, then leave it on the draining board to make my story appear believable.

At first Mum bought it, but then she noticed I was losing weight and her suspicions were aroused. One afternoon I walked in from school and instead of her normal cheery smile and 'Hi, darling,' she just stared at me. I could see the shock in her eyes. She had noticed for the first time that I had dramatically lost weight. My grey pleated school skirt was swinging around my hips whereas before it had sat comfortably around my tummy. And my red cardigan was baggy and billowing over the sharp angles of my shoulders.

'Nikki, you're wasting away,' she half joked. 'You'll have to eat more for your dinner.' But behind the nervous laugh there was strain in her voice. Maybe in the back of her mind she had noticed I'd been getting skinnier for a while, but now it was blatantly obvious.

It didn't bother me how worried she was, though. I was losing weight and it was good, good, good.

From then on Mum watched me like a hawk at every meal. The next breakfast time I used my 'I've had toast earlier, Mum' line she was on to me in a flash.

'Well, if you have, young lady, how come the burglar alarm didn't go off when you went into the kitchen, because I set it last night?' she said.

She angrily tipped a load of Frosties into a bowl, doused them in milk and slapped them down in front of me. I spent the next 20 minutes pushing them around the bowl with my spoon until she nipped into the hall to find Natalie's school shoes or something and then I leapt out of my chair and shoved them down the sink. Ha, ha, I'd won after all!

Dinner times got a lot harder too. For a long while I had been eating the meals Mum made me at night – I'd allowed myself that much, but no more. But that autumn, as the days grew shorter and the weather colder, I just got stricter and stricter on myself until there were only certain bits of dinner I would allow myself to eat.

Why was I doing it? I had started out just wanting to be thinner and a better gymnast but quite quickly my eight-year-old mind had come to see not eating as something I *had* to do. It was like a compulsion. I had to eat less and be in total control of what I was eating. And if Mum tried to stop me I had to find a way to get away with it.

By now, depriving myself was just as important as, if not more than, becoming skinny.

Dinner times became a battleground. As soon as the

front door slammed shut behind me as I walked in from school there would be the usual yell, 'What's for dinner, Mum?', that is heard in millions of homes across the country every afternoon. But while most mothers' replies are normally greeted with a 'Yeah, yummy' or at worst a 'Yuk, that's gross,' in our house Mum's evening menu was just the beginning of a negotiating session that could last for hours.

Usually Mum gave in and made me whatever I demanded because she was desperate for me to eat something and she thought that if she gave in to me, at least I would have something. But even that didn't always work. Often she would slave for ages cooking something that she thought I might find acceptable, chicken or fish, only for me to shove it away the moment she laid it down on the table.

Mum tried everything to make me eat. She tried persuading me: 'Go on, Nikki, just for me, please eat your dinner up.' And she tried disciplining me, threatening that I wouldn't be allowed to go out with my friends or to gymnastics unless I ate.

Sometimes she got so frustrated with me that she totally lost it and started screaming and shouting. But that was fine. I'd just scream and shout back.

Other times she simply sobbed and sobbed, begging me to eat while I looked at her blankly. Getting Mum crying was always a result. It meant she hadn't the strength to fight that particular mealtime and it was a victory for me. Dad was still living in the house but he was normally at work at mealtimes, which meant Mum was desperately trying to cope with me on her own – as well as watching her marriage collapse and trying to come to terms with having lost Grandad.

Although only eight, I was already an accomplished liar. 'Did you eat your lunch at school today, Nikki?' Mum would ask. 'Yes thanks. The egg sandwiches were great,' I'd say. I always gave just enough detail that Mum couldn't be entirely sure whether I was lying, although deep down she must have thought I probably was.

I'd also discovered a brilliant new way of getting thin – exercise. I started with sit-ups every single night in my bedroom. It was great because Natalie now slept in the attic room, which meant I could get up to anything in my room and no one would know.

'Night, darling,' Mum would say, tucking me into bed and kissing my forehead. 'Night, Mum,' I'd call out to her as she shut the door, already throwing back the duvet, ready for at least 200 sit-ups before allowing myself to sleep.

Soon the bones started to jut out at my elbows and my legs looked like sticks. Mum was becoming more and more worried. She was equally concerned by what she saw in my face – a haunted, troubled look and eyes that had lost every bit of sparkle. My sense of fun had disappeared and I was withdrawn, distracted and sullen.

One Sunday lunchtime all four of us went to the Beefeater for a roast. It was a birthday 'do' and so we were all making a show of togetherness.

When we got to the table, Mum, Dad and Nat all sat down while I hovered at the edge. 'Sit down, Nikki,' said Mum. But I couldn't. I had to keep moving, had to keep using up that energy inside me to make me thinner. And I didn't want to be near all that food – it felt disgusting.

I refused to sit down for the entire meal. Mum and Dad both tried to persuade me and got mad with me, but nothing could make me sit at that table. That was when they really started to worry there was a major problem emerging. And they were scared.

It was about this time that *The Karen Carpenter Story* was on television. It was on too late at night for me but Mum saw it and immediately spotted the similarities. And it was then that the presence of 'anorexia' as an illness first entered our lives.

Anorexia – the name given to a condition where people, usually women, starve themselves to reduce their weight – has probably been around since the end of the 19th century. In Victorian times it was thought to be a form of 'hysteria' affecting middle- or upper-class women. It was only in the 1980s in America that it became more recognised and clinics began treating sufferers.

The death of Karen Carpenter, one half of the brother-and-sister singing duo The Carpenters, played a huge part in increasing understanding of the illness. She had refused food for years and used laxatives to control her weight before dying in 1983 from heart failure caused by her anorexia.

It was only after the film of her life, made in 1989, was aired in Britain that people here had any idea about what anorexia really was. And even then it was regarded as a condition which only affected teenage girls. That's what made Mum think at first that it couldn't be what was wrong with me. I was only eight, so how could I possibly have it? But still she was worried.

'Right, if you won't eat your dinner, I'm taking you to the doctor – tomorrow!' she shouted at me at the end of another fraught meal.

The following evening after school – it was towards the end of 1990 – Mum marched me into our local surgery in

Northwood. Our family GP was off on maternity leave, so we saw a locum instead. Mum explained to him how I would agree to eat only certain things and how at other times I'd refuse to eat entirely or shove food in the bin or down the sink when I thought no one was watching.

The doctor was one of those types who treat children as if they're all a bit thick. 'So, my dear,' he said slowly, 'what have you eaten today?'

This was going to be a breeze, I just knew it.

'Well,' I said quietly and hesitantly, my very best 'butter wouldn't melt' look on my face. 'I had a slice of toast for breakfast, then my packed lunch at school, although I didn't have the crisps because they're not very good for you, are they?'

Mum looked at me in disbelief. 'Tell the truth, Nikki,' she hissed.

'But I am, Mum,' I lied effortlessly, thinking of the one mouthful of sandwich that had passed my lips all day.

'Well, Mrs Grahame,' said the doctor. 'I can see she's a bit on the skinny side but I don't think it's anything to worry about at this time. It'll all blow over, no doubt. You know what girls are like with their fads and fashions.'

'She's not faddy,' insisted Mum. 'I know my daughter and it's more serious than that.'

'Well, let's just keep an eye on her and see what happens,' said the doctor, his decision clearly made.

We drove home in silence, Mum feeling defeated again and me victorious once more. No way was anyone going to be 'keeping an eye' on me!

And when I wasn't doing the screaming and shouting it was Mum or Dad's turn. After their initial decision to split they had decided to give their marriage another go. Then the rows just became even more vicious and after a torturous couple of months they returned to the idea of divorce. But because they couldn't agree on what to do about selling the house and splitting the money, we all carried on living under the same roof.

In my eyes Dad was still acting like a monster. He'd gone from someone I would chase down the road every time he left the house to someone so bitter and angry that I didn't want to be around him. I transferred all the intensity of my feelings for Dad straight over to Mum. And now I'd lost Grandad and Dad, I clung to her, both emotionally and physically. I reverted to acting like a toddler. If we were watching television I'd insist on sitting on her lap and if she went out I'd stand by the window waiting for her to return. If it was evening time I'd lie on her bed until she got home.

Mum became the focus of everything for me – both my intense love on the good days and my anger and frustration on the bad.

By worshipping Dad rather than Mum I'd probably backed the wrong horse, but I wasn't going to lose out now. No, that would have to be Nat. That caused big rows between me and her then – and it still does even today.

But even though Natalie and I both desperately needed Mum, she didn't really have much left to give us. She was weak, crying all the time, and I was just so needy that she felt exhausted, which in turn made me feel abandoned.

My world was falling apart.

When Mum couldn't stand sharing her bed with Dad any more she decided that she, Natalie and I would all move up into the attic and live there. From now on I slept on a double bed with Mum as I couldn't bear to be physically apart from her. Natalie slept on an old brown sofa. All our toys were still scattered around the room, so it seemed like a bit of adventure having Mum up there with us, but it was kind of weird too.

By now I was struggling at school. The less I ate, the harder I found it to concentrate. And so much of my energy was being spent thinking about how I was going to dodge the next meal, how much I'd eaten so far that day and what Mum might be thinking about making for dinner that night, that I just couldn't focus on lessons at all.

Then at break times I started going to the girls' toilets and doing sit-ups. I would do dozens in a session before the bell, then dash back to my desk all hot and sweaty. One of the girls in my class must have told on me because one day a teacher came in and found me and said I wasn't allowed to do it any more.

That must have been when school started getting really worried about me and called Mum in for a meeting. They said they were concerned about my rapidly falling weight and that I didn't seem able to concentrate in class any more.

Mum hauled me back to the doctor again. It was a different locum, so we went through the same charade of my pretending to be eating a healthy if meagre diet and the doctor believing me. Again we were sent home, Mum even more dejected and me even more triumphant.

Dad was seldom around at mealtimes despite still living in the house, so he rarely saw the battles. When Mum tried to talk to him about me, it just ended up in another row as they tried to blame each other for my getting into such a state. Although what kind of state it was exactly, they still weren't sure themselves.

One night Dad was in the pub when my friend Sian's mum walked up to him.

'Are you Nikki's dad?' she asked. Dad nodded and this woman he'd never met before grabbed his arm with a terrible sense of urgency.

'My daughter is really worried about Nikki,' she said. 'She's hiding in the toilets at school doing exercises and refusing to eat. Are you aware of what's going on?' she said.

Dad looked blank and was forced to admit he didn't really know the extent of what was happening at all.

'Well, you need to be worried,' my friend's mum told him. 'If you don't do something, your daughter is going to die.'

CHAPTER 4

NEVER
GIVE IN

So why was I doing it? I can imagine that a lot of people reading this will find it totally weird that someone should want to put themselves through the pain and misery of starving themselves. Not to mention all the upset and stress it causes for their family.

As an eight-year-old I had no idea about the big 'why' behind it all – it was just something I *had* to do. A bit like other girls had to get every single badge at Brownies or had to get 100 per cent in a spelling test. But this was obviously more compulsive. And potentially fatal too.

Some of the anorexia counsellors I've had have said that maybe my eating disorder started as a bid to make myself literally disappear in the warring situation at home, as if by physically getting smaller I would just fade from view. And another expert said he thought I simply went on a hunger strike that got out of control. He thought I was so angry and devastated at how my perfect life had been shattered that I was refusing to eat until someone picked up all the pieces and put them back together again.

Counsellors have also quizzed me endlessly about my mum and whether she was to blame in some way but I really don't think so. Mum has always been slim but not skinny and I never remember her dieting. But I do once recall her taking me and Nat to Folkestone for a weekend just when things were starting to go badly wrong with Dad. She was really stressed and hadn't been eating properly. She stood in the hotel bedroom admiring her flat tummy in the mirror and said, 'Ooh, I've really lost weight.' But I honestly don't think that alone could have caused it – there can't be a woman in the country who hasn't said something similar at some stage and not all their daughters have become anorexic.

Another counsellor – trust me, I've seen dozens – thought that on some subconscious level I was trying to copy the way Grandad had just faded away from life. He reckoned it was a 'mourning reaction' and I was trying to identify with Grandad by losing weight myself. And while I guess there might be some truth in that, part of me still thinks I would have become anorexic whatever happened. It was in my nature from before I was born, and the events of that year only brought it on at that particular time.

I also believe that anorexia just gave me something for myself that year as my life fell apart. I felt unhappy about everything that had happened, useless at gymnastics and inadequate at keeping my family together. But not eating was something I was good at. Not eating became my hobby, something that was all mine and that I could be in control of while my family and my perfect life fell apart around me.

In fact how much I ate was about the only thing I could control in the deepening chaos. And maybe I began to realise that not eating actually brought me quite a lot of control. Very soon I was pulling all the strings in my family. Mum's every waking moment became filled with begging me to eat, pacifying my moods, sorting out my medical support and worrying about me. And while I remained anorexic, all her attention remained focused on me.

And as I'd always wanted to be the best at everything I did, long before I'd even heard the word 'anorexic' I'd set about becoming the very best anorexic ever.

I didn't tell Natalie what I was doing and she never asked. I didn't tell my friends and certainly not Dad. And when Mum asked, begged or pleaded with me to tell her what the problem was, I simply denied there was a problem.

Even though I'd started depriving myself of food to get skinnier for gymnastics, that soon went out of the window and before long losing weight became an end in itself. In fact my gymnastics was only getting worse as by losing weight I was also losing muscle. I couldn't do the flips, I couldn't jump, I couldn't do rolls any more – and that made me feel even more useless.

Then, just as you might have imagined things couldn't have got much worse at home, they did – with bells on! Dad found out that Mum had started seeing another man. Even though they were supposed to be separated despite living under the same roof, he went mad.

It wasn't even as though Mum was having some mad, passionate affair. She'd just struck up a friendship with a bloke called Tony who used to pop round to fix her old

Morris Minor whenever it broken down – which was pretty often!

Natalie and I had always quite liked Tony. We'd usually be playing out in the street on our bikes while he messed around under the bonnet. He'd talk to us and ask about school and he seemed harmless and friendly. After he had finished on the car he would go inside to wash the grease off his hands and have a cuppa and a chat with Mum. And that is how it all started. Tony's marriage had been a bit rocky and I think he and Mum were two lost souls clinging to each other for a bit of comfort.

Natalie and I worked out what had been going on when the rows in our house reached volcanic proportions.

But, despite Dad's jealousy, there was no way Mum was ditching Tony and having Dad back. Because what I didn't know then was that, all through what I'd thought of as my perfect early years, my dad had been having a string of affairs.

Natalie was just nine months old when Mum and Dad had decided to have another baby and Mum fell pregnant almost immediately. But around the same time Dad started going out most nights with his mates, leaving Mum looking after a small baby alone and expecting another.

It was only one day when she found a long blonde hair wrapped around one of his socks as she filled the washing machine that everything became clear. Dad admitted it all. It was a woman who worked in one of our local shops. What a cliché! But it was easy, I guess – and so was she.

I love it when Mum tells the story about how she threw her best coat on, strapped Natalie in the buggy and marched up to the counter of the shop, pushing in front of all the other customers.

'I hear you've been screwing my husband,' she said calmly to the woman, suddenly finding herself the centre of attention in the shop as all the other customers listened in.

'Leave him alone,' Mum said determinedly.

'Are you threatening me?' the woman sneered.

'You're bloody right I am,' said Mum, spinning the buggy round and storming out.

I've always liked to think that moment was Mum's victory over a woman with the stunted imagination, let alone morals, to shag a man with kids. But it was a hollow victory. That weekend Mum miscarried the baby. She'd lost an unborn child and her belief in what her marriage had been.

Mum said everyone was entitled to make a mistake and agreed to take Dad back so long as he promised never to do it again. He said he couldn't promise but he'd try. Some commitment, eh? Anyway she took him back.

Mum says a string of 'other women' followed over the years, which is why when she finally called time on the marriage, she really couldn't go back.

It wasn't until I was older that Mum told me about Dad's affairs, but I picked up enough information from ear-wigging their rows at the time to have a pretty good idea what was going on.

I'd always been such a Daddy's girl, I'd adored him, and finding out that my dad wasn't who I thought he was hit me hard. I felt betrayed.

Tony started coming round quite a bit in the evenings. He would hold Mum when she cried about Dad, and Grandad, and me. If he'd known at that time what he was taking on by getting involved with Mum and all of us, he would probably have run for the hills! But he was kind and caring and he stuck around. He would come round a lot when Dad wasn't there, which was another huge jolt for me and Natalie. It just confirmed for us that we were never going to get our old life back. The only thing that softened the blow was that we both liked Tony. We called him Hog because his hair stuck up like a hedgehog's bristles. He didn't even seem to mind too much when we took the mickey out of him.

Mum, Natalie and I were still living in the attic because Dad was refusing to move out of the house. There was a court battle pending over who would keep the house and it was becoming really nasty. Dad instructed one of his American cousins, a hotshot lawyer from New York, to act on his behalf. And then a few times this really scary heavy bloke came round saying, 'We're going to make you an offer – you should take it.'

But Mum had nowhere to go to, so we stayed in the house, living like normal downstairs during the day when Dad was at work, then scuttling up to the attic each evening. We'd sit up there watching television and hear Dad walking around downstairs singing manically. It was like something out of a horror film.

One night it kicked off really badly between Mum and Dad. There was screaming and shouting downstairs, a smashed teapot and so much anger. I lay in bed, the pillow over my head to dull the noise as I cried and cried.

After that night Mum applied for a restraining order against Dad. In the end, though, she let him back into the house and the court case over what they should do with our home rumbled on.

In January 1991 Mum filed for divorce and my perfect life was well and truly over. That same month Dad finally lost his job and it was obvious that sooner or later we'd have to move out of my beloved Stanley Road.

Things at school were going rapidly downhill too. I started spending most of my days sitting in the medical room with the school nurse, Mrs Bullock. My teachers didn't mind because they could tell I was very weak. I looked awful and hadn't been concentrating on my lessons for months. Mum had told them about the problems at home and maybe they thought I was just going through a difficult patch and I'd pull through soon.

Mrs Bullock became a surrogate mother for me in the hours when I had to be away from my real mum. I loved her and wanted her total attention all the time. If another pupil dared to come to the medical room with a cut knee or something wrong with them and needed Mrs Bullock, I couldn't bear it. I would pace up and down, feeling angry and anxious. This is my room, I'd say to myself. I need Mrs Bullock – she's for me and me only.

By the beginning of 1991 I had reduced what I would allow myself to eat more and more until it was virtually nothing. For breakfast it would be one small glass full of hot orange squash and four cubes of fruit salad. Then Mrs Bullock would give me tea and two digestive biscuits in the medical room, which would be my lunch. Obviously she knew that wasn't enough, but I think she too was grateful to think I was getting something inside me.

I negotiated with Mum – or should I say bullied her? – into letting me eat my evening meals out of a peanut bowl. If she ever tried to serve something up on a normal dinner plate I'd just freak, push the whole lot away and refuse to eat anything at all.

But even a peanut bowl-sized portion was no guarantee

I would eat. For a normal dinner I would allow myself ten strands of spaghetti or two small potatoes with some vegetables. And when I had eaten the amount I'd decided was acceptable, that was it, I'd stop eating and however much Mum begged, cajoled or shouted at me, nothing would change my mind.

And all the time she was growing more and more terrified and frustrated as the weight fell off me.

We went to the doctor four or five times but each time it was a locum and he was insistent it was 'just a phase' or 'girls being girls' and 'something I would grow out of'. How wrong could he be?

My doctor's notes at the end of 1990 recorded my weight as 21.4 kilograms (3 stone 5 lb). By February 1991 it had dropped to 21 kilos (3 stone 4 lb). The locum described me as: 'Very quiet, introvert and controlled. Reluctant to open up. Kneading her hands and tearing up the Kleenex given to her when she started to cry.' But he still sent me home again.

I was also suffering from Raynaud's Disease, which affects blood flow to the extremities and means you are incredibly sensitive to the cold. But by then I had so little body fat protecting me that it was hardly surprising.

One evening things hit a new low at home. Mum had cooked dinner, so again I trailed up to the table, sat down, looked at my peanut bowl and point-blank refused to eat. Normally Mum would try to persuade me at first, but this time she just lost it.

'I can't stand this any more,' she screamed. 'Are you trying to kill yourself?'

She dragged me to the floor and with one hand held me down by my hair while with the other hand she scooped up fistfuls of pasta and tried to force them into my mouth. I was screaming, clawing at her and trying to push her off me. Then I clamped my lips shut. Whatever she did, she wasn't going to make me eat.

Another time Natalie and I had gone shopping with my auntie and Mum for bridesmaids' dresses because my cousin was getting married. We were in the restaurant in Debenhams and Mum ordered us fish and chips. But when it arrived I picked at a few peas, then pushed it away.

Mum went mad. She held me down on the chair with one hand and tried to force the chips in my mouth with a fork. I was shouting and crying at her to stop but she was raging. My auntie was shouting, 'Sue, stop it! Calm down, Sue. Leave her.' But Mum couldn't. She was terrified at what was happening to me and overwhelmed with frustration that she couldn't do anything about it. Nothing she had tried was working, the doctors still weren't taking her seriously and I was fading away in front of her eyes.

As the weeks went by I became weaker and weaker and was feeling so out of it at school that one day the headmistress called Mum in for a meeting. She said the school couldn't deal with the responsibility of having me there any longer while I was so ill and I'd have to take some time off.

So that was it, no more school. But by then I was so tired and weak I was beyond caring. I became so weak and helpless that I'd get Mum to carry me around the house. I loved that. I could still have walked if I'd had to, but being carried made me feel like a baby again – it felt safe.

The state I was in gave Mum and Dad a whole new subject to row about. Dad blamed Mum, saying I'd got worse since she'd filed for divorce. Mum blamed Dad for, well, everything that had happened really.

Then, by the February of that year, I'd reduced what I would allow myself to water – which I'd only agree to drink out of one particular sherry glass from the kitchen cabinet – vitamin C pills and the occasional slice of toast or shortbread biscuit.

I was painfully skinny but not only had all my body fat gone, so had my spirit, my energy and my childishness.

Lying on our battered brown corduroy sofa watching television, I was locked in a world far away from everything going on around me. I was unable to concentrate on anything, play with toys, think or even move very much.

For a fortnight I ate virtually nothing at all. I chewed gobstoppers to keep away hunger pangs. And I screamed and lashed out if Mum or Dad tried to make me eat. I was so weak that at night I had to crawl up the stairs to bed as Mum tried to help, tears rolling down her face on to the carpet.

You might wonder why she wasn't dialling 999 or camping outside the doctor's front door, but she had been told so many times I'd just 'snap out of it' that she had lost all confidence in the system – and in herself. Her self-esteem was shot to pieces after everything she had been through and she had no strength left to fight. But one morning at the beginning of March she knew she couldn't leave it another day. She helped me into the car and drove me to the GP's surgery.

When we arrived she helped me out of the car and we found ourselves a seat in the stuffy waiting room. Mum went up to the receptionist and quietly but determinedly stated her case. 'My daughter is very ill,' she said. 'I can't cope any more. We are going to sit here and we're not leaving until someone does something to help her.'

This time it took the doctor just one look at me to tell I was dangerously ill. I was malnourished and extremely weak. But most urgent was the fact that I had become severely dehydrated.

I was so tired I hadn't got the strength to lie when the doctor asked what I'd eaten that day. And Mum was doing all the talking this time anyway. The previous day I'd had a quarter of a slice of toast for breakfast, no lunch and two slices of bread and a fish finger for my dinner. That was all.

The doctors weighed me and I was just 20 kilos (3 stone 2 lb). I had a BMI of 12.4, which meant I was severely underweight. A normal eight-year-old would be around 27 kilos (4 stone 4 lb) – that's 7 kilos, or more than a stone, heavier than I was.

The doctor promised Mum that by the following day they would have found me a specialist unit where I could be assessed and helped. He turned to me and said, 'Now go home and eat something – it'll be your only hope of staying out of hospital.'

When we got home Mum heated up a Cornish pasty for me in the microwave and I ate the lot. It was delicious. After so many weeks of eating almost nothing, it felt amazing.

But within an hour of finishing it, a huge wave of guilt surged over me. I hated myself for being so weak and giving in. You must *not* do that again, I reprimanded myself.

I went to bed feeling angry at myself and guilt-stricken about how much I'd eaten. And I was terrified of what the morning would bring.

CHAPTER 5

THE
MAUDSLEY

I was lying on the sofa wearing a billowing white dress dotted with huge purple lavender flowers when the call came saying they had found a specialist unit for me.

That morning I'd crawled up to the attic and dug the dress out of our big red dressing-up box. I had a porcelain doll that had an almost identical dress and I decided I wanted to look like her. It must be easy being a doll, I thought.

I put the dress over my head, then, exhausted by the effort, returned to the sofa, where I lay and watched Mum vacuuming around me. By this point I was so sick I could barely move.

'We've got a place for your daughter at the Maudsley Hospital in south-east London,' the official-sounding woman on the phone told Mum. 'Can you come straight away?'

'Oh yes,' Mum replied. 'I'd go to hell and back to save my daughter.' She didn't know then that hell and back was precisely the journey she would be making over the next nine years.

The following few hours were a flurry of activity. Mum rang Dad, who came straight home from work, picking up Natalie from school on his way. We drove to the station, then set off on the tube journey to the Maudsley.

The Maudsley Hospital is the biggest mental health hospital in Britain. It treats people with all sorts of horrific mental problems, including kids with emotional and behavioural problems, obsessive-compulsive disorder (OCD), post-traumatic stress, depression and other serious psychiatric conditions. When we turned up there that day, 5 March 1991, I had no idea I was being bracketed with kids so seriously ill.

The journey from Northwood Hills tube station to the other side of London was exhausting. When Mum helped me off the train at Elephant & Castle, people were staring at me. I must have looked like a kid dying of cancer. And when I saw the stairs leading up out of the station, I thought I couldn't do it – I just didn't have the energy to get up there. But somehow Mum and Dad helped me and we clambered up into the daylight and through the dirty doors of a red London bus. After about ten minutes the bus lurched to a stop and the doors flew open again. In front of us was the Maudsley.

It was certainly a serious-looking building, with two grand pillars flanking a flight of stone steps that led up to the main entrance. I felt tiny as I crept up the steps and entered the monstrous great building.

Inside we were greeted by a smiley nurse who showed Mum and Dad into a side room for a meeting with Dr Stephen Wolkind, the hospital's expert in child psychiatry.

Natalie and I were taken into another room by a nurse – let's call her Mary – who gave us crayons and paper to keep us occupied. It felt like Mum and Dad were gone for hours. After Natalie and I had coloured and drawn everything we could think of we wandered outside and sat on the low bars of a climbing frame in the fading spring sunshine.

'I wish Mum and Dad would hurry up so we can just clear out of this place and go home,' I said to Natalie. It had never occurred to me I wouldn't be back in time for *Neighbours*.

Then Natalie pushed me on the swings for a bit. I was too weak to push her. But still Mum and Dad didn't emerge from their meeting. What could they be talking about?

Finally Mary, the nurse, came out to the swings and told me it was time to go in. She led me down a corridor and into a small cubicle. Inside there was a narrow single bed, a table and a chair. She sat me down at the table and told me to wait a moment. A couple of minutes later she returned carrying a glass of milk, a couple of cream crackers and some cheese.

'Here's a snack,' she said, placing it in front of me, then sitting down herself on the edge of the bed.

I looked at the plate, barely able to hide my disgust at the big chunk of cheese plonked in the middle. Didn't these people know cheese was about *the* most 'bad' food around?

'Oh no, I don't fancy that at the moment, thank you,' I said quietly.

'Nikki, you have to eat your snack,' replied Mary. 'I'll talk to you when you have finished it.'

For more than an hour we sat in silence. A few times I tried to engage Mary's eyes, buried deep in her pudgy face, but each time she looked away. It was only later I discovered that it was the Maudsley's policy to avoid any interaction with eating-disorders patients during mealtimes. So instead I silently gazed out of the window watching aeroplanes etching white lines across the sky of south London.

Finally, another nurse came into the room.

'Right, Nikki,' she said brusquely. 'Your mum and dad are going home now, so you'd better say goodbye to them.'

Mum was standing in the doorway behind the nurse, her gaze flickering between me and the floor. I could tell by the red puffiness around her eyes that she had been crying. Even Dad looked shell-shocked.

At first I couldn't quite understand what was happening. I'd always thought we were just here for a meeting with specialists. It hadn't occurred to me for a moment that they might want to keep me here. But the look on Mum and Dad's faces told me in a second that this was exactly what was happening.

'No, no. Don't take my mum away,' I pleaded, my voice high-pitched but starting to choke with the realisation of what was happening.

'I need my mum. Please don't make her go. I need her.'

As Mum and Dad moved towards me to kiss me goodbye, I started to wail. This just could not be happening. Mum couldn't be abandoning me. Not her, surely? OK, Grandad and Dad had left me, but Mum wouldn't do that. Would she?

My screams grew louder and louder, like the howling of a wounded animal. I watched the nurse gently take hold of Mum's elbow and lead her back out into the corridor. 'No, no, noooooo,' I screamed.

I lunged forward and flung my bony arms around Mum's thighs, my screams now subsiding into loud sobs as I begged her not to leave me in this strange place surrounded by strange people.

Tears were sliding slowly down Mum's face as she tried to untangle my arms from her legs and steady herself.

'I've got to, Nikki,' Mum kept saying. 'I've got to – the doctors are going to make you better. You'll be home soon, I promise.'

But I didn't hear any of that. My head was thumping and my ears were filled with a strange howling – I didn't realise then that it was me making such a horrific noise.

Mary and the other nurse peeled me away from Mum but I started screaming and lashing out at them. I was so angry, so furious that everyone would gang up and do this to me. Why me? After everything else, why me?

I flung myself around the room, banging into the bed and table, flailing my arms and legs.

Eventually, Mary pinned me to the floor to stop me smashing my head while the other nurse gently pushed Mum and Dad into the corridor.

For a moment I stopped struggling and took a breath. Through the glass window of the door I could see Mum looking back at me over her shoulder as she walked away. She had walked away and left me sobbing on the floor. Mum, who'd been there me for every second of every day, who carried me like a baby from room to room, who cuddled me to sleep and kissed my tears. She had left me.

I lay totally still and heard the lock on the door at the end of the corridor click shut. I was eight years old and totally alone. I cried until my head pounded and I was shaking with exhaustion.

After five minutes Mary picked me up from the floor and eased me back into the chair by the table.

The two cream crackers and lump of cheese were still sat there on the plate. My whole life had been upended once again but that chunk of cheese wasn't going anywhere.

'Now, Nikki,' she said, 'we're going to work you out an eating programme which is going to make you better.'

She was fat and spoke with a strict, headmistressy voice that I could tell meant she wouldn't put up with any negotiation. I was so scared.

'If you stick to the programme and eat your food you will see your Mum in a couple of weeks,' she told me. 'As for now, eat your snack up and then we'll talk to you.'

'When am I going to see my mum?' I mumbled through my tears.

'Eat your snack and then we will talk to you.'

'But I need her. I need her.'

'Eat your snack and then we will talk to you.'

'Please let me see her. Please.'

'Eat your snack and then we will talk to you.'

And that is how it went on. Me, sobbing, begging and way beyond being able to think about eating. Them, refusing to talk to me, comfort me or even look at me unless I started eating.

At six o'clock they took away the plate of crackers and cheese and replaced it with a meat casse
role dish with mash and peas. Again I looked at it and refused to eat. Again they sat near me at the table, refusing to speak unless I ate.

'Please, when can I go home?'

'Eat your dinner.'

At eight o'clock they took the cold, congealed food away and brought a glass of milk and a small KitKat.

'When am I going to see my mum?'

'Eat your snack.'

At 8.30 the chocolate and milk were taken away and the nurse said it was bedtime. I looked over to the bed where the pyjamas Mum had sneaked into her handbag on the way here had been laid out for me.

The only time I'd ever been away from home before was at a Brownie camp and then I was so miserable I'd wet the bed. How on earth was I going to manage in this place with absolutely no one I knew around me and no idea when I might be going home?

I was shaking as I swung my legs in between the plain white sheets. I thought of my teddy-bear duvet cover. I thought of my sticker collection. I thought of Mum and Dad and Natalie all doing just what they had done last night, last month, last year – but without me.

How could this be happening?

One of the nurses sat on the bed as I lay there and closed my eyes. It can only have been exhaustion from that long day that made me able to sleep.

Next morning it all began again. I was woken by a nurse and got up and dressed myself. At eight o'clock a tray was put on my table with a bowl of cornflakes, a slice of bread and butter and a glass of orange juice on it. I allowed myself the orange juice and left everything else.

Then they set about weighing and measuring me. My weight had dropped to 18 kilos (2 stone 12 lb) – the average weight for a four-year-old. And I was a month off my ninth birthday.

The doctor's reports from that assessment say I was

'finding reality of life too hard to bear and wished to be dead to be reunited with her idealised grandfather'. I was the worst anorexic case they had ever treated at the Maudsley and there was a real concern that unless the weight went back on immediately, I could die.

'You are dangerously underweight,' Mary, my key nurse, told me. 'You will not be allowed to see your Mum until you eat. And you will not be allowed to speak to your Mum until you eat. And if you still refuse to eat we're going to take you to a medical ward, put a tube into you and force-feed you.'

No one ever asked me if I wanted to put the weight back on. No one ever considered I might not want to get better.

But I realised then that this woman was totally serious and this wasn't a battle I was going to win.

And, young as I was, I was old enough to know that my only option was to play the system.

OK, I'll comply with their rules, I thought. But as soon as I get out of here I'll eat whatever I want and get as skinny as I can as soon as I can. I'll eat whatever they serve me up and pretend I'm better.

The food's just like medicine, I told myself. I'll take it to get them off my back. So every mealtime I sat obediently at the small, square table, pushed up against a blank wall, and slowly yet surely cleared my plate.

It was real old-fashioned school food, like liver with potatoes and green beans, steak and kidney pie and shepherd's pie. All of it was disgusting but I got my head down and got on with it.

During mealtimes there was no one to talk to, nothing to look at and nothing to do. In some ways eating the food relieved the boredom – and knowing this was just a game, something I'd do to shut everyone up, made me feel like I was still in control too.

And when I ate my food everyone treated me so much more nicely. If I ate my meals I'd be allowed out of my cubicle to play with the other kids on the ward. There were about ten of them, but I was the only one with an eating disorder. The rest were just oddballs.

A girl called Janey used to run up and down the ward shouting and swearing at the nurses. She'd been kicked out of school and seemed totally out of control.

Then there was Anna, who was about the same age as me, and she had behavioural problems and Down's Syndrome. At that stage I was really into Felt by Numbers, a cross between Fuzzy Felt and Painting by Numbers. I was mad about it and for a while Mum had been buying me a box of it every weekend. When I'd finished my felt works of art I Blu-Tacked them up all around my room and they looked amazing.

One morning Anna came into my room when I wasn't there and pulled every single one of my Felt by Numbers off the wall and threw them on the floor. When I returned and saw hundreds of pieces of felt lying higgledy-piggledy all over the floor I was heartbroken. I squatted down, picked them up and stuck each tiny piece back in its correct place. It took hours.

Next morning Anna came back and did exactly the same again.

The boys on the unit were really naughty too – some had behavioural problems and others would shout and swear at any time of the day or night. And we had another couple of Down's Syndrome kids too.

I'd never come across kids with mental problems before

and it was utterly terrifying. The screaming and shouting at night, the dramatic mood swings and violent outbursts were all alien to me and I felt so isolated. If one of the kids was having a temper tantrum at night, I'd pull the sheets and blanket over my head and try to block out the noise by thinking about home.

But the other kids' rages and fits taught me something too – it got them attention and for a short while it gave them control. I think that on some level this sunk into my brain because within the year I was ranting and raving like the rest of them.

My first week at the Maudsley seemed to last for ever but within a month I understood the system and just got on with it. As a child you become institutionalised very quickly.

I made friends with a couple of the other girls and even the really weird kids started to seem more normal with every day that passed. There was a girl called Emily who used to shout all the time and couldn't stop lying. She probably had Tourette's Syndrome or something similar, but at the time I thought she was just mental. Even so, we became friends and would hang around together. Well, it was either that or being on my own all the time.

I'd been in the Maudsley for a fortnight before Mum and Dad were finally allowed to visit. When it was time for them to leave I cried hysterically again, grabbing hold of Mum's leg. After that they came every week and I got more used to the partings, but it was never easy. Mum was relieved that I had a bit more meat on me and that for the moment I was safe, but they didn't dare look any further forward than that.

Natalie came to visit a couple of times but only because she was ordered to by Mum. I could tell from the way she looked around the place out the corner of her eyes that she hated it. I don't blame her at all. She was still just a kid herself and it was a dark, horrible, looming building filled with all these nutcase kids.

I think she also felt sorry for me having to live there. As my big sister, she felt bad I was there and not her, but at the same time she couldn't help feeling glad it wasn't her too.

Spending all weekend on the ward was really miserable. All the other kids went home on a Friday evening so I'd be on my own apart from a couple of nurses who were called in especially to look after me.

Chesney Hawkes's 'The One and Only' was number one in the charts at the time and whenever I hear that song I'm instantly transported back to the Maudsley with that playing on radio and me playing the hundredth game of KerPlunk with a nurse in a deserted day room on a Saturday afternoon.

Those weekends dragged on for ever. Sometimes one of the nurses would take me out on a little trip but other times I'd just watch films or write letters to my friends.

Then, after three months, I was told that as long as I continued to reach my target weight each week I would be allowed to go home at weekends. I was over the moon.

I was weighed every Friday afternoon and if I hit my target, Mum and Dad could come and collect me. If I didn't hit the target, though, there was no way on earth I could persuade the doctors to let me go.

The first weekend I was allowed home, I was so excited. Mum and Dad came to pick me up and we went home together on the tube.

I kept thinking about climbing into my old bed, seeing

Natalie and my friends. And best of all, I wouldn't have to eat as much as in hospital. Re-sult!

'Am I going to have to eat this weekend?' I asked Mum as the train doors slid shut at Elephant & Castle.

'Yes, you are,' Mum replied firmly. 'We've been instructed by the hospital exactly what you have to eat – they have given us menu sheets and told us how much weight you've got to maintain over the weekend. So you have to eat.'

Mum and Dad would take it in turns to pick me up for 'home weekends'. Their divorce was finalised in July that year but they were still living under the same roof and on reasonable enough terms to present a united front to me. You didn't have to dig far below the surface, though, to hit a wall of mutual resentment between them.

The moment I walked out of the gates of the Maudsley on a Friday evening, rush-hour traffic roaring up and down Denmark Hill, I felt elated, free and victorious that Mum and Dad were there together to pick me up.

But by the time I'd stepped through my front door an hour and a half later my thoughts had already turned to how I was going to get out of eating between then and Sunday night. My goal for home weekends soon became purely to lose the weight I'd had to put on during the week – and I'd do my damnedest to achieve it.

Relations with Nat could be pretty fraught on my home weekends too. In the months I'd been away she had been transformed from 'Natalie Grahame' to 'Nikki Grahame's sister'. At school she felt other kids and teachers only wanted to talk about me and how I was getting on, when I might be back and if I was feeling any better.

Things were tense between Natalie and Dad too, as she

was mad at him about the divorce. She had always been closer to Mum than to him and in some ways had been quite pleased at first that they were splitting up because she felt he had been so horrid to Mum. But then Nat didn't want Tony being close to Mum either. So she was mad at Dad for allowing that to happen too.

There was certainly a lot of anger in our house back then. Some of the doctors were concerned about me returning to that environment at weekends but Mum and Dad could have been attacking each other with chainsaws as far as I was concerned – I just wanted to be at home.

Yet as the weeks rolled by, home visits became more and more about skipping meals and exercising secretly in my bedroom than about seeing my family. In fact the longer I stayed away from home the less I cared about Mum and Dad, Nat, friends, school, gymnastics, everything really. All I could think about was how I was going to lose all the weight they had made me put on in hospital. But while I was at the Maudsley I complied with their rules.

Each morning after breakfast of a bowl of cereal and a slice of toast we would go to the hospital's classroom. It wasn't like a proper school but it was OK. I did a project about flowers, learning their names and colouring in pictures. That took us up to lunchtime – and one of their stomach-churning meals.

Then, in the afternoons, we would either go to the park or play outside. The Maudsley offered us lots of things to do and sometimes we did have fun. There was a toy room, an art room, a gym and a Sega room where you could play computer games. We could watch telly and videos too. My favourite video was *Willy Wonka and the Chocolate Factory*. I watched it over and over again and loved the bit where the Golden Ticket-winning kids were allowed inside the factory. I'd look at all the chocolate and think, Oh, I wish I could eat that. But I knew there was absolutely no way I could allow myself – the guilt would be too unbearable.

There was also a day room where we'd sit around and do jigsaws or play board games like Buckaroo and draw Spirograph pictures.

In the evenings I'd write letters to Mum. Each week she sent me writing paper and stamps and I'd spend hours drawing pictures and writing notes for her and my friends from school. By now I'd been gone a matter of months and almost every day letters decorated with childish colourings and stickers arrived from my old classmates. I glued them up all around my room.

Evening was also the time for us kids to visit the tuck shop. Of course all the other children were beyond excited about that – but I hated it. The doctors encouraged Mum and Dad to give me 50 pence a week to spend on sweets. But why on earth would I want to do that? I was already eating massive meals every day. I didn't want to spend money on sweets in the evenings. I wanted to buy comics and magazines but the staff weren't having any of that. It was Chewits, Chewits and more Chewits. Sweets felt like a punishment to me.

There were some good times at the Maudsley, though. One time they took us camping in the New Forest for a few days. One of the nurses, Clive, left a trail of red paint through the woods and we had to follow it. It was such a laugh just doing normal kids' stuff.

But even that trip had its moments. Mary was there and one morning she said to me, 'It's snack time, Nikki. You can have a packet of crisps and a fizzy drink.'

'I can't eat crisps,' I said. 'I can't.'

Mary barely looked up and just threw four biscuits at me instead.

The following evening everyone else was making warm bananas with melted chocolate around the camp fire. 'Can I have my banana cold, on its own, please?' I asked. Mary tossed the banana in my direction with a look of disgust.

They also took us on trips around London and to the Water Palace in Croydon, an indoor water park. It was fun, but there was a lot of crying and shouting too.

At the hospital there was an occupational therapist called Charlotte. Her job was to help me express my feelings through art and crafts. I liked making things but I just wasn't interested in her constant questions about my mum. Did she watch what she ate? Had she encouraged me to diet? Did I get on with her? It all seemed so irrelevant. Why couldn't everyone just leave me alone to eat – and not eat – exactly what I wanted? What none of them realised was that I couldn't give a toss about getting better. I just wanted to get out.

The staff did try really hard to make us kids feel comfortable. There was a young nurse called Billy who everyone thought was really cool. And there was lovely Pauline who used to cuddle me when I was sad.

Clive was cool too. But one morning he said to me, 'You're filling out a bit.' Surely anyone – most of all a qualified nurse – would know that is not the sort of thing you say to an anorexic. That had a massive effect on me. I already hated what they were doing to my body. I could feel my thighs become softer and see my tummy getting rounder and it disgusted me. I was gutted that they were undoing all the work I'd done to my body over the past year. So for Clive to then say I was filling out threw me into a new depression.

But worst of all the nurses was Mary. I remained terrified of her until the day I left the Maudsley. She would stand behind me during meals and make me scrape every last scrap of food off my plate. If I didn't finish it, she'd tell me off. I was still just a child and found her really frightening.

If any of us played up we were given a certain number of 'minutes' to stand and face the wall. Mary was always handing out the minutes to me for being cheeky by saying 'Shut up' to the nurses or even a couple of times 'I hate you' when they made me eat something I couldn't face.

One of the nurses would read me a story when I got into bed but when she turned the light out there were no cuddles or goodnight kisses like at home. Often I would lie there and quietly cry. About missing Mum, missing Dad, being stuck in hospital and another destroyed Felt by Numbers.

Other nights I'd feel stronger and make plans about what I'd do when I got out of there, how I'd set about losing the weight they'd made me put on and how I'd get back in control of my life. All I could focus on was the day they would let me home. To reach that day, though, I knew I just had to get on with doing what I was told and so I did start gaining weight.

After a couple of months of eating all my meals properly, sitting at the table in my cubicle, I was allowed to eat in the main sitting area, although my table was still shoved so that I was facing the wall with a member of staff sitting next to me.

When I'd done that OK for a month, I was allowed to eat in a downstairs office, although still it was only a blank wall and a nurse for company.

Then finally, four months after arriving at the Maudsley, I was allowed to eat my meals with the other children in the main dining room. Chatting and giggling during meals again was fantastic. I felt normal. There were three tables in the children's dining room: the Dinosaur table, the Happy Eaters table and the Care Bears table. They put me on the Happy Eaters table! What a joke that was. If only it had been funny.

It had taken me virtually my entire stay at the Maudsley to work my way up to that table but it meant I was one of the kids who behaved during mealtimes and, most importantly for my doctors, I was eating my meals.

At the beginning of September, after six months at the hospital, I was told I would be going home. I'd gained 6 kilos (13 lb), to bring my weight up to 26 kilos (4 stone 1 lb) and although still skinny I was closer to the average weight for a child of my age.

But although on the outside I appeared to have recovered, inside my head I was still as intent on starving myself as the day I'd arrived there. If anything, I was more determined than ever. The big difference was that I was now far cleverer at fooling people about what I was thinking.

To celebrate my last day at the Maudsley the staff treated all the kids on the unit to a McDonald's. I ordered a hamburger, chips and a strawberry milkshake and hated every minute of it. For me the entire trip was a nightmare, although the other kids were having a great time. I ate and drank with a smile on my face, making sure everyone thought I'd come through my problems and was as right as rain again.

But in my mind there was no doubt – as soon as I was home the starving would begin. And this time it was going to be serious.

CHAPTER 6

I DON'T
BELONG HERE

Brand-new, neatly pressed grey skirt, new red woollen cardigan and new Kylie pencil tin. It was the beginning of the school year at Hillside Infants when I emerged from the Maudsley in September 1991.

After six months in hospital I'd gained more than 3.2 kilos (7 lb). There was colour in my cheeks, a slight curve around my thighs and tummy and a shine to my hair. And I hated it. I hated every millimetre of fat they'd made me put on my body and I wanted it starved off my bones as quickly as possible.

I found it hard to settle back into school. In fact I loathed it. I hadn't been away that long but, at nine years old, things move fast. My old friends Joanna, Emily and Erin had found new best mates and I felt I was constantly hanging around the edge of conversations.

And I felt different. I was different. In the six months I'd been away I'd seen things my classmates didn't know existed – kids with severe psychiatric problems, others torn from their families, girls who had been abused by their dads. And I too had behaved in ways I'd never thought possible, being rude, aggressive and hysterical when pushed to the limit. The way other kids acted in hospital had rubbed off on me and I'd seen how being naughty and rude could get you attention when you needed it.

Everyone I bumped up against at school wanted to know where I'd been and what I'd been doing, even though I'm sure they all knew already.

Kids would come up to me in the playground and say, 'Where have you been?'

'I've been at private school for a while,' I replied, not batting an eyelid. I'd become a pretty accomplished liar.

But even though I was back at school, I still stood out as different. Mum had to pick me up every lunchtime, take me home and try to get me to eat my lunch before bringing me back for afternoon lessons.

'Why do you go home at lunchtime?' one nosy parker after another would ask me. Sometimes I'd just ignore them, other times I was more inventive. 'I've got diabetes and can only eat certain things,' I'd lie. It was none of their business. It was none of anyone's business.

As the weeks went passed I suppose it became a bit more normal but I felt as though from now on I was never going to be plain Nikki Grahame ever again. Oh no, I was always going to be Nikki-the-girl-who-got-so-skinny-she-had-to-leave-school-and-go-into-hospital-Grahame. I hated it.

Things at home were no better either. Mum, Natalie and I were still living in the attic bedroom while Dad was downstairs on his own.

The only good thing about being home was that I was able to control my eating again – and that meant only eating what I wanted. Within weeks of leaving the Maudsley I'd cut right back on what I was eating – just like I'd planned all the time I was away.

At first, breakfast was cereal and a slice of toast. Then at school I got a free packed lunchbox which Mum took me home to eat. (Since the divorce she'd been struggling for money, so we qualified for free school meals.)

Dinner would be something hot like spag Bol or fish pie. Again, at first I'd eat what Mum put in front of me but within a couple of weeks I started hiding food again and was back to all my old tricks – and more.

Mealtimes became a war zone. I'd seen so much bad behaviour, fighting and swearing in the Maudsley that I had emerged from there a very different child. I knew what kind of behaviour could get results because I'd seen it close up day after day. So I'd shout and swear at Mum in a way I'd never have thought of doing before. I hadn't even known the words existed.

'You can shove that up your fat fucking arse!' I'd scream when she tried to put a meal in front of me.

Mum must have wondered where this monster had come from.

Part of it was copying what I had witnessed in hospital but I think being away from my family for so long had made me more brutal. I didn't care who I upset with my antics any more. The slightest thing could tip me into a full-scale tantrum. And, as I got older, I was physically stronger and less scared of Mum or anyone else who might try to force me to eat.

I had to go to my GP every week to be weighed and I

knew that there they would quickly realise what I was up to, hiding food and refusing meals. But that didn't stop me. I'd only been home a month when Mum first suspected I had vomited up my dinner one evening and marched me back to the doctor.

To be fair to myself, I never made my anorexic career out of vomiting. It was just something I did if I felt really uncomfortable about the amount I'd eaten.

A bigger problem for me was my obsession with exercise. After school I ran up and down the slope outside our house until I was breathless. And I never sat down in the evenings, ever. I would pace up and down the living room while Mum and Natalie watched television. And when they'd finally had enough of me disrupting their viewing and were shouting at me to stop, I'd stand by the fireplace. I couldn't bear the thought of sitting down – you don't burn any calories like that. Then, once everyone was in bed, it was more sit-ups, hundreds of them.

Once again I was feeling very low. I was unhappy at home and school and took my misery out on both myself and those around me. I hit myself and bit myself during temper tantrums if Mum tried to make me eat. My arms and legs would get covered in bruises and I pulled my hair out in clumps.

And I was spiteful to Natalie too. I wouldn't let her near any of my toys and would lash out violently in our fights.

'I just want to be dead,' I said to Mum one evening. 'Why can't I be dead?' And I meant it.

Then, in the run-up to Christmas, Dad finally moved out. I felt split down the middle. Part of me was glad he was gone because I was still so angry with him for everything that had happened. But another part of me was devastated that any hopes of my life returning to how it once was were totally dashed.

What was worse, Dad's old employer, the bank, had called in our mortgage, so it was just a matter of time until we would all have to be out and the house sold. It was a Monday lunchtime and Mum had picked me up from school for lunch when she broke the news. We were sitting in the kitchen when she turned and fixed me with one of those despairing looks that left even my nine-year-old mind in no doubt there was more trouble coming down the line.

'I'm so sorry, Nikki,' she said, 'but we're going to have to sell the house. Your Dad's not working any more and the bank want their money back.'

It was just awful. I immediately started to cry. Stanley Road had been about the only stable thing in my life over the past three years and now that was being taken away from me too. It felt like the unfairness of it all was never going to end.

There were so many memories of that house and its amazing garden. There were the good memories: water fights with Natalie in the back garden and playing hide and seek in the attic. And, more recently, there were the bad memories: the screaming matches between Mum and Dad and the tears rolling down Mum's face as she stood at the kitchen sink staring out past those dreadful orange curtains she loved so much.

If I ever become ridiculously rich I'll buy that house in Stanley Road again and move back there. Maybe one day I'll get the life back that I lost.

But that lunchtime, sitting in front of a tired-looking ham sandwich, I just couldn't take in what Mum was saying. 'But leave here, Mum? We can't. No way. *No way*.'

But whether I liked it or not, soon afterwards there was a For Sale board up in the front garden and Mum was packing up our clothes and toys into old banana boxes. Dad leaving and the house going up for sale hit me hard. Life seemed so unsettled again, so I went back to focusing on the one thing I could control – eating. I cut the amount I would allow myself more and more until I was on tiny portions.

Mum tried to keep a close eye on me during mealtimes but I was hiding food again. Chips would go up my sleeve, pasta and meatballs inside my knickers. I was an expert at it by then and it only took Mum to lose concentration for a moment and food would disappear from my plate.

I was also negotiating with her again about what I would and wouldn't eat and as I gradually wore her down I was getting away with smaller and smaller portions. She still feared that to fight me might mean I ate nothing at all. I think the state I was in when I was admitted to the Maudsley had so terrified Mum that she would agree to anything if she thought she could prevent that happening again.

She couldn't, though. I liked to give her the illusion she had some control over what I was doing but in reality she had none. It was me and me alone who would decide how much I would eat.

Mealtimes became horribly bitter and fraught. I would scream and throw tantrums if Mum served up something I wouldn't eat. The first time I threw an untouched plate of food at the wall, she gasped in shock before going mad at me.

'How dare you?' Mum finally yelled, visibly taken aback at what her little daughter had turned into.

I didn't even reply, I just pushed my chair away from the table and stamped upstairs to my bedroom.

But within a couple of weeks that behaviour had become the norm. Anything I didn't like went straight up the wall until you could tell what we'd had for dinner recently by checking out the stains Mum couldn't scrub off the walls of her once cream-coloured dining room.

Christmas 1991 has entered family folklore because of one of my terrible outbursts. Tony had assured Mum there was no point in rushing out early to get a turkey, even though we had my auntie, uncle and three cousins coming over for lunch on Christmas Day. 'Everyone just makes a big fuss before Christmas,' he laughed. 'There'll be plenty of turkeys left if we wait until Christmas Eve *and* they'll be half-price. You'll see.'

Well, what we didn't see when we turned up at the shops on Christmas Eve was a single turkey – not one. All we could find was one very sad and scrawny-looking duck. Not that it bothered me – I wouldn't be eating much of it.

Mum spent hours cooking for everyone, trying to make it an extra-special Christmas after the grim year we'd all had.

But as soon as I saw the duck lying on my plate I knew I was in trouble. I couldn't bring myself to eat it. I just couldn't eat all that fat. Mum could sense the danger too as my face took on that haunted, troubled look that I would get so often at mealtimes.

Everyone was chatting and joking around the table when suddenly there was a loud smash. I'd picked up my plate and thrown it across the festively decorated table straight at the wall.

'I'm not fucking eating it!' I screamed, watching the gravy sliding down the wall like a slow-moving oil slick.

'For God's sake, Nikki,' Mum screamed. There was

silence as my auntie and cousins stared intently at their Brussels sprouts, not daring to look up. But suddenly Mum, Natalie and I broke the silence by all starting to giggle hysterically at the same moment. Then everyone joined in and we were all laughing uncontrollably. I think we were probably laughing at the sheer awfulness of everything – it was a real laugh-or-cry situation. Now we always call it the Flying Duck Christmas.

But it wasn't normally like that. By then there was rarely much laughter at mealtimes in our house. It was far more likely to be screaming and shouting, particularly when I'd just hurled another dinner plate across the room.

Soon I was eating virtually nothing again and my weight fell dangerously low. I was mentally and emotionally tormented too. I felt isolated and alone at home and school and I found it hard to concentrate or even think about anything other than food. I became totally focused on what I was trying to do – not eat. I was locked in a vicious circle because the less I ate the weaker I became and the more incapable I was of finding any pleasure in anything. Food and avoiding it occupied my mind every waking hour.

At the beginning of 1992 I was pulled out of school again. In less than four months since I had been discharged from the Maudsley I had lost three kilos (nearly 7 lb) and was down to just 23.3 kilos (3 stone 9 lb) – 75 per cent of the weight I should have been.

I was pale, sickly-looking and covered in a layer of lanugo hair, which anorexics get when they are seriously ill. It's a fine hair, almost like fur, which grows all over your body in a bid to keep it warm when there isn't enough body fat left to do that. I had loads on my back and all down my arms. It was horrible.

The whole family was attending family-therapy sessions in the hope it might help me but when I was there I refused to get involved. These people still didn't get it – I didn't *want* to eat and get better. I couldn't let myself do that.

My medical notes show that I then went down to consuming just one glass of water and a biscuit each day. It was critical.

Soon after that I stopped eating entirely. I just couldn't do it any more. Eating was giving in and I refused to do it. I was going to be strong and deny myself everything. At mealtimes I stopped sitting down at the table. Instead I would stand in the corner of the room and watch as they all tucked in. I'd watch Natalie's every move as she nudged the food on to her fork, lifted it to her mouth, chewed then swallowed. It looked so simple but I just couldn't do it. The guilt would be too much for me. I'd feel like I had done something too awful and I couldn't let that happen.

By this time Mum, Dad and my GP were frantically worried about me again.

Our family doctor, Sara, was back from her maternity leave and was brilliant at trying to find me specialist care. But that wasn't so easy. Letters flew backwards and forwards in an attempt to secure the funding from my local health authority for a bed in an eating-disorders unit. But then there were no beds available and I was put on a waiting list. It dragged on like that for weeks and all the time I was getting thinner and weaker.

Then one week I ate nothing except vitamin C pills. During all the times I had starved myself before I had never felt hungry, but this time even I felt the need to eat – yet still I couldn't do it. Something inside me just wouldn't let me give in to food. 'You can't do that, Nikki,'

I'd hear in my head. 'You'll be giving in. You have to stay strong.' And I did. I stayed strong in my head and I didn't eat. But physically I was weaker than I'd ever been.

My GP's notes show that when I visited her on Friday, 24 January I hadn't eaten anything since the Wednesday. I was terrifyingly thin. On the Saturday and the Monday I was back at the surgery but still I wasn't eating. I was so hungry I was unable to think straight. I told Mum I wanted to die and threatened Natalie with a fork.

Mum was buckling under the strain. One or other of us was in tears most of the time and the tension was unbearable. And still the battle to find a bed at a suitable unit continued.

Then I stopped drinking too. I became more and more dehydrated and was desperate for a drink but I just couldn't allow myself to give in to that either.

I remember watching Tony and Mum sitting in the kitchen drinking tea and I was just desperate for it, desperate – but I couldn't do it. I couldn't give in.

One morning, truly desperate, Mum took me back to our GP again and pleaded with her for help. The doctor told my mum to drive me straight to the nearest hospital.

I was nine years old and weighing just 19 kilos (just under 3 stone) and I hadn't drunk any fluid for a week. I was now a critical emergency case because I was so severely dehydrated and was rushed to the local Hillingdon Hospital and placed on the Peter Pan Ward, a general children's medical ward.

'It'll only be for a night, won't it, Mum?' I asked as we climbed into the car to go there.

'We'll see, darling,' Mum replied. 'We'll see.'

CHAPTER 7

HILLINGDON HOSPITAL

As Tony drove us to the hospital I stared numbly out of the back window of the car. I was too tired to talk and too weak to pay much attention to the people going about their everyday lives, scurrying up and down the busy streets.

Then something in a shop window caught my eye. It was a huge poster, the height of a man, advertising bottles of water. In the picture, water was splashing out of the bottle and falling into a glistening pool beneath it. I stared at the image, transfixed by the wetness. Oh, I so wish I could drink that, I thought. I'm so thirsty. Because I hadn't drunk anything for three days I was seriously dehydrated, but still I hadn't been able to permit myself even a drop of water.

I knew from being in the Maudsley that once I was in hospital they would be making me drink and eat – and part of me was relieved. I would be able to hand over control to the nurses and it would be like having a holiday from myself.

We pulled up outside Hillingdon Hospital and I looked up, half scared and half comforted by the solidity and plainness of the huge building.

Inside, a lovely nurse introduced herself as Geraldine, the ward sister. She helped me with my overnight bag – stuffed full of comics, clothes and my teddy bear – as we walked along the ward and into the cubicle which was to become my virtual jail for the next three months.

'Now, Nikki, we're going to start off by getting you a nice drink,' Geraldine said, smiling. I didn't even bother to fight the suggestion. But I did lean down, unzip my bag and pull out my sherry glass. 'Can I have it in this, please?' I asked, holding up the tiny tumbler. 'I only drink out of this glass.'

'Really,' replied Geraldine. 'Well, I think you're going to need a bit more than that, dear. You've got to drink a litre of lemon squash by midnight or we'll have to put you on a glucose drip.'

She was really lovely but clearly wasn't going to take any nonsense from me, and her threat worked a treat. As she poured out the first large glass of lemon squash from a plastic jug, I held out my hand and grabbed it.

The first mouthful tasted amazing. It felt like I could distinguish every single ingredient and I loved it. I was so thirsty that soon I was gulping down the squash. But however much I drank they just kept topping up my glass in a bid to rehydrate me.

The next step was for staff to weigh and measure me, take my blood pressure and assess my mental state. The notes on my admission sheet make grim reading: 'She shows feelings that life not worth living, sad, tearful and irritable, obsessed with weight and once thought of drinking her sister's chemistry set in attempt to kill herself. Digs forks into herself.'

Certainly I'd reached a point where there didn't seem anything in my life worth living for.

After all the tests, Geraldine sat on the edge of my bed and handed me a programme of what my life would be while I remained at Hillingdon. I still have the two pages of typed notes which were to provide the format for my every waking moment during my stay there. They are decorated with my childish felt-pen pictures of a rainbow, balloons and a flower, but not even my pretty doodlings can take away the harshness of the regime.

During stage 0, which lasted until I had increased my weight from 19 kilos (3 stone) to 19.95 kilos (3 stone 2 lb), my day consisted of:

Bedbath, not hairwash
Bedpan
Schoolwork for half an hour each day
Mum to visit for half an hour each day
Dad to visit for 20 minutes every other day
Reading half an hour each day
No other visitors.

And that was it – my entire day's activities. All of it was to take place in my hospital bed, which I was not permitted to leave even to use the toilet.

There were hours and hours every day where there was just nothing at all for me to do except lie on my bed and stare into space.

Stage 1 – until I reached 20.3 kilos (3 stone 3 lb) – introduced the 'perks' of a hairwash once a week and drawing and colouring for half an hour each day. Everything else remained the same.

Stage 2 – until I reached 20.8 kilos (3 stone 4 lb) – increased schoolwork, reading and Mum's visit to one hour each per day and Dad's to 20 minutes daily. Natalie was also allowed to visit once a week with Mum.

And so it went on with extra privileges at each stage. But it all came accompanied by the threat that if I lost weight at any point I would be fed through a tube.

I'd been told enough times about 'tube feeding' and it sounded terrifying. The mere thought of having a tube shoved up my nose and all the way down into my stomach made me gag. Worse still, it meant I'd have no control at all over the number of calories they were pumping inside me.

Mum and I had talked about tube feeding too. 'If you ever have to be tube-fed I won't be able to visit you,' she'd said. 'I couldn't face seeing you like that.'

The doctors at Hillingdon must have thought that the privileges they were offering plus the fear of tube feeding would be enough to make me eat. But they can't have dealt with anyone with such ruthless self-control before.

I decided in my head how much I would allow myself to eat, and then nothing more. And no amount of privileges or threats would make me change my mind. There was no way I was giving in just to have an extra half-hour's colouring or an extra half-hour with Mum. Hugging my mum? By then I could take it or leave it. That's what being locked up in hospitals had done to me.

I didn't even make it to Stage 4 and after my weight had crept out of the critical level to reach 21 kilos (3 stone 4 lb) it stayed pretty static until I left there.

All my meals were brought to me in my cubicle and served up on one of those narrow tables that swing across the bed. I wasn't even allowed to go for a shower or to the toilet, so my whole life was contained for three months within those cubicle walls.

It was cripplingly boring and enough to send anyone mad, let alone someone who was obviously struggling to keep their senses together, as I was at the time.

I guess they thought that if my life was so unstimulating I'd start to find food interesting and give in to it. But they hadn't reckoned on my cast-iron will.

For breakfast I would allow myself to eat a Weetabix with water and black tea. For lunch it would be half a jacket potato and dinner would be something like minced turkey. They made no effort to force me to eat and would just leave the food in front of me until the next meal if I hadn't touched it. Meal after meal I would pick at few vegetables or anything else I felt I was 'allowed', then leave the rest for hours on end until eventually it was cleared away.

I suppose they didn't feel the need to encourage or force me to eat because they thought the combination of privileges and punishments was enough.

So I sat there for hour after hour, day after day, my head aching with boredom, but still refusing to eat up all the food in front of me.

I'd sit and stare out of the window or peer through the gap in the curtains at the comings and goings of the nurses up and down the ward. But if one of them caught me looking she would just pull the curtains tight shut – looking out was far too much like entertainment.

Bed-wash in the morning, when the nurse would come round with a bowl of warm water and some soap, became one of the high points of my day. At least it was some human contact.

'Hello – do you like working in the hospital?' I'd ask my bed-wash nurse, in a desperate child's attempt to strike up a conversation. I'd do anything to make them stay for just 20 minutes and talk to me. Most of them were pretty on the ball, though, and knew I was just trying to relieve the boredom. And that was against the rules. So they'd just give me a friendly smile, finish the wash and walk away, leaving me in silence in my cubicle jail all over again.

When I arrived at Hillingdon I was still young enough to be scared about being told off by nurses and doctors. But as the weeks rolled on and I became more and more bored, I became rebellious and cheeky. I started getting off my bed to do star-jumps when no one was around. But I was usually caught by the nurses and sent back to bed.

One day, some charity workers came to our ward, handing out toys to all the kids. There were He Man and Action Man figures for the boys and Barbie dolls for the girls.

I was sitting in my cubicle, trying to hear what all the excitement was about, when a lady from the charity poked her head through my partially opened curtain and said, 'Hello, dear, would you like this?' She handed me the most beautiful Barbie I'd ever seen. She was wearing a pink ball gown and came with her own hair brush.

'Oh, thank you, she's lovely,' I murmured. And I'd never been so grateful for a present in my whole life.

She really was beautiful. I sat on my bed and brushed her long, blonde hair with the tiny pink hair brush and unfastened her clothes, then put them back on her again, until she looked perfect.

I felt so lucky. I had my very own doll to play with.

It was about half an hour later that Alison, a ward sister, came into the cubicle and saw me dancing my doll up and down the bedcovers.

'You're not allowed that,' she said, before walking over and snatching it from my hand. 'It's got to go.'

Hot tears swelled in my eyes as Alison stomped out of my cubicle, Barbie's glossy blonde hair bouncing on her shoulders as she disappeared from sight in the sister's hand. 'I hate you,' I gulped as she pulled the curtains shut behind her. And at that moment I did.

I was getting harder, tougher. They were treating me like a prisoner and I was starting to act like one.

I counted the hours until visits from Mum and Dad. They were the only thing that broke the boredom. I didn't normally have much to say when they were there but it felt good being near real people again.

Mum would come to see me every day. I used to look out of my bedroom window and wait for her Morris Minor to pull into the car park. Just seeing the familiar curve of its bonnet and knowing Mum was nearby made me feel better. But as soon as her allotted visiting time was up, that was it and she was sent packing again.

It was a very tough time for Natalie. That was when she learned to cook – and look after herself. Mum was so caught up in trying to get me better that it was hard for her to look out for Natalie too. Even now I think Nat hurts a lot when she remembers how she would have to walk home from school and cook her own dinner if Tony wasn't around. Then she'd spend the evening tidying the house and watching telly on her own until Mum got back from visiting me. She was trying so hard to be the perfect child, to make everyone else feel better in this awful situation – it was only later when her anger and resentment for all that came pouring out.

Dad used to visit too. Once he smuggled me in copies of the *Beano* and *Dandy*, which I'd loved reading at home. I lifted my blankets over the bed-table to create a den, then sat underneath reading the comics with a torch.

Yeah, I've fooled them. They won't know what I'm doing, I thought. But it was only a couple of nights before I was spotted, the comics were confiscated and Dad was banned from visiting me for the rest of my stay at Hillingdon.

They were incredibly strict there and Mum and Dad had to agree to their rules. In any case they were terrified that if they brought me home I would die.

The nurses were very tough on me too. One day I asked one of the agency nurses if I could have a bath. I knew I was chancing my arm but I was desperate. She let me walk all the way down the corridor on my own, which was a treat enough. Then, in the bathroom, I soaked for 20 minutes, feeling my weightless body resting effortlessly in the water.

But when Sister Alison came round and discovered what the agency nurse had done, she went mad. I never saw that nurse again and think she might have been sacked.

If I needed the toilet I had to ring a buzzer and a nurse would appear and snap at me, 'What do you want?' Five minutes later a bedpan might be brought.

One afternoon a nurse called Heather had gone off to get me a bedpan but after ten minutes she still hadn't reappeared. I was desperate for a wee and after another five minutes I couldn't hold it any longer. I picked up the bowl used for my bedbath every morning, squatted down and weed into it.

Sure enough, Heather chose that exact moment to walk back in. My cubicle was opposite the nurses' station and as she opened the curtains all the other ward staff could see me. They were giggling and nudging each other as I squatted there in full view. I felt so humiliated that I crawled on to my bed and cried.

Some people may find it difficult to believe that nurses could be unkind in the ways that I have described but I don't think they were nasty – they just didn't have any time for me. I was on a medical ward alongside kids with 'real illnesses' and they must have thought I was a self-indulgent little madam taking up a valuable bed. That's certainly how I felt they thought.

There was a boy in the cubicle opposite me with leukaemia and they must have made comparisons between us. He used to wave at me when he went past the window of my cubicle and apparently he wanted to come in and visit me but he wasn't allowed as it wasn't on my privileges list. Instead he made me a card and one of the nurses delivered it.

In the first few weeks I spent a lot of time crying for Mum, Dad and Natalie. But I'd already survived the Maudsley and I was getting tougher all the time.

Natalie wrote me a letter once and was telling me that she was totally in love with Marti Pellow, the lead singer of Wet Wet Wet. She copied out all the lyrics to their song 'Goodnight Girl'. It was in the charts at the time.

The night after I received Nat's letter I woke in the early hours and could hear the song playing quietly on the radio in the nurses' station. I lay there and thought about my love and promises – for Mum, for Natalie, for Dad.

Then I rang my buzzer. When the nurse came, looking

tired and a bit tetchy, I said, 'I want to get well – can you bring me a glass of milk, please?'

She returned with a large glass of milk and I drank the whole lot down in one go. It must have been a month since I'd drunk milk like that and it tasted good.

It was an amazing moment. That could have been my happy ending and this book would be over here. But it wasn't to be that simple. Next morning when I woke all I felt was guilt and self-loathing at having drunk the milk. It was clear to me I didn't want to get better that much.

I went back to refusing food, and spent more days and weeks watching time pass by outside my cubicle window. My weight had gone up a bit after I arrived at Hillingdon but once I felt they were trying to push it up too far I just refused more and more food.

I didn't hit a couple of stages on my chart, so – as threatened – out came their nasal tube. As soon as I saw a nurse carrying the long, white tube towards me one afternoon, I felt physically sick. At the side of my bed she coated the end of it in gloopy KY Jelly and then began to insert it into my nostril. The pain was acute.

'Keep swallowing, Nikki,' the nurse said as she thrust the tube further and further down. But I could feel it coming out through my mouth and I was gagging. There were huge globules of KY stuck at the back of my throat and I was crying, begging her to stop.

When she finally realised she couldn't get the tube any further down my throat, she whipped it back out, making me gag and choke. It was a size-10 tube – one of the large adult ones – so I begged them, if they had to do it, to use something smaller. In the end they agreed to one of the feeding tubes they use for babies.

When the nurse tried to insert that one it was only slightly less painful and I still cried as I felt it slip down into my stomach. Once it was inside me, the nurse then attached the tube to a bag of milk feed connected to a pump which began flooding the liquid into me. I pulled a hand mirror out of a drawer, opened my mouth and watched as the milky feed slipped down into my body. There was nothing I could do to stop it. I'd lost control and I was devastated.

I did soon start to do something, though. The next time they tried to tube-feed me, I started writhing around the bed, pushing the nurses away and clamping my hand over my nose. For 20 minutes I screamed and shouted, adamant I would not let them get the better of me again by tube-feeding me. Fighting made me feel good, as though I still had some control over my life, like I was still alive. But what happened next was to change all that.

I'd been lashing around so much on the bed, I hadn't seen another nurse enter the cubicle with a huge hypodermic needle in her hand. It was only when her hand was by my thigh and jabbing the point towards me that I had any clue what was happening.

'This will just help you sleep,' the nurse said as she broke the surface of my skin with the needle.

Maybe I should have screamed out in protest at this, the first of literally hundreds of times I would be beaten into chemical unconsciousness over the next few years. Maybe I should have fought harder at being treated like a troublesome zoo animal. Maybe I should have screamed as my last ounce of fight was being drugged out of me. But in reality all I thought was, Oh my God, I wonder how many calories are in that?

The sedative was of a thick, syrupy consistency. That has *sooo* got sugar in it, I thought, before I slumped backwards against my pillows, unable to care any more.

Clearly I'd become too big a problem for them. Pacifying me or negotiating with me had become too much bother, so they went for the easy option – a quick jab in the leg and a perfectly docile patient.

It was like something out of *One Flew Over The Cuckoo's Nest* – I was being drugged into submission. But for them it worked and meant they could at least get a nasal tube in quickly while I was out for the count.

I still ripped out a couple more nasal tubes during my time at Hillingdon but, by using sedatives and tube feeds, within three weeks they had lifted my weight out of the danger level. Even so, with it still hovering around 21 kilos (3 stone 4 lb), they realised the Hillingdon regime just wasn't working for me. They needed somewhere that could help me get to the root problem of my anorexia and try to bring an end to it. It was felt a medical ward wasn't the best place for that.

And so, at the beginning of April, I was transferred to a psychiatric unit for young people. My weight was still desperately low and getting better was a very long way away.

CHAPTER 8

COLLINGHAM GARDENS

'Celery? Yuk. Not even an anorexic who knows celery contains no calories at all likes celery!'

I turned my nose up in disgust at the first meal laid out in front of me at my new 'home'. Then, when no one was looking, I lifted my T-shirt with one hand and with the other hand slipped the celery beneath the waistband of my jeans and into my knickers. Done in a flash and no one had spotted a thing. This place was going to be a walk in the park.

It was 7 April 1992 and I'd been transferred straight from Hillingdon to Collingham Gardens Child and Family Centre, a psychiatric unit for children. Again, at that time I was the only kid there with an eating disorder, but at least they had the specialist expertise that might help me.

And, as I soon learned, they were wise to anorexics' food-dodging tricks. It was only half an hour after that first celery salad and my new key nurse, Erla, said I could go and play in the cosy room with some of the other young patients.

We were rolling over the sofas when I suddenly felt the stick of celery slide down my trouser leg and out on to the carpet. I kicked it behind the sofa and wandered off to the other side of the room as casually as I could. But Erla wasn't daft and within minutes she had found the offending item and knew exactly who was to blame. She pulled me to one side and knelt down, staring me straight in the eye. 'While you are here, young lady, you do not hide food. If you hide any item of food whatsoever your entire meal will be replaced and you'll have to start it all over again.'

I was terrified, both of Erla, a big, imposing woman who seemed to growl rather than speak, and the prospect of double portions for misbehaviour.

Until that point my first impressions of Collingham had been good. It was housed in one of those huge mansions that line the back streets of Earl's Court, west London.

One of the care assistants from Hillingdon, a lady called Pat, had taken me for a day visit before I was admitted properly. The other kids in there mainly had behavioural problems or learning disabilities. Some had been in care, others had been abused by their parents. But even though we'd all been through some really bad stuff in our lives, we still managed to have a good laugh together. We all kind of picked up why each of us was there without ever really discussing it, and we just got on with kids' stuff instead.

Everyone seemed a bit more normal than at the Maudsley. What a relief that was! Also, the Maudsley was a secure unit whereas at Collingham we weren't locked in and that gave it a far more casual atmosphere.

There were some really cool boys there too. I was a couple of weeks off my tenth birthday when I arrived and just beginning to realise boys could be nice to hang around with. There was Simon, who had been abused by his dad, and David, who had been thrown out of school for getting into trouble, and Mikey, who had behavioural problems. But none of that mattered. To me they were just fun and a bit cheeky and I could be a total tomboy hanging around with them.

At first I even quite liked the regime at Collingham. They started off by giving me meals like salad with a bit of bread and butter and I felt OK about that. They'd make up the calories with FortéCal, a glucose drink which contained 450 calories in each 200-millilitre bottle. But I was OK with that as I knew exactly what FortéCal contained – it didn't feel like anyone was trying to trick me into having more calories than I wanted.

I stopped having tantrums and became a lot calmer. I was happier because I felt I had some control again over what was going inside me.

But things went a bit wrong the day Mum and Natalie made their first visit to see me there. I had been in only a week and was having my lunch. They'd given me just a salad and everything was fine. But when the nurse brought over a Complan high-calorie build-up drink to go with it, I went potty.

'You've filled this mug up too far,' I screamed. 'Are you trying to con me? I'm not drinking it,' I yelled. 'You might as well take it away.'

I was still sitting there 40 minutes later when Mum and Nat arrived at the door of the unit. I heard a nurse saying to them, 'We're very sorry, Mrs Grahame, but I'm afraid Nikki has refused to eat her lunch, which means she won't be able to have any visitors this afternoon.'

A raging anger which had been lying inside me for months suddenly burst to the surface and I became like a demon. I screamed and swore at the nurses, waving my arms around like an out-of-control windmill. 'I hate you!' I shouted. 'You're all horrid. You won't let me see my mum. I hate you.'

One of the nurses walked slowly towards me, making soothing noises and holding her hands out, but I wasn't having any of it. I lashed out at her, kicking her shins and flailing my arms about.

I ran towards the stairs to try to get down to where Mum and Nat would be. But by now I was out of control and on reaching the top of the stairs I flung myself forwards, down the steep staircase. I don't know if I even thought about what I was doing – I just wanted my mum and I needed someone, anyone, to listen to me. I hurtled downwards until I rolled to a stop halfway down the steps, crying and shaking in a pathetic heap.

The nurses ran down to pick me up but I still wouldn't let them near me. I hate you!' I kept screaming. 'I *need* my mum.'

I smashed my head against the banister and pulled at my clothes and hair with my hands in a frenzy of screaming and sobbing. It took nearly a quarter of an hour for me to calm down enough for the nurses to be able to help me up the stairs and back to my cubicle.

Things were only going to get worse at Collingham, though. To begin with they must just have been getting me used to eating again because after the first fortnight the salads stopped and they started giving me the same food as all the other kids – and that was terrible.

Chips were on the menu twice a day. Now, I can understand why they did it. They were catering for children and their thinking was 'kids love chips'. Except me of course. I was the only one on the ward with an eating disorder and being given chips was about the worst thing I thought possible.

As soon as I smelt the deep-fat fryer warming up in the kitchen my stomach would turn in revulsion. Normally the chips were slapped on the plate with burgers or fish fingers or, when Erla was in charge, Cornish pasty! All that pastry as well as chips. It was foul.

My stance hardened. Now my day fell into a routine of meals that I would eat and those I would refuse. I would always eat breakfast because it was always the same, a bowl of cereal, a piece of toast and cup of tea. It was safe for me – no surprises.

After breakfast I had to have half an hour's bed rest. Like at Hillingdon, the staff knew I would take any opportunity to exercise, even if it meant just stepping on the spot in the corner of a room. And bed rest was the only way they could stop that.

Afterwards, I'd have time for a quick play with the other kids before snack time at 10.30. But I'd never eat that snack, which meant I'd have to sit there with it in front of me until lunchtime at 12.15, when they'd take it away. It was all part of a carefully worked-out plan. I'd realised that if I ate that snack – usually a Complan drink and a couple of biscuits – I'd then have to have another half an hour's bed rest, before just 45 minutes' play, then lunch. For the sake of that 45-minute play, it was not worth drinking a 450-calorie Complan drink. I might as well sit it out until lunchtime.

I rarely ate lunch either – again, it just wasn't worth it to me because lunch finished at one o'clock, followed by an hour of bed rest, then an hour of play before the afternoon snack at three. I wouldn't eat a full lunch in return for just one hour's play in the afternoon. No way.

I saw the afternoon snack differently. It was normally only a Complan build-up drink and a biscuit, followed by half an hour's bed rest, then two hours' play before supper. Two hours running around made eating the snack worthwhile. I'd use that two hours to stomp up and down the corridors or run around the garden, anything to burn up some calories. That playtime also provided some mental stimulation after having spent most of the day sitting at a table staring at food I was never going to eat.

By the evening meal I was usually back to not eating again. Dinner finished at quarter to seven, bed rest for an hour took it to quarter to eight and then bedtime was half past eight. Again, it just wasn't worth it to me and I might as well just sit in front of my untouched meal until bedtime.

I sat at my meal table for hours on end, bored out of my nut. Occasionally some of the nurses would try to encourage me to eat but most of them just ignored me – that's what they had been told to do as I wasn't supposed to get any interaction or attention until my plate had been cleared.

The Queen singer Freddie Mercury had died six months earlier and I'd been given the band's recently released *Greatest Hits Volumes I and II*. I was a massive fan of Queen – I always had been since Mum and Dad used to listen to their records at home when I was little. While I was at Collingham, Mum even took me on a day trip to lay flowers outside the house where Freddie had lived.

Every day at Collingham, to pass the time, I'd sit at the dinner table and go through in my head the lyrics of each Queen song in the exact order they appeared on the albums. I knew every single lyric to every single song. Lunchtime would start with 'Bohemian Rhapsody' running through my mind, then 'Another One Bites The Dust'. Often I'd still be sitting there three hours later in front of a cold plate of sausage and chips when 'One Vision' finally came to a crashing finale in my head.

But we did have good times at Collingham too. The manager there was called Paul Byrne and he was lovely. He took me under his wing and looked after me. He was good to me and for the first time in years I could laugh again. Paul played all those 'Dad' tricks that other kids got at home. Once I was in the bath and he dangled a broom down from the floor above and banged on the window. I nearly jumped out of my skin. Another time he put custard in my bed – it was disgusting but very funny. And he was always jumping out on me from behind curtains and doors.

Paul made Collingham fun. When he was around I could even forget about food for a while. But he was strict with me too and if I didn't eat he would really shout at me. 'Come on, Nikki, stop staring at your plate and eat.' But if I did eat it I got loads of extra treats. He'd get one of the nurses to take me to the pottery room or let me go with the other kids when they walked down to the local shop for a magazine.

One day, he said if I ate everything they gave me until Wednesday lunchtime he'd take me to the zoo. I did it and he took me. It was brilliant.

There was a really cosy day room at Collingham with amazing board games and a Nintendo and there was also a classroom where kids who were well enough had lessons. To help us with our French lessons Paul fixed up for us all to go on a day trip to Boulogne. It was so exciting going over on the ferry and trying out our 'Bonjours' on every shop owner we met.

The only downside for me that day was the food. All eight of us piled into a restaurant and of course everyone except me instantly ordered burger and chips. I couldn't face the burger and thought omelette at least sounded a bit healthier. But when it arrived it was the size of a dustbin lid and oozing bright-yellow grease.

Paul took one look at my plate, then at my face and laughed out loud. 'Serves you right for trying to be smart and not having burger like the rest of us,' he chuckled. 'You can eat the lot now!' But he didn't make me eat it all – so long as he knew I was trying to eat he never pushed me too far.

Another time we went on a camping holiday in the New Forest, like I'd done at the Maudsley. We had a camp fire, made dens and bridges and one of the nurses dressed up as a ghost. It was so much fun. Best of all, I got away with eating hardly anything.

After I had been in Collingham for a few months I had to move rooms and share with a girl called Lucy. I'm still not sure why exactly she was there but she was pretty strange. She was a real goody two-shoes and would grass me up to the nurses at any opportunity.

For months I'd been getting away with offloading loads of food on to the boys' plate at mealtimes. Whenever it was lamb chops, say, I'd slice off all the fat and lob it on to my mate Lee's plate and he'd swallow the lot. It was a perfect system. But once Lucy saw what I was up to she wasted no time telling the nurses. Paul came in and screamed at me, 'What do you think you are doing, Nikki? Well, you won't be getting away with any more of your little tricks.'

I was so angry at Lucy for dropping me in it and we didn't speak for days. But after a while we made up and sometimes we even got on OK. Once I persuaded her to get up with me really early in the morning to jump out on the nurses turning up for their morning shift. We hid at the bottom of the stairs at the crack of dawn to play our trick and when we leapt out on the nurses as they came in, they all screamed. Once they'd recovered from the shock they saw the funny side. They were cool. And I think they must have realised there weren't a lot of other laughs for us kids in that unit.

Collingham was only open on weekdays but at first I wasn't trusted to go home at weekends, so Paul would drive me back to Hillingdon Hospital instead. On a Friday evening, as we sat in traffic jams in the Sunshine Variety Bus, I'd make him listen to my Queen tapes.

The weekends back at Hillingdon were grim. I'd spend hours tidying up the playroom because it was good exercise and something to do, then I'd lie on my bed watching Queen videos and singing to myself, trying to kill the hours until it was time to return to Collingham on Monday morning.

At Collingham I had my own bedroom. It was quite big and I decorated it with colour posters of Freddie Mercury I'd bought in the Virgin Megastore and my collection of helium balloons. Every time Mum visited I'd drag her out to a card shop for another balloon. I was also really into stickers and had them all round my room – the furry ones and scratch 'n' sniff ones that I got out of Frosties packets (without eating the Frosties, of course).

The only problem with my room was that it was right next to the nurses' station, which had a massive observation window so that they could keep an eye on me at any time of day or night. I also had to sleep with the door open in case I was up to any exercise or being sick. That meant I had no privacy, even when I was sleeping. It was like living in a goldfish bowl.

After I'd been at Collingham for two months, Mum was allowed to come in and sit with me during meals. They were trying to work out some kind of strategy to help her cope with me when I eventually went home. Everyone was just terrified that otherwise, as soon as I was discharged I'd just go straight back to my tricks and tantrums, Mum wouldn't be able to cope and I'd get really sick again.

First of all at mealtimes Karl, my clinical nurse, sat down with us. But once he was happy that Mum could be strict with me if she needed to be, he would leave us alone. Of course as soon as he was gone I started pushing my luck again. I'd still try to wrap Mum around my little finger.

But I was making progress and my weight did start increasing. In my mind, though, I still firmly believed being skinny was perfect and that was still the way I wanted to be.

What the doctors didn't know was that I had been using my time wisely at Hillingdon and Collingham, devouring every women's magazine and newspaper article I could find about losing weight. I'd become a child expert on food and nutrition and could recite the calorific values of hundreds of different products. And I'd worked out exactly how much exercise would burn off how many calories too. I had an almost encyclopaedic knowledge of slimming.

So when I did start to go home at weekends I was already several steps ahead of Mum – even though I was only ten. The moment I arrived home on a Friday evening I'd have a set amount in my head that I would allow myself to eat that weekend. And no matter what instructions Mum had been given by Collingham, it wouldn't make any difference.

I was tricky too. One weekend at home I invited my old boyfriend Nicholas Richards round for tea. We'd been at Hillside School together and written to each other during my stays at the Maudsley, Hillingdon and Collingham. I was so looking forward to Nicholas coming round but I still couldn't help obsessing about how to reduce the calorie count of our tea.

'Oh, but Mum, can we have Quavers instead of the normal Salt 'n' Shake crisps? I love Quavers,' I said. Mum was just delighted to think I was eating crisps. What she didn't know is that a packet of Quavers is 85 calories and Salt 'n' Shake is 146. Mum could be such a soft touch.

And I'd still argue with her about everything she prepared for dinner. If she tried fish fingers, for instance, it would be the same old argument.

'Collingham say you have to eat three of them, Nikki,' she would say.

'Fine,' I'd reply like a right little cow. 'But if you give me three I won't eat anything. If you give me two I'll eat them all.'

What could she do? I had her over a barrel.

Mum was still very brittle. She would cry a lot about

what I was doing to myself and everything that had happened. I may only have been ten years old but I could sense she was weak and I used that to my advantage.

Another thing Mum was always trying to feed me was waffles. I hated them and would squeeze them on to kitchen paper to blot all the oil off before I ate them. Mum would huff and puff about it but it was either that or they went straight in the bin. I'd hide food in my knickers too and on a bad day there would be plates thrown at the walls again as well.

I think I regressed whenever I went home because it was easier to bully Mum than the nurses. I knew Mum was desperate for me to eat – my life depended on it and by now she felt hers did too. But in hospital the nurses, even the nice ones, weren't as emotionally connected. Whether I ate or not, at the end of their shift they would go home and put their feet up in front of *Corrie*.

Because I liked Collingham, though, my mood was much better and I was far calmer there than at home or Hillingdon. The only tantrum I ever had was the day Mum and Natalie were turned away at the door. They never gave me sedatives or tube-fed me there, so I must have been far easier for the nurses to handle than I'd been at Hillingdon.

Collingham was a very warm, caring place and I liked it for that. It didn't necessarily help me sort out my anorexia but maybe that would only happen when I was ready. But my weight did gradually creep upwards.

I was allowed home for Christmas and I knew I was only weeks away from getting out permanently. I still didn't want to eat but I knew I had to go through the motions to get everyone off my back.

They finally discharged me on 14 January 1993. I

weighed 28.5 kilos (4 stone 7 lb) and was 132 centimetres (4 feet 4 inches) tall.

As Mum helped me load my bags into the boot of her car outside the unit, I felt I had won another battle. I was being allowed home – free at last. But to me it was clear that even if victory in this battle was mine, there was still a long, painful war ahead.

CHAPTER 9

TOO UNCOOL
FOR SCHOOL

'Ninety-eight, 99, 100.' I took a quick breath of air as I finished my second set of sit-ups, then jumped off the floor and started pacing up and down the room.

It was three o'clock on a freezing February morning and it was still pitch-black outside my bedroom window. But, like the night before, and the night before that, I'd been awake for the past three hours exercising silently while Mum and Tony slept in the room next to mine.

I'd start with sit-ups, then walk up and down the room until my head spun. Then I'd do lunges and star-jumps, although they were more tricky as sometimes the floor shook and Mum would wake up. My bed looked inviting and sometimes I felt so tired I could die but I had to keep going, had to keep burning off those calories.

As soon as I returned home, away from the watchful eyes at Collingham, I had thrown myself back into an almost constant exercise regime. Again, I couldn't even sit down in front of the telly in the evenings. Instead I'd stand in the corner of the room, stepping from one leg to the other.

I'd gone back to Hillside School but was finding it really tough to settle back in. I didn't feel I belonged there – or anywhere – any more. I'd only just got things back on an even keel after the Maudsley when I'd had to leave for Collingham. And this time it was even harder to fit back in.

Before, I'd always been a leader in my group but all the friendships had changed since I'd been away. There was a girl called Amanda Turbeville, who had joined the school while I was away. Joanne and Emily and Erin were all hanging around with her now and I was totally left out. That's what it's like with girls at that age – you're either in or you're out and I was most definitely out.

Maybe my old friends thought I was just a bit too weird or uncool to hang around with now. I don't know what it was but I felt rejected all over again.

Mum told me to stick at it and things would get better, so I kept turning up, hanging around the edge of my old group and waiting for acceptance. And waiting.

It didn't help that I was really behind in my schoolwork too. We'd had lessons at the Maudsley and Collingham but they were only really giving us a basic education as best they could in the situation. I was never destined to be a great academic. I'm more of a doer than a thinker and it didn't really bother me that I was behind except it was just something else which marked me out as different.

As the months rolled by Mum would encourage me to ask friends round for tea but there really weren't many girls for me to invite. Then I made one new friend, a girl called Lena, who was Russian and had just moved to the country and couldn't speak English very well. She was stunning, with long, dark-brown hair, but the other girls were mean to her because she was different. We were both outsiders and clung together. Lena would come round my house after school and we would play games and make circuses. We kept each other going for a long time.

Things at home were tough too. While I had been in Collingham, Mum had moved into a new house in Tolcarne Drive, five minutes' walk from our old home. It was a nice house and Mum had bought me a lovely new bed and decorated the walls with Forever Friends teddy-bear wallpaper and curtains. But I still desperately missed my old bedroom and our old house.

Tony was living with us permanently now, which also bothered me as it was just someone else battling for Mum's attention.

Everything felt wrong. Mum was upset too as she knew in her heart that I'd been happier at Collingham than I was at home. It was true. Collingham had given me a stability that I didn't feel at home. And despite the bad times I'd had fun there too. There wasn't much of that at home.

I was continuing as an outpatient at Collingham, which meant once a fortnight Mum and I would get on the tube down to Earl's Court for a weigh-in. Also, once or twice a month, I was having outpatient psychiatric treatment with Dr Matthew Hodes at St Mary's Hospital's Department of Child Psychiatry at Paddington Green. I hated those sessions – just another nosy parker asking me a load of questions I didn't want to answer. Sometimes I wouldn't even sit down in his room.

We had family therapy sessions too. Natalie had to take afternoons off school for them, which she hated too – to her it was just another example of me causing more upset in her life.

For about six months I trundled on at a fairly steady weight. I was still exercising and very fussy about what I would agree to eat, but at least I wasn't losing a lot of weight.

If it was a meal I 'allowed' myself, like two fish fingers and one potato, things were usually fine. But if Mum made something with more fat, like macaroni cheese, it was back to the same old tears, screaming and tantrums. She wasn't allowed to fry anything and pastry was a definite no-no. It must have been a nightmare for her every single evening. Before Mum even turned the oven on I would demand to know what she was planning to make. Then there would be the lengthy period of negotiation until we found some way of cooking it that we could agree on.

Collingham had left Mum with strict instructions about how much I should eat every day. But I knew she would bend the rules so long as I was getting some calories every mealtime. I was all too aware that her greatest fear was me throwing my plate at the wall or simply refusing to eat anything. I used that fear to blackmail her into giving me my own way. Once Mum started preparing the meal, I would stand behind her supervising, watching every single ingredient go in and calculating the calories in my head. But at least I wasn't losing weight. And my mood was a bit brighter during that spring too. Things settled down at school a bit in the early summer and I even got invited to a few of the girls' birthday parties.

But shortly after that, things took a turn for the worse again. Everyone around me suddenly started growing up – and I was being left behind.

'Have you started yet?' a girl in my class asked me as we sat in the playground one morning break time. It was the same conversation all the girls in my class had been having for the last couple of months – periods, time of the month, 'coming on'. They couldn't shut up about it – they were obsessed.

'Er, no, not yet,' I replied, looking intently at my scuffed school shoes.

The doctors had told me that my puberty might be severely delayed by my anorexia. At first it hadn't bothered me. Who'd want to go through that yukky business every month anyway? But as more girls in my class began to have this mysterious experience and turned into young women I felt more and more of an outsider.

Then at PE I noticed how loads of them were starting to get pudgy bits around their chests – they were growing boobs. They'd arrive at school on Monday mornings wearing bras, the tell-tale straps showing through their white cotton school shirts.

'Are you still wearing a vest, Nikki?' Amanda asked one warm day, peering at my childish white vest through my summer blouse. I was mortified. My chest was still as flat as a pancake.

That Saturday Mum took me to British Home Stores and bought me a little cami top which I wore just to make myself feel better. By now I was 11 and wanted boobs and periods. I wanted to be normal but the doctors were warning me that, because of the ramifications of anorexia, it might not happen for years, if ever. In the meantime I had to continue living in the body of a child.

I started slipping back mentally and physically. I could feel it sweeping over me over a few weeks. I felt so isolated again. I became quieter and introverted and as hard as Mum tried to reach me by talking to me and trying to comfort me, there was nothing she could do. I dealt with my torment the only way I knew how – more exercise and less food.

As soon as I got home from school I would lock myself in my bedroom. Sometimes I'd lie on the bed and cry. Other times I'd just exercise – it was the only thing that made me feel better.

The dining-table screaming matches escalated again. Each mealtime started in the same way. Mum, Tony, Natalie and I would be sitting down together but Mum would barely be able to concentrate on her own food as she would desperately be trying not to take her eyes off me for a moment in case the food started disappearing down my top or trousers.

I'd begin by pushing the food around my plate and separating it into piles so nothing touched anything else. Then the food would just sit there getting colder and colder while I stared silently at the wall or floor, withdrawing further and further into myself.

Mum would beg me, 'Please eat it, Nikki. You said you'd eat this. Please?'

As the minutes passed she would become more forceful. 'Look, if you don't eat, you'll have lost weight when you go for your weigh-in next week and they won't let you home again. You'll be sent back to Hillingdon Hospital.'

Sometimes that threat would work, because I was still haunted by the regime at Hillingdon and hated the thought of going back there.

I began drinking litres and litres of water and would put bars of soap in my pockets to make me heavier for my fortnightly weigh-ins at Collingham. As long as I could get away with these tricks there was less need to eat at home.

But soon, even the threat of Hillingdon meant nothing to me. I wouldn't even look up when Mum mentioned being sent back there. There wouldn't even be an eyelid flicker. I don't care about Hillingdon, I thought. I don't care about anything. I don't even want to be alive, to go through this, any more.

Tony, too, tried hard to make me eat, praising me when I did eat a mouthful, persuading me when I wouldn't. But there must have been loads of times when he thought he'd wandered into a total nightmare.

After half an hour or so Tony and Natalie would drift off into the other room, leaving Mum and me sitting there, my plate still piled up between us. Some evenings it felt like we were enemies on either side of a battlefield. And sure as hell I wasn't going to be the one to give in first.

Things got so bad that after a couple of months Mum made me eat my dinner wearing just my knickers so she could tell if I was hiding food. I felt the cold really badly then because I was so skinny and I would be covered in goosebumps, but it was the only way she could see what I was doing.

An hour or more would drag past and still I'd refuse to eat. That was when Mum would sometimes lose it with me and start shouting at me in her frustration. 'Just eat it, Nikki!' she'd scream. 'You're killing yourself and you're expecting me to sit back and watch you.'

Once she had started I'd join in too, screaming and lashing out at her. 'I'm not fucking eating it. Understand?' I yelled back. 'I don't want your food. You can fucking stuff it.'

Even after I had finished my food, or the whole thing had been abandoned, I'd then have to sit in front of Mum for an hour in case I was sick.

If I'd eaten everything, I'd be allowed out to see Lena and some of the other kids from our road who used to hang around on their bikes. But if I felt I'd eaten too much I'd make my friends stand and wait as I vomited it all up.

Other times I just ran out of the house straight after dinner, before Mum could stop me, and threw up against someone's garden wall. One night she tore round the streets in her slippers looking for me by following a trail of vomit.

I was never a bulimic, though – someone who constantly controls their weight through vomiting. For me, being sick was simply a last resort if I'd been made to eat something that I really couldn't cope with.

I knew Mum was finding it draining because I was constantly outwitting her. She was truly stuck in the middle. Collingham had given her strict guidelines about what I *should* and *shouldn't* do. But I was giving her ultimatums about what I *would* and *wouldn't* do. 'It's your choice, Mum,' I'd say. 'I'll either eat what I agree to or nothing at all – you decide.'

Collingham had told Mum that if she allowed me to leave food on my plate she was helping me kill myself. So every time I didn't eat a full meal, which was most days, she was consumed with guilt.

Mum was trying to please everyone and constantly feeling like she was failing everyone.

Her every attempt to outwit me failed. Collingham had told her to buy double-cream milk to help build me up. She knew I would point-blank refuse to drink it, so she had to pour it all into semi-skimmed milk bottles when I wasn't around. But she didn't get away with that for long as I could tell the milk was thicker and creamier and it made me gag. Then she tried buying higher-calorie Tesco cakes and putting them in boxes of McVities low-fat cakes.

'These don't taste the same, Mum,' I said after the first mouthful. It was like I could taste calories and she couldn't get away with anything.

Mum was tired of the constant battle. Every day she was reliving the same nightmare but there was no alternative. If she gave in to me, the chances were I'd die. I was making her life a misery.

All the counsellors had told Mum she had to be strong for me. Because while anorexics like to think they are in control, their behaviour is actually totally out of control. And that is why they need to feel their family is strong, like a fortress protecting them.

Deep down, I guess I did want Mum to be strong to protect me. But I also wanted her to be a push-over, to give in to my outrageous food demands and tempers. It was like I was constantly testing Mum to see exactly how strong she was. And sometimes she did cry, and sometimes she did lose it. And then I could see the despair in her eyes as she realised she wasn't being as strong as she ought.

Natalie was becoming so angry that everything at home revolved around me and what I had or hadn't eaten. Mum's every waking thought was consumed with me and whether I'd live or die. There wasn't much time or energy left for Natalie and she resented me like hell for that. She started rebelling in her own desperate bid for attention. She would be rude and stroppy to Mum and would stay out late, giving Mum even more to worry about. Natalie and I were getting on worse than ever, bickering all the time. Our house was so full of anger and violence that it was impossible to believe that we'd once been so happy. How could things have slipped this far?

During that autumn my weight started falling quite quickly as I became more and more withdrawn and unhappy. I'd slipped back into this hellish cycle where I could only make myself feel better by not eating, but not eating was just making me feel weaker and more sick again.

I began bunking off school and hanging around the shops. When Mum found out she went mad. It didn't stop me, though. I was angry, threatening suicide, rebelling and being a complete pain in the arse.

The fortnightly trips to Collingham to get weighed became even more of an ordeal. I'd tried bars of soap but now I'd fill my pockets with paperweights and anything else heavy I could find to boost my weight. But even the combination of that and drinking several litres of water wasn't enough to disguise the fact that it was slipping dangerously low.

At that point I think Mum in a way gave up on me – she was exhausted and just felt there was nothing she more could do. Then one day in December I simply refused to go to see Dr Hodes at Collingham and be weighed. Mum tried persuading me, then we started screaming at each other, but still I wouldn't budge. I refused to leave my bedroom.

'Please come, Nikki,' Mum begged. 'Otherwise they'll send you back to hospital and it's Christmas soon.'

'I don't care!' I screamed. 'I hate you, I hate hospital and I hate my life – I wish I was dead.'

I'd been saying things like that more and more, talking

about killing myself. I don't know whether I seriously meant it at that age or even understood what death meant. But I certainly knew I wasn't happy in the life I was in.

Mum had made an appointment for me at Collingham and I knew I would be readmitted. I had no idea how long I'd be away for this time, so the night before the appointment I persuaded Mum to let Lena and my other friends Suzanne and Jennifer come round for a Christmas party sleepover.

We lay in our sleeping bags on the lounge floor, chatting and giggling. At times like that I almost felt normal.

When Mum and Tony went to bed we lit a cigarette and passed it round between us. I knew it could be months before I saw my friends again and there was nothing I could do about it. I was being thrown along by events out of my control.

The next morning Lena, Suzanne and Jennifer went home and Mum helped me pack a suitcase for my stay in hospital.

As we walked down to the station I looked at all the toys and decorations in the shop windows. It would be Christmas in a fortnight but try as I might I couldn't see much to celebrate.

CHAPTER 10

RAW ANGER

'Here we go again,' I mumbled to myself as I forced my emaciated frame back up the steps at Collingham Gardens.

It was a bitterly cold day and the gusts of wind stabbed at my body, now unprotected by even the merest layer of fat.

There was a huge Christmas tree in the entrance hall at the unit, and tinsel neatly wrapped around the staircase, but I was long past enjoying that sort of thing. I was down to just 23 kilos (3 stone 8 lb) and didn't care about anything much at all.

I was put straight on total bed rest and not even allowed to walk down the corridor without permission. Yet it was almost a relief to be back. It felt like coming home. Again, someone else was going to take control for me for a while. All I had to do was comply.

And it was good to see Paul Byrne again, even though I knew he and the others were going to make me eat. A few days before Christmas there was a big dinner for all the kids and they made me finish the lot – turkey, sprouts and stuffing. It was agonising.

As Christmas got closer all the other kids gradually drifted away with their parents and the unit prepared to shut down for the holiday. But there was no way they would allow me home for a fortnight. Instead I was transferred to the Chelsea and Westminster Hospital to be kept under observation. I was allowed home for just Christmas Day and Boxing Day.

Mum and Tony came to collect me in the car on Christmas Eve. It was another bitterly cold afternoon but when we arrived at our front door I didn't even step inside. Instead I started running up and down the road to burn off some of the calories they'd been ramming down me at Collingham. It might have been Christmas for other people, but to me it was just a chance to exercise.

When Mum finally persuaded me to go inside, I stood shivering next to the open fire in the living room, keeping the exercise going by rocking from one leg to the other.

Mum looked at me in despair. 'I see nothing has changed then, Nikki,' she said.

Christmas was OK. It was good to be home and to see my friends, but hanging over me all the time was the thought that I had to go back to the Chelsea and Westminster after Boxing Day – and there they were going to make me eat again.

Back in Collingham after New Year, things weren't as good as they had been during my first stay.

A lot of the old nurses had moved on and the new ones weren't as much fun. Many of the kids were new too. They were a nice group, but they weren't my real mates. Yet again I felt like everything had changed around me and I was the odd one out. That was becoming such a familiar feeling. At first it hit me hard, so I had a wobbly start back at Collingham, exercising furiously whenever I could until I dropped another kilo.

I'd heard the name 'Rhodes Farm' bandied about for the past couple of years by other anorexics and experts, especially when I was at Collingham. People always spoke of it with a certain awe. The place was regarded as the Alcatraz of anorexic centres – no one got out of there without being made to put on weight.

'I'll never go to Rhodes Farm,' I said confidently. 'Not me.' Cockily, I thought I'd always be able to outwit the system.

At Collingham they had me straight back into counselling sessions too, which I still loathed. One session I spent the whole hour listening to my Walkman rather than answer their boring questions.

I made the decision I just had to get out of there as quickly as possible, which meant going along with whatever they wanted me to do – and that was eat. So I started eating whatever they put in front of me and gave myself a break from my constant battling.

I began to make some progress, clearing my plate at mealtimes and my mood improved too. And the less miserable I felt, the more inclined I was to eat. And the more I ate, the better I felt. Somehow I'd drifted out of the bad cycle I'd got stuck in at home and was in a better phase. I even started concentrating more in classes.

Paul said if I could reach 34 kilos I would be allowed home at weekends again. The alternative was misery weekends at the Chelsea and Westminster, and I'd have done anything to avoid those.

So I pretty much complied and ate what was put in front of me, and my weight crept up. Of course there were still times when I'd try to hide food but there were none of my tantrums and plate-throwing routines. I was much calmer at Collingham.

There were other treats too if I ate my meals. One day Paul took me shopping to Kensington High Street because I'd been making such good progress. For some reason we wandered into a Thorntons Chocolate shop – bizarre, I know! They had a raffle on and Paul got me a ticket. And what do you reckon? I won an Easter egg and it was huge. I felt so proud when I carried it back into Collingham. I didn't eat it of course – I just kept it in my room – but it was great to look at.

Although I was eating more, I was still obsessed with exercise. Mum would come and visit me at weekends and if I'd been eating OK she would be allowed to take me shopping. But what Paul and the other nurses didn't know was that once we were out of the front door I'd break into a run, desperate to burn off a few calories. Mum would be left trailing behind, trying to keep up.

But I knew she wouldn't shop me to the nurses as that would mean she'd be barred from visiting. So again I had her over a barrel.

By the spring I had reached that golden 34 kilos (5 stone 5 lb) and was allowed to spend weekends at home again. But of course it was back to dodging food and exercising every weekend. If I didn't take every opportunity to do that at home I'd feel guilty, as though I'd failed in some way.

Even when Mum came to collect me on the tube I'd run to the top of each escalator at the station for the exercise.

'Please don't do that, Nikki,' she would say.

'Oh, don't worry about it,' I'd tell her. 'Let's just get home.'

In April it was my thirteenth birthday. Hurray, I was a teenager at last. Still no boobs or periods but I felt sure they had to come soon.

Just after my birthday I was allowed a weekend at home, so to celebrate I went with Lena and Jennifer to an under-18s disco. It was brilliant.

Still in a better frame of mind, I continued to gain weight. They were giving me enormous meals – plates piled high with chips, and custard on every pudding. There was no choice but to eat them. If I didn't eat it or tried hiding anything then I'd just get the whole lot replaced and would have to start all over again.

On 21 June I hit my target of 38.2 kilos (6 stone). I was 142.2 centimetres (4 feet 8 inches) tall. Two days later I was discharged and allowed home.

Mum and Dad had been having loads of sessions with the doctors at Collingham while I was there about how they were going to prevent me losing all the weight again the minute I came out. They were trying to build Mum up, to teach her how to be strong with me when I was in a rage or negotiating myself down to one cream cracker for my dinner.

Mum had to make it clear to me that she was never going to let me die. The doctors thought that once I truly understood this I would feel more secure and stop trying to control situations myself by refusing to eat. It was a good idea in theory. But in practice, no chance.

When I got home the weight fell off faster than ever before. My willpower kicked in and just wouldn't let me give in to eating anything more than an allowance set by myself. It was like everything that had gone before, with bells on. It was during this autumn that my illness reached its peak.

There were still some meals that Mum could cook me which I was OK about. A slice of roast beef in a gravy from a packet was allowed because I knew there was 120 calories in the gravy and roast beef was only 100. With that I'd have one potato cut into four (120 calories) and carrots (virtually none).

I remember thinking to myself, I wish I could eat food, not numbers. But I couldn't. My entire life was dictated by calorific values.

Mum was trying to get tougher with me and would make lasagne (500 calories) or macaroni cheese (500 calories) as 'punishment meals' if she thought I'd been hiding food or exercising a lot. But I knew exactly how many calories a lasagne contained and would just go mental about it.

So it was the same old battles. Several times I scalded myself on my stomach when I tried to hide spag Bol and other food down my knickers. Another time Mum found pasta inside my school sock. Most of my clothes got food stains on them somewhere before Mum returned to insisting I ate in my knickers.

I threw Complan drinks in the plant pots, shoved food behind the cooker until we got rats, and would often fill my mouth with food but then spit it out when no one was looking.

If Mum even considered giving me the kind of portions I had meekly eaten up while at Collingham, the whole lot went straight over the dining room wall. Poor

Mum spent so many evenings wiping off all the pasta sauce and grease.

I was being sick, throwing food around, hiding food and doing everything I possibly could to get my weight back down again.

Mum looked so sad and so hopeless. But I still thought this was all her fault and she deserved my outbursts – she shouldn't be making me eat when I didn't want to.

Our neighbours just hated us because of all the screaming and shouting. They kept complaining about the noise but they were the least of our worries. It was a house so full of anger that nothing would keep us quiet.

I was angry at Mum, angry at Natalie and angry at myself. Some days I would hit my stomach again and again, screaming, 'I'm so fat. I hate myself.'

All the time my weight was dropping perilously low.

I was still attending outpatient appointments at Collingham, but even they were unsure how to save me. Whatever good work they did while I was in there was all undone immediately I returned home.

By the start of October my weight was down to 29 kilos (4 stone 8 lb). I'd lost 9 kilos (1 stone 6 lb) in just four months. I was sullen, spiteful, having temper tantrums and rowing with everyone. I was vomiting up food soon after meals, and even several hours later if I felt the need.

Mum says the haunted, troubled look had taken over my face again and she gave up the fight herself – she couldn't see anything left that she could do to help. Then, one morning at the start of October, she told me we were going to an appointment at Great Ormond Street Hospital for Sick Children in central London. Great Ormond Street is a general hospital, I thought. This will be a walk in the park! I was so angry inside and so full of pain that I wasn't bothered what happened to me next. It couldn't be any worse than the present.

On 16 October 1995 Mum, Tony and I trooped up to the Mildred Creak Unit at Great Ormond Street, which specialised in psychiatric and eating disorders. When we walked in, it looked more like a youth hostel than a hospital – it was really cosy with posters on the walls and lots of armchairs. A group of kids were sitting around having their afternoon snack and chatting.

The nurse took me into a side room before guiding Mum and Tony down a corridor away from me. She returned a few minutes later with a glass of lemon squash and a couple of biscuits.

'I've brought you this for your afternoon snack, Nikki,' she said.

I took one glance, smirked at her and replied, 'No thanks, I'm going home soon.'

How wrong I was – it was to be almost three years of pain, sadness, anger and loneliness before I properly returned home once more.

CHAPTER 11

DEATH
PACT

I'd been at Great Ormond Street Hospital for about a
week when Nina arrived. Tall and super-skinny, with
dark-brown hair which fell either side of her angular face
in long plaits, she looked amazing.

She was dressed really grungily in brown corduroy
trousers and a Radiohead T-shirt. She was so severely
anorexic and so cool. I was desperately jealous. Nina was
the first anorexic I had ever met and to finally find someone
else who felt and thought like I did was incredible. In the
four years I'd spent at the Maudsley, Hillingdon and
Collingham, I'd always been the only anorexic. That had
just made me feel even more of an outsider.

So meeting Nina was fantastic. She was like me, but
better, because she was skinnier. Nina was 12, just a year
younger than me, and we became best friends instantly. We
thought we'd be soul mates for life. The staff put us in the
same room and that first night we stayed up talking for
hours, sharing our secret thoughts and dreams. It was

obvious to us that we both had the same problem, although we didn't really discuss it then or later.

It was just as well I found a friend, though, because the rest of the kids on that ward were, quite frankly, nuts. They weren't anorexic but they were some of the most seriously messed-up kids in Britain at the time. What I didn't realise then was that I too probably qualified as seriously messed-up. But all I could see was myself surrounded by total oddballs. Sometimes it was funny the way people behaved but other times it was just horribly scary.

At one end of the ward there was a girl called Isobel who spent every day propped up in a big wheelchair. She was very pretty but she didn't speak or communicate with the outside world at all. She needed to be fed through a nasal tube, was incontinent and had to be carried or pushed in a wheelchair everywhere she went.

But the incredible thing was that there was nothing physically wrong with her. Nothing! What she had was a psychiatric problem called Pervasive Refusal Syndrome, in which kids just shut their body down and go back to being babies. When her parents came to visit she would lie there and scream and scream. Isobel was at Great Ormond Street for two and a half years, then one day, all of a sudden, she started talking and walking. She returned home and went back to school. It was unbelievable.

Then there were a couple of kids at the Mildred Creak Unit with Attention-Deficit Hyperactivity Disorder (ADHD) – to me they just seemed incredibly naughty and would run up and down the corridor screaming and shouting at all times of the day and night.

Then there was a great big fat boy called Jonathan who we

used to call Pugsley after the character in *The Addams Family*. He used to lie in bed all day and the nurses would have to bring his food to him because he claimed he couldn't move. They even had to wheel him into the schoolroom.

And there was another boy called Shane. He had this weird thing going on in his head where he claimed he couldn't see or walk. I used to fight with him all the time. I could tell he was a liar and couldn't see why everyone made such a fuss about him. When I saw him crawling past my room for a wee, I'd follow him down to the toilets, then look under the door and see him standing up for a pee. I knew I was right.

Honestly, these kids were nuts and sometimes when they were having fits or tantrums it was terrifying. I'd come from a pretty ordinary middle-class home in a nice area with nice friends and there I was in a scene like something in a horror film. Often I felt Nina and I were the only sane ones in there. Although looking back, we probably had a lot of problems ourselves.

At first they only gave me portions I was happy about, so I pretty much ate what was served up to me. My first dinner there, the day I arrived, was spaghetti hoops (a Great Ormond Street speciality), mashed potato (another of their favourites), one sausage and for pudding a fruit salad. So, although that was a lot more than I'd been eating recently, it was still bearable.

After dinner, one of the nurses searched my bags for laxatives, which some anorexics use to flush food through the body, and razor blades, in case I was thinking of killing myself.

Breakfast the next morning was OK too – one Weetabix, a piece of toast and a cup of tea.

I felt I was doing really well and told myself I was fine again now. They should let me home in two days, I thought. But if they don't, I'll start refusing things. What I didn't realise at first was that they were just warming me up with small portions and there was no question of them letting me home for quite some time. When I saw how wrong I was I began to refuse food.

All of the kids in the unit would sit around the dining table together, watched by a nurse. There would be Isobel with her drip feed and Pugsley Boy Jonathan, whose bed had to be wheeled right up to the table. Every mealtime would be the same. 'Come on, you need to make a start, Nikki,' the nurse would say over and over. But I'd just carry on sitting there, staring miserably at my plate and shaking my head.

I'd eat on Mondays because afterwards I'd be allowed down to Radio GOSH, the hospital's station. But other days I just wasn't interested.

The policy at Great Ormond Street was that I had to stay at the table until I had eaten everything on my plate. I wasn't allowed into the schoolroom or day room until it had all gone.

If, after a couple of hours, I was still refusing to eat, everything left would get carried over to the next meal. So if I refused a snack, later on I'd have to have lunch *and* a snack. And if I refused lunch as well, that evening they would give me dinner, lunch and a snack.

If it got to bedtime and I still hadn't eaten anything, I'd got away with it – and I did. But then they'd threaten me that if I did the same the following day I would be tube-fed. So I'd go a few days eating a bit more before refusing again. It was a case of staying one step ahead of being 'tubed' for as long as possible.

Nina and I were equally obsessive about food and our conversations went round and round. 'What do you think will be for lunch?' 'What will they make us eat for dinner?' 'How many calories do you think were in that casserole?' 'How many sit-ups will it take to work off that cheese sandwich?'

But there was one big difference between us – Nina was cooperating with the nurses. She would beg for smaller portions and say things like, 'Please don't make me eat this,' but in the end she would give in. Great Ormond Street was her first admission and she was still compliant and polite, like I'd been at the Maudsley.

But my time there and at Hillingdon had made me fearless and far harder to control. I'd watched kids have screaming fits and rages and learned from them. I was well on my way to becoming a psycho child myself.

After being kept away from my family for the best part of four years, I really wasn't sure where I belonged any more. I'd been drugged up and dragged face to face with the horrors of mental illness and I felt deeply damaged by it. I was going into fits and tantrums more and more often and crying a lot of the time. My mind was utterly tormented. And although my anorexia had begun with a desperation to be skinny, now it was almost as much about beating the system as about being thin. It was Me against Them.

One afternoon Mum took me down to the hospital shop to buy a helium balloon for my collection. I was standing in the aisle waiting for her to pay when I saw a plastic bottle of paracetamol pills. I wasn't even thinking about what I was doing, or why, when my hand instinctively reached out, picked them up and slipped them in my jeans' pocket.

I might have been only 13 but I knew exactly what taking the contents of that little bottle could do and it felt very possible. After Mum had left for the day I called Nina over to my bed and turned out my pockets.

'Where did you get them?' Nina asked, staring at the bottle of pills and immediately realising the seriousness of the situation.

'I nicked them downstairs and I'm keeping them,' I replied. 'I'll put them in the second drawer of the cabinet between our beds in case either one of us ever really needs them. For if things ever get too bad.'

'OK,' Nina whispered. 'It's our secret. But we've got to promise that whichever of us needs to take them will tell the other one first.'

'Pact,' I replied solemnly.

'Pact,' repeated Nina.

We should have been little girls making pacts no more serious than about which boys we fancied. But it was too late for that. We had already been propelled into a hideous other world far removed from childhood.

I was still eating as little as I could get away with and was weak and listless. One day, Nina and I were allowed to go to nearby Covent Garden as a treat but I had to be taken there in a wheelchair because I couldn't afford to use up any energy by walking. When we got there I bought a Baileys-flavoured Haagen-Dazs ice cream and ate the lot – it was fantastic. But the guilt I felt afterwards was overwhelming and I didn't eat a thing the next day.

After I'd been at the unit a month the doctors called a meeting with Mum and Dad because they were concerned I hadn't really gained any weight since my admission. Dasha Nicholls, the registrar, said to Mum, 'Things aren't getting any better, Mrs Grahame. We might have to think about tube feeding.'

When Mum told me what they were proposing I felt sick. I hadn't forgotten the tube feeding at Hillingdon and exactly how painful and disgusting it had been. But worse still, I knew it meant I'd have no control over how much I was eating. But even though that threat was there I still refused to eat. I knew I couldn't cope with the guilt I'd suffer if I gave in to their food.

One morning I saw a nurse approach my bed pushing a trolley. On the trolley was a long tube. I knew exactly what this meant – they were going to tube-feed me through my nose.

Dr Bryan Lask, my specialist doctor, came over and talked me through it. Dr Lask is a professor of child psychiatry and one of the leading experts in his field but he always talked to me as an equal. I really liked and respected him, so I listened.

In the end I agreed to be tube-fed so long as I was allowed to follow a 1,000-calorie-a-day diet. That's about half what a girl of my age should have been eating but I think Dr Lask hoped to be able to increase the amount later and felt that in the meantime anything was better than nothing at that point.

The deal was I would eat normally during the day but whatever I didn't eat in proper food would be made up for at night through the nasal tube. For instance, if I ate 100 calories of crackers at lunchtime and another 100 calories of fish at dinner, they'd give me the remaining 800 calories by tube during the night.

It was a metre-long tube made of pure silk, which meant it was much softer and less painful to push into me than the hosepipe-like one they favoured at Hillingdon. A vanilla-flavoured milky liquid containing calories, fibre, protein, fat and vitamins called Ensure was pumped through the tube and down into my stomach.

After a couple of weeks my weight stabilised and Dr Lask wanted to increase my daily intake to 1,500 calories. I went schizo. I felt I'd been betrayed and was furious. 'There's no fucking way you're doing it!' I screamed at the nurse as she tried to fit up a larger bag of milk feed.

I went on yelling and throwing my body around until Dr Lask had to be called. Finally we agreed he could increase the calories by 100 every other day.

But the day it hit 1,800 I went mad again. As soon as the nurse inserted my tube that night I ripped it straight out and tore it in half. The pain as the tube came shooting up my throat and down my nose was hideous. But I didn't care. It was a victory to me.

I was raging. A second nurse came and had to hold me down while they inserted another tube. But again as soon as she stepped away I pulled it out with one sweep of my arm and threw it across the room. That happened again and again until I'd destroyed six tubes. One of the nurses told me later that each tube cost £45. On top of everything else I was costing the NHS a fortune – but I couldn't have cared less.

For weeks I would rip out up to six tubes a day. I did it so often I became anaesthetised to the pain. Even now my nose still clicks because of the damage I did by pulling those tubes out so roughly.

Sometimes six male nurses would hold me down, trying to keep my arms from the tube, as it was connected to the feed bag and pump. I was like a mad thing. Screaming, kicking, punching them, pulling their hair and scratching their faces to get them off me so I could grab hold of that hateful tube before it started poisoning me with calories.

I was obsessed with keeping that tube away from my body. On different occasions I punched a couple of nurses quite hard and spat in the registrar's face. Another time Nicky Harris, the ward sister, had to sit on me to hold me down because I was demented with anger.

By now I was little more than a bag of bones but my desperation to stop them from feeding me gave me an inner strength. And I would never give up. It was like I was being driven by some demon to claw and punch and spit – anything to win.

In the end the nurses got sick of fighting with me time and time again and one morning as I started screaming and lashing out, I suddenly felt a sharp prick in my bum. The sensation of drowsiness I'd known at Hillingdon soon surged over me and within a minute I was lying there unable to fight any longer. It was Diazepam, a sedative and muscle-relaxant which basically just knocks you out.

That became the norm. They didn't have the staff to spare six nurses to hold me down six times a day as they tried to feed me – there were another nine kids on the ward who needed looking after too. A 'chemical cosh' was both quicker and more cost-effective, I guess.

In addition to the emergency Diazepam jabs, I was already on a daily cocktail of other drugs designed to knock the fight out of me and make me compliant. I was on Thioridazine, a tranquilliser, Amitriptyline, an anti-depressant, and Chlorpromazine, an anti-psychotic drug which was supposed to reduce my anxiety.

I went from being a real live wire, always slightly hyper

and ready for a fight, to a total zombie. I was 13 years old and one of the living dead. My eyes were glazed, my expression blank and inside my mind it was like stumbling through a deep fog. It was like living my entire life buried under a huge pile of blankets, warm and comfy but suffocating too. I knew things were going on around me but every noise was muffled, every sight fuzzy and every sensation dulled.

I'd fall asleep in classes or halfway through a sentence when Mum came to visit. I couldn't concentrate on anything.

At first I tried to fight the drugs by drinking litres of black coffee but then the nurses worked out what I was doing and limited me to one cup a day.

Whenever the drugs wore off, though, I'd become even more angry than before. I was like a wild animal who'd broken out of its cage and wanted revenge knowing that it would soon be recaptured. I'd hit myself and the nurses, claw and spit. Often I'd go up to the playground on the roof, where there was an area for kids to shout and let off steam. I'd scream for hour after hour until patients all over Great Ormond Street Hospital could hear me.

Even in my most docile state, I never totally gave in to the system. At every opportunity I would turn off the machine next to my bed which pumped the milk feed into my nasal tube. The milk feed dangled next to my bed in a bag connected to a machine, but I soon worked out how the machine worked. I would press a button at night to see exactly how many millilitres had gone through and how many were left to go, then lie awake for as long as I could manage to watch those calories flooding my body.

Sometimes I switched off the machine but that was only

ever a brief victory as the nurses would soon spot what I'd done.

A craftier trick was to unscrew the connector which linked my nasal tube to the bag of Ensure liquid, then let the milky fluid drip from the tube on to my mattress. Sometimes I'd lie all night in a soaking-wet mattress that stank of vanilla-flavoured milk. But even that was preferable to having it go inside me.

One time I kept the tube disconnected for three days, letting the feed drip each night on to the carpet beneath my bed. But when my room started stinking of rancid milk it became clear what I'd been up to.

The machine pumped feed into me at 250 millilitres per hour. But then they replaced it with a super-duper new machine that they were very proud of as it could pump in 400 millilitres per hour. When they used that I could feel the liquid pouring into my stomach. I felt like a car being filled up with petrol. I felt bloated and sick as the rich liquid swilled around my stomach.

One night as they hooked up the new pump to begin feeding me, I just lost it. I couldn't face another night of it and I exploded with rage, ripped the machine off the stand and lobbed it across the room. That was the end of their smart new machine. Well, until it returned from the menders.

All that time, every mealtime, after a bit of a cry and a half-hearted attempt to negotiate with the nurses, Nina would dutifully put her head down and eat. I felt she was betraying our special bond. And couldn't she see she was putting on weight? It was frightening and only made me more determined to never let that happen to me.

I became so angry about how much they were

pumping into me at night that I started refusing all food during the day.

My weight was now dangerously low. At around 27 kilos (4 stone 3 lb) it was less than half what a 13-year-old girl should weigh.

Dr Lask decided to give me an incentive – if I complied and reached 29.5 kilos (4 stone 9 lb) by Christmas, I could go home for the holiday.

As desperate as I was to go home, I wanted even more to win my battle to be skinny – so I carried on fighting. I couldn't give up anyway, because the guilt would be too great if I caved in after having achieved so much.

The big weigh-in was set for a week before Christmas. As I stood on the scales and looked down I could see I was 2 kilos (4½ lb) short. My first feeling was simply joy that I'd kept the weight off so well. And I didn't believe they'd really keep me in over Christmas.

Mum and Dad were called in for another big meeting with the doctors. As soon as Mum came into my room afterwards I knew it was bad news. 'Sorry, Nikki, but they're going to make you stay in over Christmas,' she said. It took a couple of seconds for it to sink in, then I went mad. I didn't feel anything but rage. I whacked my head against a wall and scratched my face with my fingernails. I raged for an hour with no one able to calm me down until I finally collapsed, exhausted.

This is it then, I thought. I'll show them how much trouble they have caused not letting me go home and not letting me starve myself to death. This will teach them that all their efforts to keep me alive were just a total waste of time.

I turned and walked quietly back to my room and dug

out the paracetamol pills from my bedside drawer. I got a cup of water from the kitchen, then sat on my bedroom floor and swallowed the lot. The water ran out after the first half a dozen and I was gagging as I forced the rest down my throat.

I didn't think about Mum and Dad or Natalie. All I could think was how sorry everyone would feel when they saw what they had made me do.

I wandered into the day room and lay down on a sofa. The next thing I remember is being carried down to a medical ward. I opened my eyes and there was Nina, in tears as she looked down at me. 'Nikki, I can't believe you've done this without telling me,' she said. 'What about our pact?'

I felt so tired I couldn't answer. I just closed my eyes and thought how nice it would be for all this pain to be over.

Nina had seen me lying on the sofa, totally out of it, and guessed what I'd done. When she checked the drawer and found the pills missing she had alerted the nurses straight away.

Mum and Dad were called and came straight to my bed on Victoria Ward, a medical ward at Great Ormond Street, where my liver function was being monitored. Although I probably hadn't taken enough pills to kill myself there was still a danger that with my critically low body weight I could have seriously, even fatally, damaged my liver.

'You could have died, Nikki,' Mum kept saying. 'Please don't leave us, Nikki. Me and your dad love you so much. We want you to live.'

After a couple of days I rallied but I still wasn't eating and I felt more depressed than ever. The thought of returning to the nasal tube just filled me with fury all over again.

Then one morning Dr Lask came and sat by my bed. 'OK, Nikki, you've got your way,' he said. 'We'll give up on the nasal tube for a while – but you have to eat.'

He explained they had decided that Mum would have to visit all day, every day, to look after me, bath me and try to get me to eat. The nurses couldn't cope with me on their own any longer and, besides, the doctors thought I might respond better to treatment if Mum was around more.

But still I wasn't eating enough and in the last couple of days before Christmas they became desperately worried about me again. I was refusing fluids too and they feared I was becoming dehydrated. All over Britain kids of my age were working themselves into a frenzy of excitement about Christmas. But I was being given a stern warning that if I didn't get food or drink inside me soon, I was going to die.

On Christmas Day, Mum, Tony and Natalie came up to visit me. I've got a photo of me and Nina from that day. I'm wearing a blue Oasis T-shirt and my brand-new Ellesse trainers, which I loved. But I look so haunted and sad in that picture. At that point I was totally out of it from all the drugs they were giving me to keep me quiet plus the paracetamol I had taken. It was a struggle to even stand up, I was so ill. But in my mind I was stronger than everyone.

The four of us sat at the table for a Christmas dinner but it was pretty hard to find much festive cheer. After pulling a cracker with Natalie I sat there utterly miserable. I ate an orange, then watched as everyone else piled into their hospital turkey and sprouts.

Mum must have been desperately forcing out that

'ooooh' noise everyone makes while pulling crackers because one look at her pale and frozen face revealed her true terror. She knew full well that it would need a miracle for me to still be alive the following Christmas. In fact the way I was going I'd be lucky to make the New Year.

That evening Dad came up to visit me with Trudi, his new girlfriend. We all did a jigsaw puzzle, although I stood up the whole time – sitting burned no calories.

On Boxing Day morning Mum made the three-hour round trip to see me again. I was so weak and sleepy I couldn't even speak to her.

'I'm going to go now, Nikki,' she said, stroking my head. 'I've got Tony's son and his girlfriend coming for their lunch, so I'd better get back.' Her brittle tone told me that she was trying not to cry but I couldn't do anything. Certainly I couldn't reassure her everything was going to be OK. I didn't know – or care – whether it was. And I didn't want her leaving me for a moment – I was supposed to be her main concern. I stood at the door of the ward looking lost and alone as she walked away, knowing that would make her feel guilty.

Soon afterwards Dad came back to visit. He bounced in the room beaming at me, just like the Dad I had adored all those light years ago. 'Hello, Nikmala,' he said. He helped me off the bed and we went into the day room to watch telly. I lay down on the sofa, my head on Dad's lap, his arm around my shoulders. It felt so safe, so warm.

We must have been there for about half an hour when Emma, one of the really cool nurses, came in and sat down next to Dad.

'Having a good time?' she asked Dad, smiling, before her gaze moved down to where I was lying.

Suddenly her expression froze and she leaned forward and grabbed my wrist, feeling for a pulse.

'Oh my God, she has passed out,' Emma shouted out to the corridor. 'Quick, get one of the doctors in here *now*.'

Dad was horrified. He thought I'd been lying there quietly enjoying the telly but I'd actually slipped into a coma. It was caused by the combination of the drugs I was on, the paracetamol overdose and my critically low weight.

Mum was just taking off her winter coat in the hall at home after getting back when the phone rang. She knew it would be Great Ormond Street.

'You're going to have to come back,' said the nurse. 'Nikki is critically ill.'

I was rushed down to Helena Ward, another medical ward, for immediate observation. It turned out I was severely dehydrated. The nurses were desperately trying to insert a drip to try get some fluid back into me when Mum and Natalie arrived.

Time and time again the nurse searched for a vein to put the drip into. But I was so ill and so weak that my veins were almost impossible to find. Even when she found one, it was so weak that it collapsed.

By the time Mum and Natalie got back to the hospital, I was still unconscious. Mum was terrified that this time it really was the end.

'What's happening?' she asked desperately. 'My baby's dying, isn't she?'

'We've got to get a line into her otherwise we can't guarantee anything,' the doctor replied. 'She is severely dehydrated. If we don't get fluid into her within the next 15 minutes we could lose her.'

Most other people would have been cracking open another tin of Quality Street in front of the Boxing Night Bond movie. But inside Helena Ward my family was facing up to the reality that I might finally have succeeded in starving myself to death.

Mum clung to the side of the bed as if by holding on tight enough she could keep me there.

Finally a nurse found a usable vein and they hitched up the drip and gradually began to rehydrate me. But I still wasn't out of the woods and my condition remained severe.

Mum stayed all night with Natalie. She held me next to her, willing me to live. 'You've got to fight, Nikki,' she kept saying. 'There is a life out there for you.'

Poor Natalie was so exhausted that in the early hours of the morning she climbed into bed next to me. But even her warmth couldn't bring me back to my senses.

It was almost 24 hours before I finally woke up, surrounded by doctors. There was my social worker Peter Honig, Dr Lask, Dasha Nicholls the registrar, my key nurse Sam and Dad all standing around my narrow hospital bed.

As I opened my eyes all I could feel was a dryness in my mouth and a grogginess in my head. But then a far stronger feeling hit me – anger. Because to my side was a bag of glucose connected to a drip which they had finally managed to feed into my arm.

'What've you been doing?' I said. I reached up to the bag, trying to see the calorie count written on it, but I was still so disorientated I couldn't work out what it said. So instead I reached for the needle that was piercing the back of my hand and yanked it out.

'Calm down, Nikki,' said one of the nurses as she set about trying to reconnect it. But this vein had collapsed too, so there was nothing she could do but try to find a new one. I wasn't having that, though, and went into the most horrific rage at Dr Lask, Dad and the nurses. 'Did you knock me out so you could fill me with this shit?' I shouted, feeling utterly betrayed.

Dr Lask must have been called in from a day off because he was still wearing a hand-knitted jumper that he must have been given for Christmas. He kept trying to calm me down and talk to me as I thrashed around the bed, clawing at any nurses who dared approach me with a needle.

After a while, exhausted, I slipped back to sleep. But I drifted in and out of consciousness, picked up snatches of the conversation going on around my bed between Dr Lask, Peter Honig, Dasha Nicholls, Mum and Dad. I wasn't even sure who was saying what – it was just words and voices rolling around in my head. They were saying things like: 'It's a huge risk' … 'But we haven't got a choice' … 'Stitch it in?' … 'Gastrostomy' … 'General anaesthetic' … 'Tube'.

The words bounced around my head like bumper cars at a fair. But there was one they kept coming back to: 'gastrostomy'. In my fuddled state I was trying to work out what it could mean. But they can't do anything to me now, I thought. I'm dying now. I'm winning, so what can they do to stop me?

It was a couple of days later, when I'd come back to my senses, that Mum explained to me the true, horrific meaning of gastrostomy. 'They're going to give you an operation to stitch a tube directly into your stomach,' she said quietly. 'Because you keep pulling the nasal tube out, there's no other option left. You won't be able to pull this stomach tube out. They have to do it to keep you alive.'

What Mum didn't tell me was that Dr Lask had described me as the worst case of anorexia he'd had to treat in 32 years and that my chances of long-term survival were slim. I was also to be the first anorexic patient ever at Great Ormond Street to have a gastrostomy – and the danger of my undergoing anaesthetic and surgery at my critically low weight were extremely high. They were only doing the operation because they thought the alternative was certain death.

I felt sick as Mum talked on and on about the op and how it was all for the best. I was scared by the prospect of surgery but terrified to think there would be nothing I could do to stop them feeding me once the tube was fitted. Then they would have won the battle for control over my body once and for all.

By the next morning, when Dad arrived on the ward a couple of hours before I was due to go down for surgery, I was hysterical.

'Please, Dad, please don't let them do it', I begged. 'Please, I'm going to be good from now on. I'll eat, I promise.'

Dad looked so confused. He desperately wanted to believe me and he didn't want me to have this hugely risky operation either.

'Go and get me a Complan build-up drink from the kitchen now and I'll drink it. You'll see, I'm serious,' I said.

Dad walked out of my room and returned five minutes

later with a large glass of chocolate Complan – a nutritious high-calorie drink.

He handed it to me saying, 'OK, if you drink this maybe I can persuade them not to do the op. But you've got to drink it.'

It tasted delicious. It was so long since I'd drunk anything like that and I loved it. And I didn't even feel overwhelmed with guilt like I would have done normally – because I knew it was my last chance to avoid the operation.

I swallowed the lot and kept it down. I had to.

'So they won't do it now, will they, Dad?' I asked.

I'd barely finished speaking when Dr Lask walked into the room, saw the empty glass and went berserk.

'What on earth is going on here?' he demanded, staring at Dad. 'Nikki is supposed to be on nil by mouth in preparation for her general anaesthetic. Are you trying to sabotage this operation, Mr Grahame?'

Dad flared up in retaliation. 'She is going to eat again,' he said, pointing in my direction. 'She has promised me, haven't you, Nikki?'

Dr Lask didn't even look at me to see my response. 'Nikki has had the last two weeks to show she could eat without a tube but she hasn't taken that opportunity,' he said. 'Why should we give her the benefit of the doubt now?' Then he spun round and left the room.

I don't think Dad realised I was on 'nil by mouth' and I'm pretty sure he didn't give me the drink to stop the operation going ahead. I reckon he was just hoping I had turned a corner and might start eating again. He was as desperate as I was that I shouldn't have a bloody great tube stuck into my stomach.

But the operation went ahead anyway. They must have

stuffed me full of sedatives again because I don't remember much more until opening my eyes and seeing the stars on the ceiling of the lift. That meant I was going downstairs for surgery. Dad was on one side of the bed and Mary, one of my nurses, was on the other.

As I stared hazily up at the stars sparkling above my head I thought, This must be what it feels like to be in heaven. Comfy, warm, safe. Kind of nice.

I looked across at Dad. 'It's all right, Nikki,' he said, squeezing my hand. 'Go back to sleep.'

CHAPTER 12

ZOMBIE CHILD

The stars were still twinkling in the dimmed light of the lift when they brought me back up to the ward from the operating theatre.

I felt groggy and my head seemed to be weighing a ton. But the strongest feeling was an incredible pain in my stomach.

Back on the ward, I lifted up the sheet and looked down at my tummy. There was a bandaged area on the left of the lower part and sticking out of it was three inches of clear plastic tubing. This was clamped to another tube stretching under the sheet and up to a feed bag suspended beside my bed. I felt disgusted as I watched the milk feed slowly seep into my body, but even I didn't have the energy to fight it at that moment.

My weight had been so critically low that the doctors had started tube-feeding me as soon as the operation was complete. They had just hours to get calories back into my body before it went into total shutdown.

I was pumped full of so many sedatives that I don't remember anything more about the next few days, until I was wheeled out of my bed just before midnight to sit with the other kids in the television room.

It was the countdown to New Year 1996.

'Ten, nine, eight...' everyone was shouting. I just sat there in silence, my face blank. I was so doped up and weak that I was like a scrawny shop dummy, propped up in a wheelchair watching expressionlessly as the rest of the world celebrated being alive.

They'd barely finished the countdown when my eyes closed again and they wheeled me back to bed.

After that I was sedated for more than another week. So in total I was in a zombie-like state for a fortnight, unable to speak or hear, and with a catheter fitted to drain away my urine and faeces.

I was again on Diazepam, Chloropromazine, Thioridazine and Amitriptyline, plus Carbamazepine, a mood stabiliser. The drugs were syringed into my feed tube three times a day, but if I started to come round they quickly topped them up.

I was totally at their mercy. For the time being, they had won.

Mum visited me every day during that fortnight and Dad came a lot too, although I had no idea at the time that either of them were there. Mum would brush my hair or sit and look at me or read the papers. Dad would wander up and down, talking to kids who didn't have visitors.

After two weeks I'd put on a couple of kilos – enough to bring me out of the danger zone. Only then did they gradually reduce the sedatives.

When I finally came round I opened my eyes and saw a

blank wall. They'd turned my bed around to make it easier to get to my tube. I stared at the dried brush strokes on the wall for a few minutes before slowly scanning the room.

To my left was a bag of milk feed still attached to me, the pump forcing the Ensure liquid into my body. On the other side of me sat Evelyn, one of the Dutch agency nurses who worked on the ward.

I moved my hands over my tummy and hips and could immediately feel I had put on weight. That immediately triggered a full-on rage. I'd been lying there zonked for a couple of weeks and all the time they had been fattening me up like a pig.

I can't believe they've done this to me, I thought. After all the hard work I've put in to be thin and they've treated me like this. Well, this is it now. The fight really begins. At that moment I was so angry I could have fought a giant.

The first thing I did was try to yank the tube out of my stomach. I grabbed hold of it and pulled as hard as I could. It was stitched in, so there was no way it would come out, and the pain was so agonising I screamed. But I still kept pulling.

Nurses ran into my room and tried to get hold of my arms but it was like my superhuman strength had come back to me and it took two of them to hold me down while another stuck a sedative jab in my bum.

And so it continued over the next few days. Whenever I regained consciousness I would straight away pull at the tube or try to prise it out with my fingers. But as soon as the nurses heard my gasps of pain they'd be there with their syringes to sedate me again.

I poked and prodded that wound every moment I was conscious. I became obsessed by the hole in my stomach and couldn't keep my hands away from it. Within days it was infected from so much fiddling, oozing a green goo.

Even that didn't stop me, though. I'd just dig my fingernails deeper into the pus and flesh, trying to unpick the stitches which held it into me.

There was about an inch and a half of tube inside my stomach and another six inches hanging out which was attached to my feed bag. My constant quest was to get my fingers to the bottom of that inch and half inside me. Some days I got my fingers right down into my stomach by poking about so deeply. The pain was excruciating but I couldn't stop myself. I stretched the hole by pulling it so much and have left a permanent scar.

One morning, about two weeks after the operation, I was sitting at the dining table with some of the other kids when suddenly everything felt distant. I could still hear them all chattering but I felt a hundred miles away. The next moment I was lying on the ground, jerking and twitching.

The nurses and other kids ran around me, trying to put me in the recovery position while a Crash team was called from Accident and Emergency.

At that moment Mum arrived at the unit but the nurses wouldn't let her in because everything was in a state of total confusion. 'Let me in,' she was shouting, banging on the door. She thought I must have dropped down dead. She'd been half expecting this moment for so long and now she was terrified it was going to happen with her unable to reach me in time, stuck behind a locked double door.

I lay on the floor, unaware of anything, for several minutes before coming to. Then, a couple of days later, I was watching television with Mum when the same thing happened again. More seizures and blackouts followed.

The doctors were really worried. But so they should have been. It was a problem they had created by giving me so many fucking drugs.

Over the next couple of months I had nine seizures – they started with something like an epileptic fit and then I'd black out. I was taken to a neurology ward for tests but they couldn't work out what was causing them. Then they stopped as suddenly as they had started.

My life fell into a routine where they would attach the feed bag to my stomach tube every evening. About half an hour beforehand they would give me a sedative to shut me up and then hope I would sleep through the entire feed.

I became desperate to fight those drugs. They were stripping out of me what little energy I had left. So, when they'd given me my evening jab, I would sit bolt upright in bed chattering to Nina long after she had drifted off to sleep. Then I'd be up and down to the toilet dozens of times – anything to prevent myself nodding off.

The drugs always won in the end, though, and soon I'd be slumped against my pillow. But I often woke in the night and if I saw the feed still pumping into me, all hell broke loose.

As the weeks passed, though, I realised that if I really wanted to win this battle I needed a plan more sophisticated than just screaming and shouting every time they tried to feed me. Soon my every waking hour was dedicated to dreaming up methods to beat the tube.

Each night after the feed had finished, a nurse would disconnect my stomach tube from the feed bag tube, slip a cap on the end of it, then tape it up against my skin to stop it getting caught when I rolled over in bed. That process normally woke me up and I'd lie there dozily watching her do it. One night, though, I noticed some of the feed came dribbling back out before she capped the end of the tube. Aha, I thought, this is worth trying.

As soon as the nurse moved away from the bed I ripped the tape off my tummy, slipped the cap off the tube, rolled on to my side and held the tube pointing downwards. Soon the feed was pouring out of it like vomit on to my mattress.

Brilliant, I thought. I'm back in control.

From then on I was doing it every night. The feed went everywhere, over my clothes, my pyjamas, my duvet. Even my teddy bears got soaked. The carpet was sodden under my bed where I hoped no one would notice. Within days the entire room stank of stomach juices. I stank of stomach juices. It was disgusting and made me wretch but I didn't care.

After a week the nurses worked out what was going on and as soon as they heard me moving around after a feed they'd be straight over armed with their syringes.

But still I didn't give in. There were fewer nurses on during the night shift and I knew that if one of them was busy with Isobel or one of the other demanding kids, there wasn't much one of them could do to stop me on their own.

Some nights they would have to call for emergency doctors and nurses from other wards because they couldn't cope with me. I was like a demon child again. Because if I knew there was a chance of getting that feed out of my body, I'd do anything to achieve it.

They decided they would have to return to feeding me

during the day as then there were more staff around and it was easier to control me.

But it remained a constant battle and I never, ever got tired of fighting. I was stronger than they thought and I was determined to prove it.

By now, winning had become an end in itself. Yes, of course I still wanted to be as skinny as I could but beating the system had become my main obsession.

When I was being fed by the pump during the day, I would have to pull it along on a stand with me everywhere I went.

On days when I was well enough I would have lessons in the Great Ormond Street classroom. In I would go, pencil case in one hand and pushing the stand with the other. As the weeks and months rolled by I lost all sense of time, as had happened in all the other institutions I'd been in. One minute I'd be making Christmas cards to send home, the next it was Easter baskets, then Halloween pumpkins. Sometimes it felt like those art and craft lessons were the only thing connecting me to the rest of the world's calendar. I never did much other school work beyond art but I liked listening to what was going on.

Then one day I came up with a brilliant plan. The next morning I put on four pairs of socks before I arrived for morning classes. Sitting behind my desk, I carefully disconnected the bag from my tube and let the feed drip on to the floor. After a couple of minutes I wiped up the milky pool with the outermost pair of socks still on my feet. Then I leaned down, slipped the dripping-wet socks off and put them in my pocket. Five minutes later I did the same again with the next pair of socks. And again. And again.

Brilliant. That was 20 minutes' worth of calories wasted. Another victory to me.

I got away with that for a couple of months before one morning one of the members of staff helping out in the classroom screwed up his nose and sniffed suspiciously.

'I can smell Ensure,' he said after a couple of minutes. 'Nikki Grahame, if you have disconnected your tube...' he went on, walking menacingly towards me. As he reached where I was sitting he looked down to see a large, milky puddle under my desk. So that was the end of that.

Then I came up with another scheme. Isobel, the girl who had reverted to being a baby and couldn't walk or talk, was tube-fed through her nose. Her milk feed was 1 calorie per millilitre and mine was 1.5. Every morning the milk feeds would come up from the dietician's office on the hospital trolley. I would wait until the nurses were busy with one of the other kids, then go down to the trolley and swap the labels so that Isobel was getting 1.5 cal per mil and I was getting just one. Genius!

After a couple of weeks Isobel started putting on weight and I started to lose weight and no one could understand how. I got away with that for a good few months until one morning I wasn't quite careful enough and one of the nurses noticed a corner of a label had peeled up. Everything fell into place and it was all over.

As a punishment I was put on total supervision, which meant I had a nurse with me all the time – even when I went to the loo and had a shower.

But even then I came up with new scams. At night there were only two nurses on duty but if Isobel woke up and needed looking after, both of them would be occupied with her for quite a while.

I'd seize my opportunity and sneak into the nurses' station, to rifle through their drawers and pigeon-holes, looking for any notes on my treatment. I'd read my notes and see if there were any plans to increase my calorie intake. Any information like that would help me in my battle.

Because they didn't trust me they began feeding me through my bag at mealtimes so they could keep an eye on me while I sat at the table with the other kids.

I desperately needed a new way of sabotaging their schemes. One night I was lying in bed when 'ding' went a bell in my head – I'd had a brainwave. I already knew that if I pushed out my stomach muscles after a feed some of the milky fluid would drip out of the tube. But it was never enough to make much difference. And that was when I came up with the idea of using a syringe to suck it out. Clever, eh?

Next morning when the nurses were doing bed rounds I wandered casually up to the trolley and snatched three syringes. Then, straight after mealtime, I dashed back to my room, plunged the syringe into the end of my tube and sucked out some liquid. It was so easy. I squirted the fluid – a mixture of Ensure and stomach juices – into an empty water bottle. Within a couple of minutes I'd removed almost a litre of liquid from my stomach.

Before long I was nicking syringes at every opportunity. Immediately after every mealtime I would hurry back to my room to start work. I was never allowed to close my bedroom door in case I was up to something, so I'd have to stand with my back to the corridor, pretending to look inside my wardrobe as I sucked the feed out of my stomach. Once I'd transferred it into an empty water bottle, I'd open my bedroom window and lob the bottle out.

It all went brilliantly for a couple of months. My weight wasn't going up and I was delighted. Then one morning one of the office staff from downstairs turned up on the ward and I could hear a commotion going on outside my room.

Five minutes later my key nurse stormed in. I loved Sam so much and felt we had a special bond – I even became obsessively clingy about her and didn't like her treating the other kids. But this time I knew I'd upset her really badly from the red flush across her face.

'We've had someone from the office downstairs up here complaining,' Sam said, her normally laid-back voice stretching in irritation. 'She says she can't see out of her window any more because the fire escape next to it is piled high with plastic bottles filled with what appears to be rock-hard milk and stomach juices. Would you care to explain, Nikki?'

Of course I didn't fucking care to explain. I'd been sussed out. I stormed out the room in a seething rage. From then on, only one syringe was allowed on the ward at any time as they couldn't risk me stealing them again.

I still tried to force liquid out of my stomach after feeds by pushing out my tummy muscles. But it was only drips and drops. Even so, the stench of vomit and stomach juices became overpowering in my room. And the carpet by the side of my bed was hard with dried stomach juices.

For more than a year I didn't eat anything properly at all. It sounds incredible but the only things that went into my mouth were water and one cup of black coffee a day.

Finally they decided to give me another chance and put me on three very high-calorie glucose drinks, called Forté

Juice, each day. Each carton was the equivalent of a meal, so it was a pretty big deal for me. But they were still making up the calories by tube feeding as well.

For a while it worked OK, although as my weight crept up I became increasingly unhappy. By June 1996 I'd reached 40 kilos (6 stone 4 lb) and I hated it. I could feel the fat gathering around my hips and stomach and it repulsed me. In the ward bathroom there was a mirror but it only showed down to my waist. I'd stand up on tiptoes trying to see my whole body but it was difficult. What I could see was bad enough, though.

One night I was lying awake in bed when the bell in my head sounded again. An even more ingenious plan.

I slipped out of bed and sneaked into the open kitchen on our unit. I picked up an armful of Forté Juices and then went to the toilets, where I squeezed each of them down the sink until they were all empty. Then I hid them in my wardrobe until the next morning, when I stuffed one up my jumper before leaving my room.

At breakfast I sat down and waited for the nurse to bring my normal morning carton of Forté Juice. I opened it but as soon as she turned away I switched it with the empty carton. For the next 20 minutes I sat there sucking a straw, pretending to empty the carton. 'Finished,' I said holding it up at the end.

'Well done, Nikki,' the nurse replied. But I hadn't drunk a thing. It was another massive win for me. Later on I emptied the still full carton of Forté Juice down the toilet, leaving me another empty carton for the next mealtime. I got away with that every mealtime for months. The weight was really dropping off me again. I was back on top and it felt brilliant.

By this time I was sharing a room with a girl called Parjeet. She was a small, skinny girl who had anorexia but also had to permanently walk around with an oxygen tank because she had breathing problems. It was more a psychiatric problem than a physical one, though.

We never got on. Maybe it was 'professional' anorexic jealousy. There were no more late-night chats like Nina and I had enjoyed. It must have been awful sharing a room with me and my mad tantrums and screaming. But it wasn't great sharing with Parjeet either. Her oxygen pump used to wheeze away all night and she would grass me up at every opportunity. One day she discovered my secret stash of Forté Juice cartons and went running to the nurses.

I didn't even find out what she had done until the next mealtime when I sat down and the nurse poured my Forté Juice into a glass. I knew the game was up from the smug look on the nurse's face. I was so angry they'd found me out that I flew into a rage. '*Fuck that!*' I screamed, pushing the glass across the table. 'I'm not drinking it!' And I didn't.

I hated Parjeet for that. But I knew she'd do anything to stop me from being thinner than her.

From then on I refused Forté Juice at every mealtime but it was hardly a victory as they just put me back on full tube feed instead. For a while I was gutted. But I never gave up. I kept on pushing feed back out of my tube and exercised like crazy every moment I was alone. At the same time I made sure they thought I was gaining far more than I really was. Sam had a set routine for weigh-in days. She pulled the scales slightly away from the wall and made me jump on. But what she didn't realise was that I was still close enough to the wall to lay my palm flat on it and push down with all my strength while she was looking at the reading.

I could add a good 3 kilos (6½ lb) by doing that and pretty much decide how much I wanted to weigh on any particular day. I refused to be weighed by anyone but Sam. All I had to do was throw a tantrum if anyone else was on duty and they would decide it was easier to wait for Sam's shift.

I did all the obvious stuff too. I'd drink loads and loads of water before they weighed me to make myself heavier. A 1.5-litre (1¾ pints) bottle of water weighs about 1.5 kilos (3½ lb) and I could easily drink two or three of those before a weigh-in.

But that's one of the oldest tricks in the book – any dimwit anorexic could tell you that 'waterloading' is vital to boost a weigh-in. What is amazing is that Great Ormond Street didn't realise I was doing it and the doctors couldn't understand how the scales said I was putting on weight when I was looking skinnier than ever.

Then one day my luck ran out. I was sitting in the classroom when the ward sister, Nicky Harris, came to the door and said, 'Nikki, come with me, we need to weigh you.' I knew at once there was no fooling Nicky. She took me to a different room and placed the scales slap bang in the middle of the floor. They showed I was 4 kilos (9 lb) less than at my last weigh-in.

It was another battle they'd won, but the war went on.

CHAPTER 13

GET ON
AND DIE

I felt like a prisoner who keeps digging escape tunnels
only for each of them to collapse or be discovered.

Every attempt to keep the calories out of my body
failed. I was more depressed, angry and obsessed with
being thin than ever before.

I was having weekly sessions with the unit's counsellor
but that wasn't helping my mood. I still couldn't see any
good raking over a load of stuff I'd been asked about a
million times before. Sometimes I'd sit in the armchair in
front of the counsellor, close my eyes and pretend to be
asleep. Other times I'd stare out of the window or hum for
the entire hour.

Mum visited me almost every day for the 17 months
that I was at Great Ormond Street. To get there and back
could take three hours, but she never complained even
when I was a total bitch to her. Sometimes if she was late
I would scream down the ward at her. Other times I
wouldn't speak or even acknowledge her for the whole

Above left: Daddy's girl – and blissfully unaware of what I would endure later in my childhood.

Above right: Big sister Nat taking care of me.

Below left: Happier days, before I got ill. The family all together before my parents' marriage fell apart.

Below right: A bleak day for my family: Granddad's funeral.

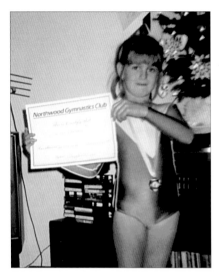

Above left: Fanatical gymnast – as with everything I do, I felt I just *had* t
be the best.

Above right: My ninth birthday – a weekend when I was allowed home
from the Maudsley.

Below left: Ready to go back to school after six months at the Maudsle
hospital.

Below right: My childhood was spent going in and out of institutions. Th
is one of the occasions when I was allowed out.

above left: Wasting away. My tenth birthday, spent at Collingham Gardens – a birthday cake would have been the last thing I wanted.

above right: At Great Ormond Street – you can see the naso-gastric tube I was forced to have.

below left: At Huntercombe with Mum – I was 14 in this photo, and 60% of the weight I should have been.

below right: Celebrating another birthday in 1995.

I have made some amazing friends who are always there to support me.

Above left: With Carly – my best friend, my sister, my soul mate.

Above right: Rachel is a true friend and we bonded over our love of indie music.

Below left: David – one of my old school friends – enjoying the sun in Brighton, 2008.

Below right: Julie has been like a mother figure to me and I'm so glad I have her in my life.

amily is the most important thing in my life.

bove: My mum has been my rock – solid, dependable and always there
catch me when I fall.

elow: My sister and I haven't always seen eye-to-eye. Here we are
lebrating 'The Grahame's Annual Christmas Party' in 2010.

Above: The birth of Nat's son, Sunny Wren, has brought us closer together. From the moment I saw Sunny, I adored him unconditionally.

Below left: Nat and I finally made it to 'In the Night Garden' after the car episode!

Below right: My lovely mum in Oz, having the time of her life.

After a horrible breakup in 2009, I went off the rails and went to countless festivals and gigs to celebrate my freedom.

Above: Nadia and I partying hard in Glastonbury, 2010. I've got no idea what we were thinking!

Below: Rachel, Bret Anderson and me at Latitude Festival in 2011.

Above: Partying with Carl and Didz.

Below: Darren, one of my closest friends, is someone who is very special in my life and always there for me.

time she was there. She'd sit at a table and I would move my chair around so my back was facing her. I felt so angry that she had sent me there and that she could take me away at any time but instead chose to leave me there being pumped full of calories morning, noon and night.

Several times she turned up only to be greeted by me screaming at the nurses, 'Tell her to fuck off. I don't want her near me. Unless she has come to discharge me she can fuck off.' It wouldn't be anything specific that she had done. I'd just be having 'one of my days'.

When Mum visited she was allowed to take me up to the hospital's roof garden or, if I was stronger, out for a walk. But Mum wasn't my mum any more. She was just an excuse for me to lose weight. As soon as we got up on to the roof I'd run up and down like a loony, trying to burn off calories. And if we went out of the building I'd speed walk along the streets, leaving her desperately trying to keep up, begging me to stop.

Some days we went to the park but once we were in the gates I'd instruct Mum, 'Sit there while I do 20 laps.' Each time I shot past her she'd try to start speaking but I'd just ignore her and race off on another lap. In my mind the sole purpose of her being there was to give me an excuse to get out of the unit and to exercise, and she had to realise that. And there was nothing she could do to stop me.

'If you tell the nurses what I've been doing I'll say I don't want you visiting me any more,' I'd threaten her. I was so, so cruel to Mum because I was using her huge love for me as my weapon.

In the past, she would sit with me during my meal and I'd hide food in full view of her. 'If you tell, though, Mum, you know you won't be coming back again,' I'd snarl. It was the same when I was allowed home for day visits. They never trusted me enough to let me stay there overnight and I think Mum was relieved as she knew she couldn't control me.

Mum would be tortured with guilt every time she gave in to me because she knew she wasn't doing the best for me, but she was terrified I'd ban her from seeing me. I think she was scared of me physically too. In my constant anger I lashed out at her regularly. I gave her black eyes and bruises on her arms and legs. But the next moment I'd be hugging her and crying, desperate for a cuddle from my mummy. It must have been so confusing for her, like being stuck in an abusive relationship with someone who says they love you but can't stop hurting you.

Some people would say she should have stopped visiting me if it was only endangering me, but she couldn't just abandon her youngest daughter in an institution surrounded by seriously mentally ill kids. In any case, the doctors had warned her that my hideous behaviour was a way of testing how much she really loved me. If I was ever going to get better I had to know deep down that she would always be there for me however much I pushed her away.

I was so self-obsessed. Even after Mum had a car accident and hurt her back, the first thought in my mind was, Who's going to come and visit me now she's too ill?

Mum also felt she had to keep visiting me because she truly thought I would be dead soon. I was so out of control that she couldn't see any other conclusion to the hell of the past five years.

Yet only once can I remember her really getting angry and losing it with me. One day I dragged her out for a walk to Covent Garden. Well, she was walking and I was jogging up ahead, burning off every calorie that I could. It was only when I stopped at a corner that Mum caught up with me, out of breath and boiling hot despite a chilly breeze. She started screaming at me like I hadn't heard her do in years. And all the nervousness in her voice had disappeared, replaced by a raw anger.

'I'm sick of this, Nikki. I've had enough,' she said. 'Why don't you go and die? Starve yourself to death. Run yourself into the grave if that is what you really want. Because I can't cope with it any more. I'm sick of you dragging me around like a dog on a lead.'

I stood there totally stunned, aware of people in the street staring at us, but unable to take my eyes off Mum's flaring eyes.

'Because this isn't just your life you're screwing up here, you know,' she went on. 'It's mine and your Dad's and Natalie's and Tony's too. But you're the one getting all the help and all the attention and you're still choosing not to get better. So just do whatever it is you want.'

Then she spun round and, propelled by fury, rushed back to Great Ormond Street. For the first time in years I was the one scurrying along behind, desperately trying to catch up and win favour. For a short while the tables were turned.

When we got back to the hospital one of the nurses grabbed Mum and said, 'Well done, Mrs Grahame – someone saw you in the street standing up to Nikki. This is what you have got to do.'

They'd been telling Mum for ages that she had to get angry with me but she had found it too hard.

That day was a big turning point for Mum. I didn't ban

her from visiting for standing up to me, so it taught her that she did have some power in our relationship. And it taught me I could have a strong mother.

Dad used to visit at least a couple of times each week. Some days I'd get him to take me swimming and I'd pound up and down the pool while he stood there watching me, uncertain how to stop me. Other times he would run around the park with me a couple of times, thinking if he let me do a bit of exercise it would stop me overdoing it. But however many laps we did, it was never enough for me.

Some afternoons Dad would bring a football and we'd go down to the park for a kick-around. He thought it was a bit of father-and-daughter bonding, like the old days. But it wasn't – we were there for just one reason and that was for me to burn up the calories.

Natalie was really supportive too and would visit me on a Friday evening, coming on the tube straight from college in Stanmore. We got on better then than we had for years. Maybe it was because we had been apart for a while or maybe we were simply growing up. Whatever it was, at least we had stopped acting like banshees every time we were in the same room.

At that time, Natalie was hanging around with a load of hippies, learning the guitar, smoking spliffs and getting her nose pierced. I'd got into all that too through Nina, so finally Nat and I had something in common. She'd turn up with tapes she had recorded for me of bands like Kula Shaker, Blur and Oasis and I thought she was dead cool. On her sixteenth birthday I sent her a card and inside I wrote, 'I'm so proud to have a sister who is 16.' I meant it.

All this time my weight was gradually increasing and every day my flesh felt a little more padded. I knew it was time for desperate action.

To hell with the pain, I thought. I'll cut it out. My next perfect opportunity was during a visit to the Great Ormond Street classroom. We were doing art and crafts and there was a box of scissors lying on a table. I didn't think for a second. I pulled down the waistband of my trousers, pulled the tube out as far as I could and snipped just where the plastic entered my stomach.

I felt victorious again.

The next time a nurse came to feed me, she pulled up my top looking for the end of the tube. I watched the look of shock on her face as she realised it had gone.

'What've you done, Nikki?' she said in horror. 'If we don't reopen this gastrostomy immediately the wound will close up with the rest of the tube inside you.'

Yeah, like I was bothered about that!

But they weren't giving in either. I was hauled back to my bed, where a group of doctors and nurses hurriedly planned their next move.

They decided to insert a new style tube. It worked by being inserted and then injected with a little water to create a balloon just inside my stomach which I wouldn't be able to pull back out. Imagine it like pushing a round balloon through a letterbox, then blowing it up so you can't pull it out again. The feed was to be pumped through another tube attached to the balloon. Fairly simple really, but apparently very effective.

The inflatable tube worked for a good few months before I came up with my counter-attack. Oh my God, I thought. Why didn't I think of this five months ago? It was obvious – all I had to do was deflate the balloon and then it and the tube would simply slip out. But what I needed for that was a syringe. They were still counting the syringes on our ward, so that was no good. Then a week or so later, by sheer good fortune for me, Parjeet became critically ill and was taken to the Accident & Emergency Department.

We may not have been buddies but as her room mate I was allowed to visit her. I was sitting chatting to her when out of the corner of my eye I spotted a syringe lying on a trolley. The whole time I was talking to Parjeet, my eyes kept going back to the syringe. I was determined I wasn't leaving that ward without it. As I got up to go I wandered over casually, slipped two syringes into my pocket and walked back up to the Mildred Creak Unit.

That night after lights out I stuck the syringe up the tube and sucked out the water. The balloon deflated immediately and with one gentle tug it was out. No pain, nothing. I'd won again. Brilliant.

The following morning I woke up and looked at my stomach under my pyjamas and the hole had already closed up. This time I had really won, I knew it. I was so proud of myself, I felt jubilant.

Half an hour later, at breakfast, the nurse came over with her breezy morning chorus, 'Right, Nikki, time to connect your feed now.'

That's what you think, I thought, smiling broadly at her.

Again she lifted my top and again the tube had disappeared. Her face was a picture of confusion.

'Where's your tube gone?' she said.

'Oh, I don't know,' I said innocently. 'It's just gone.'

Afterwards I heard the nurses panicking about how they

were going to explain it to their bosses. That was two tubes I'd managed to magic into thin air without any of them noticing.

When Dr Lask arrived on the ward later that day even he looked exhausted with me.

'OK, Nikki, I'm going to have to book you in for another operation,' he said.

But I'd already planned my response.

'No,' I said. 'I'll eat. I want to eat.'

It was the early spring of 1997 and by then I hadn't put anything solid in my mouth for more than a year but I just couldn't face another day of the tube.

Dr Lask agreed to give me one last chance to prove myself.

They started me off on Forté Juice high-calorie drinks, then after a fortnight introduced baby food because it was easy for me to digest. It was disgusting and Mum and I would wander around the hospital shop looking for jars which looked slightly more appetising than the usual chicken and potato mush.

It was a really weird sensation having food in my mouth and it took a while before I moved on to soup and bread and biscuits. But it wasn't long before the bread and biscuits were going in my knickers and I was back to my old ways again.

One afternoon Dr Lask called a meeting with Mum and Dad. 'I'm sorry, Mr and Mrs Grahame,' he said. 'But I honestly don't think there's anything more I can do for Nikki. We've tried everything over the past 17 months but nothing has worked.

'She has driven herself to the point of death, is destroying her body, will probably deprive herself of ever having children, but we can't stop her.'

Dr Lask was one of the leading authorities on anorexia in Britain but even he couldn't save me.

'Nikki is not the worst case of anorexia I've ever had to deal with in my 32-year career,' he said slowly. 'She is *by far* the worst.'

Mum was desperate, begging him to try a bit longer.

But Dr Lask was adamant that keeping me in a hospital environment was starting to do more harm than good and felt I might fare better in a more relaxed setting. He recommended a foster home called Sedgemoor in Taunton, Somerset, which might kick-start me into getting my life back.

Mum and Dad were worried at the thought of my being so far from home and away from medical support with foster carers. But, like me, their options had run out.

So on 27 March 1997, a month before my fifteenth birthday, I walked out of the Mildred Creak Unit for the last time. I weighed 29 kilos (4 stone 4 lb) and was 150.1 centimetres (4 feet 11 inches) tall. In the time I'd been there I hadn't managed to keep on any weight at all.

Mentally I'd made no progress either. I still wanted exactly the same things as the moment I'd walked into the place – to be as skinny as possible and to fight as hard as possible anyone who prevented me achieving my goal.

Great Ormond Street had admitted defeat – they couldn't cope with me any longer and were sending me away, to somewhere it would be even easier to avoid food.

I was triumphant.

CHAPTER 14

SEDGEMOOR

Fields and trees skidded past the back seat window of our Volkswagen Golf as I sat staring out on that long drive down the M4 to Somerset.

I gazed out, excited to be in the real world again after so long in Great Ormond Street. But it felt scary too, being sent so far from home without Mum or Dad or Natalie. Yet I was pleased there'd be no doctors and nurses telling me to eat any more. Now I could starve myself just as much as I wanted.

The doctors had decided that as the hospital just wasn't making me any better it might be better off to put me in a more normal home-like environment. But going home was not an option. Towards the end of my time at Great Ormond Street there had been a mammoth meeting between my doctors, social worker, family therapist and Mum and Dad. As soon as I was called into the meeting room for the last ten minutes I could tell by Mum's blank expression that something bad had happened.

'We've been talking and have decided you won't be going home until you are at least 18 years old,' Dr Lask explained. 'If you go home we have no confidence that you won't just go straight back to starving yourself.'

It was a total body blow. It made everything so pointless. If I was never going home – because that's what it seemed like to me – what exactly was the point of being alive? I started screaming and went into one of my temper fits, throwing my body around as people tried to restrain me, arching my back and whacking my head against the wall. It went on for almost two hours before eventually I collapsed from exhaustion and fell asleep.

The doctors felt foster care at Sedgemoor was a better option for me than home in that relationships I'd create with foster carers would not be as intense as with Mum and Tony and might prevent me relapsing. But the doctors were also aware my family was in no real state to take me back either. My anorexia had taken a terrible toll on them all.

Mum had borne the brunt of it and was in a bad way. Depression had swept over her gradually. She was still in a low place after Grandad's death and the divorce. But it was knowing that there was nothing she could do to make me eat which really plunged her into torment. Worse still, whenever I was with her I seemed to be an even more successful anorexic.

It is quite common in families where there is an anorexic child for something called 'reverse parenting' to take hold. Basically it means the kid is in charge while Mum and Dad do what they are told by them because they're so scared their child might die or shut them out if they don't. That is exactly what was going on between me and Mum.

Then Mum had a car accident and suffered constant back pain for months which only added to her depression. On top of that she heard people gossiping about her, questioning whether she was to blame for my anorexia. 'Well, Sue's always been thin herself,' they were saying. 'Makes you wonder if she encouraged it.' If those silly old cows had seen just one of Mum's amazing sponge puddings they'd have known there was no way that was true.

But rather than fight back, Mum just shrank into herself. There was no fight left in her.

And if all that wasn't enough to deal with, Natalie was still furious about all the attention being lavished on me and was staging a full-on teenage rebellion. Mum felt she had failed me and Natalie and so was a failure as a mother – as well as as a wife. She was tearful a lot of the time and found it harder and harder to do even the simplest jobs around the house. Gradually it reached the point where she was spending every day just lying on the sofa, unable to face the world.

She'd get up in the morning thinking, Right, today I'll go down the town, do some shopping, come home and have a good tidy-up. She'd shower, put some nice clothes on and come downstairs, up and ready for the world. But once Natalie and Tony were out of the house her resolve would start to slip and her strength would ebb away.

Some days she would make it out of the house and round the corner. But by then the outside world would all seem too much and she would run home crying and gasping for breath. She'd collapse on the sofa, crying in front of the telly, and only get the energy to tidy herself up when Natalie was about to come in from college. The only time she could get herself out of the house was to visit me.

For a while she managed to lie quite convincingly to Tony and Natalie about how she was feeling, but she was sinking fast.

She and Tony were sitting at the kitchen table talking and for the millionth time trying to make sense of it all. Then Mum calmly walked over to the draining board, where she kept the big bottle of ibuprofen pills she needed for her back pain. She undid it, tipped a handful of pills into her palm and shoved the lot into her mouth. She swallowed as many as she could get down her, then did it again.

Tony leapt across the kitchen, snatched the bottle from her hand and slapped her on the back in an effort to bring the pills back up.

Obviously if she had really wanted to kill herself she wouldn't have done it in front of her boyfriend. So I think it was really Mum's way of showing how desperate she felt. She couldn't cope any more.

The GP put her on anti-depressants and she had group therapy with other anorexics' parents at Great Ormond Street. It all helped but nothing was able to help her shake off that constant feeling of sadness.

So all that meant that going home just wasn't an option. Which was why I was speeding down the motorway to Taunton.

Sedgemoor was then one of Britain's biggest residential care businesses, which placed kids in a number of children's foster homes around Taunton. Then the kids all attended a special school nearby.

Some of the kids had been kicked out of school, others had run away from home because they didn't get on with their parents, some had family problems and some were total delinquents – really rough, tearaway kids.

There were two other girls living in my house. Vicky was a big fat girl who had ended up there because she didn't get on with her mum and had been thrown out of school for behavioural problems. She couldn't stop nicking stuff. It was obvious she came from a really rough home, and she stank. She'd go into my room when I wasn't around and steal my CDs and shower gel. They even had to lock up the food in the kitchen otherwise she'd have had the lot.

My other housemate, Karen, was lovely but very, very disturbed and into self-harming. She spent most of her time in her room listening to really depressing music with candles burning all around her bed. When they called her down to dinner she would often have candle burns all up her arm and hot wax over her clothes.

We had three women carers: Margaret, who was a bit unfriendly, Wendy, who was a real soft touch and didn't know the first thing about calories or food (result!), and Kath, who was OK. Each morning one of them would drive us to school, where we did proper coursework, aiming towards our GCSEs. I felt more normal than I had in years.

The first day you arrived at Sedgemoor, the staff would hand you £1,500 to buy a stereo and television for your room and anything else you wanted to decorate it with. And there was still loads of cash left over for new clothes and make-up. I think the idea was to kit yourself out for a new life. If you stayed six months you got to keep all the stuff you had bought. But if you didn't stay, you lost it all.

Each week we got an additional allowance of £5 to

spend on magazines or to go bowling or to the cinema.

After having to obey the rules and regulations at Great Ormond Street for so long, foster care was like arriving in heaven. I had so much freedom, I didn't know what to do with it. First off, I dyed my hair pink. I was still into that hippie look that Nina and Natalie were into.

Then one Saturday afternoon I went into Taunton and got my nose pierced. It was so cool. Then I had five holes pierced in one ear and four in the other.

We were living quite near Glastonbury, so on Saturdays we would get the bus there and go shopping, returning with bagfuls of multi-coloured flowing skirts and lacy white tops.

And one day we went to Stonehenge because it seemed a cool thing to do. I didn't drink because of the calories but I smoked a couple of spliffs with some of the other girls. I didn't like it much, though, because it made me feel lethargic, which I hate.

Nina, my friend from Great Ormond Street, visited me for a day at Sedgemoor. It was brilliant to see her, but secretly it was even more brilliant to see her looking fatter than me. However much we loved each other, we were still hugely competitive.

Most girl friends would have spent the day together agonising over which nail polish to buy or slobbing out at the cinema, but not me and Nina. We filled our day running around the streets of Taunton, trying to burn off calories.

It had been arranged that once a month Larry, my key social worker, would take me back to Great Ormond Street to be weighed. When I left there, Dr Lask had threatened me that if my weight fell dramatically I would be straight back in for emergency feeding. But even that thought wasn't enough to make me eat enough. The house I was staying in wasn't an anorexic unit, so the staff there had little idea about dealing with me and I got away with loads of dodges.

Also, because it was foster care, we could make our own breakfasts and lunches if we wished, which for me was perfect. At first I had one Weetabix for breakfast with water and black coffee. For lunch I had a Weight Watchers' soup and a packet of Ritz crackers. Then for dinner it would be steamed vegetables and some fruit or a low-fat yoghurt. Before bed I would have an Options drink which the carers thought was hot chocolate – they didn't realise it was only 40 calories.

Sure enough, when I went for my weigh-ins at Great Ormond Street my weight had dropped. I was allowed to return to Taunton but told I had to start eating and my weigh-ins were increased to once a fortnight. I didn't want to go back into the Mildred Creak Unit permanently, but once I started losing weight again I liked it and I couldn't bear the guilt of eating more than I felt was enough. Soon I was skipping breakfast entirely. Because it was like living in your own home I just went back to the crumbs-on-the-plate trick, claiming I'd already eaten if anyone challenged me.

I started buying low-calorie crisps and having them for my lunch – that was about 90 calories. And for dinner I'd have a tray of button mushrooms – they are only 13 calories per 100 grams (3½ oz). Then I found something even better – water chestnuts at just seven calories per 100 grams!

The carers would cook evening meals but I'd just say I

didn't fancy it and they let me off. They saw me eating my water chestnuts or Weight Watchers' soups and thought that was OK. They had no idea about calories.

I cut back and back until for about a month I lived on nothing but Weight Watchers' soups, black coffee and cigarettes. I'd started smoking every now and again out of our bedroom window at Great Ormond Street with Nina. We'd nick cigarettes from the nurses' station and think we were really cool. In foster care, everyone smoked and I was soon on 20 a day. I'd read they suppressed appetite and made you skinnier, so what wasn't there to like about smoking?

I'd been at Sedgemoor for two months when one morning in May I was due to return to London for my next weigh-in. As I'd barely eaten for a fortnight, I knew I was going to be in big trouble. I was painfully thin again and feeling incredibly weak. I couldn't even run down the street because my legs would ache, and my clothes billowed around me because I was so scrawny.

I was lying on my bed thinking, How am I going to get through this one? when my eyes settled on the metal doorstop in the shape of an owl that held my door open. It must have weighed a few kilos but I picked it up and wedged it down the front of my navy-blue flared dungarees. (I'd chosen them as the best clothes I had for disguising how much weight I'd lost.) Perfect, I thought, slipping on a chunky wool jumper over the top.

All the way back up the M4 we went with the doorstop stuck inside my dungarees.

When I arrived at Great Ormond Street one of the nurses took me upstairs and put me on the scales. I'd slipped off my boots but was still fully clothed. But when

I looked down at the numbers on the scales I saw instantly that my weight was dramatically low – I'd lost 6.5 kilos (1 stone) in just seven weeks. The nurse diligently wrote my weight down on her chart, then scurried off to find a doctor.

Mum had met me at Great Ormond Street and as I trudged out into the corridor she put her arm round my bony shoulders. We had a couple of hours left until the doctors decided what we should do next so we decided to wander down to Covent Garden for a bit of window shopping.

It was only a ten minute walk but by the time we got there I was exhausted. We were crossing the Piazza when my feet, too tired and clumsy to move properly, tripped up on the cobbles and I landed in a heap on the ground. I must have looked such a pathetic figure – a little bag of bones, pale, scraggy and sickly, too weak to even pull herself to her feet. A few people stared at me as I sat there and I didn't even have the energy to look away.

Mum saw the horror on the faces of passers-by as they looked at me, and tears started rolling down her face. As another couple of shoppers turned to stare at me, Mum just lost it. 'What are you looking at?' she screamed. 'Stop staring at my daughter – can't you see she's ill.' It was just awful.

But of course people were going to look at me. Why wouldn't they? I was a walking skeleton, except I could scarcely even walk.

Mum helped me up and we went back to the hospital. There the nurse told us to go straight to the Middlesex Hospital for a bone-density scan. Anorexics tend to have very low bone density, which means they are vulnerable to fractures and osteoporosis. The doctors wanted to assess my risks.

We climbed into a taxi with Larry, my social worker from Sedgemoor, and off we went. The doorstop was still in my dungarees as I quietly congratulated myself on getting away with it so brilliantly.

CHAPTER 15

HUNTERCOMBE

I lay on the padded bed as the scanner glided up and
down my body, checking out exactly what damage I
had done to my bones.

Then, all of a sudden, the nurse froze as she stared at
the screen.

'What on earth is that?' she said, pointing at a dark
object on the monitor.

She pulled up my T-shirt and as her eyes fixed on the 3-
kilo (6½ lb) lump of iron that had been secreted inside my
dungarees all day, everything became clear.

My fate was sealed – although naively I didn't yet
realise it.

Outside the Middlesex Hospital, Mum, Larry and I
picked up another cab, which jerked its way through the
afternoon traffic.

'Which train for Taunton do you think we'll make?' I
asked Mum as I gazed dreamily out of the window.

She looked at me, a mixture of fear and frustration in
her eyes.

'We're not going back to Sedgemoor, Nik,' she said. 'The doctors have said you are too ill – you have to go straight to Huntercombe Manor.'

I didn't need to ask what Huntercombe Manor was. It was well known on the 'anorexic circuit' as a specialist centre for teenagers and adults with severe eating disorders and in desperate need of refeeding and help. I'd been threatened with it loads of times when I was at Great Ormond Street.

There was only one place 'worse' than Huntercombe and that was Rhodes Farm. No one came out of Rhodes Farm without being fattened up. Huntercombe was supposed to be tough too, although I knew a few people had managed to beat the system there.

But I still didn't want to go. I went mad in the cab, shouting and throwing myself around the back seat. God knows what the driver must have thought, but I didn't care.

Mum held on to me, trying to calm me down. 'Please, Nikki, we want you to live,' she kept saying. 'We want you to live.'

'I hate you!' I screamed, pushing her violently away from me. 'All you want is to ruin everything.'

But as we pulled up on the gravel drive outside Huntercombe Manor, even I, through my angry tears, couldn't fail to be awestruck by the place. It was like a scene out of *Four Weddings and a Funeral*. Set on the outskirts of Maidenhead, in Berkshire, Huntercombe was a beautiful old house surrounded by stunning grounds of neatly trimmed grass, mature shrubs, an orchard and even a secret walled garden.

We climbed up an imposing flight of steps into a main

hall where the floor was laid with deep carpet and the walls lined with huge oil paintings. There were grand murals everywhere, even on the ceiling.

It was probably the most beautiful building I had ever been in. But I didn't really care about any of that then. I'd been locked away inside so many hospitals and institutions that I couldn't give a toss what they looked like inside or what the staff and other patients were like. The only thing that mattered was what they were going to do to me there.

As I walked through the hall I saw a girl that I knew from Great Ormond Street going through the door for an evening out with her parents. I didn't even say hello but grabbed her arm and asked, 'Gemma, how much are they going to make me eat?'

'Probably about a thousand,' she replied grimly.

'No, I won't eat more than three hundred. I won't.'

Gemma gave me half a smile as she walked off with her mum. All us anorexics followed the same code. It wasn't about being friendly and having a chat about old times and mutual friends. The only thing that mattered was calories – how many and how to avoid them.

Three hundred calories a day was the top limit of what I'd been allowing myself during the past few weeks at Sedgemoor. It is a pitiful amount and not enough to survive on. That's why I was literally skin and bones the day I arrived at Huntercombe, my translucent skin drawn tightly across the jutting bones of my face.

I must have looked like the living dead because as my eyes met those of another girl of about my age standing in the hallway, she literally flinched in horror. I saw her take a small gasp, unable to take her eyes off my emaciated frame, and she stepped backwards slightly, as if repulsed by me.

It is strange that after such a violent reaction she should become my best friend at Huntercombe and probably the person who helped save my life.

'Hi, I'm Carly,' she said, in a girly little voice which seemed quite at odds with the troubled, world-weary look in her eyes.

Carly had been at Huntercombe for nine months and was approaching a normal weight, although still skinny by most people's standards.

Hello, I thought, instantly assessing her weight. Not as thin as me, I decided with satisfaction.

Then one of the staff came over and guided me up a flight of stairs to a kitchen where they sat me down at a table and brought me a banana and a glass of fruit juice. Carly followed me into the room and sat down opposite.

I wasn't allowed to talk to anyone until I'd eaten my snack, so Carly just sat there watching me in silence. But she didn't need to say anything. Just being there was enough to tell me that she would be a real friend.

The next step was to be weighed and measured. My weight was then just 27.7 kilos (4 stone 5 lb) and I was 152 centimetres (4 feet 10 inches) tall. I was 60 per cent of the weight I should have been at that age and height.

Huntercombe had an adolescent unit and an adult ward. I'd arrived as an emergency case and there were no beds free in the adolescent unit, so I was put in with the grown-ups. I'd never met an adult with an eating disorder before and it was really shocking. There was a woman called Jane, who was 20, who looked so thin and so old already that it was sad to watch her move around the ward. Then there was another woman, Fran, who was not just painfully skinny but sad-looking too.

But the good thing about being on the adult section was that there was more freedom. The first night I went into my bedroom, closed the door and started exercising immediately. I must have done 300 star-jumps that night and no one noticed.

Obviously it was good for shedding calories but it also kept me warm. My body weight had fallen so low that I was constantly freezing and the high ceilings and old-fashioned windows at Huntercombe meant draughts howled through the place at night.

When I finally lay down in bed, I rolled on to my side and put my hands between my thighs for warmth. But when my knees met there was a gap above them – I was that thin.

When I woke up, at 5am, I was still freezing cold, so I got up and inspected my new room properly. I opened the door of my new wardrobe and inside noticed a full-length mirror. I immediately pulled off my clothes and inspected my naked body for the first time in three years – there had been no full-length mirrors at Great Ormond Street or Sedgemoor.

I was so shocked at what I saw that I couldn't quite believe it was me at first. I had to keep touching my legs and stomach to make sure it wasn't an illusion or one of those magic mirrors that I remembered looking in with Dad when we went to Blackpool Pleasure Beach.

The figure looking back at me was little more than a skeleton with just a thin layer of tissue paper for skin, drawn over the stick-like bones. I stood staring for a good couple of minutes, considering what I'd become.

And my verdict?

Brilliant, I thought. It's been worth every moment of all that hard work.

I pulled my clothes and Dr Martens boots on and thought, I'm going for a jog now.

Now I'd seen what I'd achieved through all those years of starving myself, I was more determined than ever that I couldn't let anything destroy all my good work.

But I knew that meant I was going to have to fight even harder than I had ever done before.

I slipped quietly out of the door downstairs and started running around the garden, hoping no one would wake and notice me.

I managed a few days of dawn jogs before one morning one of the nurses came rushing across the grass towards me.

'What do you think you're doing, Nikki?' she scolded. 'Come inside right now. And if you do this again you will be put on total supervision.'

I later found out a girl called Paula, a total bitch, had seen me out of the window and snitched to the nurses.

I'd only been there a couple of days and I was already loathed by all the girls on the adolescent unit. I was the thinnest, most ill-looking girl they'd ever had there and they hated it. When it came to anorexia, I was the best. They could see it and they were jealous. At this time I was so immersed in my anorexia that I was unable to think or concentrate on anything else. I was desperately sick, but didn't realise it.

I'd been at Huntercombe less than a week when Mum came to visit and brought with her my old schoolfriend Lena. We'd kept in touch by writing letters to each other but I hadn't seen Lena for almost two years. When she walked into my room I was stunned. She had turned into a young woman – she had boobs! And hips! She was wearing a pair of trendy white patent wedges, an A-line skirt and a skimpy little top. I looked at her and thought, Wow, you look like a model in a magazine.

There was me in my tie-dye trousers and pink hair with a ring through my nose, looking like a skeleton being propped upright by a pair of Doc Martens.

We were both 14, but I knew then that we were worlds apart. I thought, You're not the little girl I used to run up and down the street with in a shower cap and a swimming costume, knocking on people's doors and running away. You're not the little girl who came for sleepovers in a tent in the garden on Halloween. You're doing your thing now and I'm doing mine. So I just ignored her for her entire visit.

I wasn't jealous of Lena and what she looked like. I couldn't even think that far – all I could think about was what was happening to me right there, right then.

'Mum, please get me out of here,' I pleaded as Lena stared at me with a mixture of shock and revulsion. 'Take me back to Sedgemoor. I can't stay here. They're going to make me fat. They're going to make me eat.'

Then I'd repeat the same thing over and over again.

Mum and Lena left after a couple of hours. They were barely outside the building when Lena burst into tears. 'She's dying, isn't she?' she said to Mum.

Mum couldn't say 'no', but she couldn't bring herself to admit the answer might be 'yes' either. Lena was just a kid herself and had never seen anything as shocking before.

'Nikki didn't even notice I was there,' she said. 'She's so

175

caught up in her illness. That's all that she can see.' Mum nodded. Lena was absolutely right.

I didn't care about any of them then – Mum, Dad, Natalie, Lena. All I cared about was not eating.

After a fortnight I was moved into a bed on the adolescent unit and then my battle really began.

There were two kitchens in the unit: a downstairs one for residents on the road to recovery, who were allowed to prepare their own food, and an upstairs one where nurses supervised everything. That's where I, Carly and the other four really sick kids – Debbie, Hannah, Paula and Simon – all ate. Simon was the first boy I'd ever met with an eating disorder. He was from North America but had to come to England because it was the only place he could get treatment.

Simon and I were the sickest. Hannah was pretty ill too but she hated me as she knew I was her main competition and much skinnier than her. Paula and Debbie were just weird. Paula used to regurgitate all her food and Debbie wasn't really a proper anorexic – she just pretended to be by not eating, because she wanted attention.

Every week the Huntercombe dietician, Yvonne, would plan out our individual diet sheets.

When I arrived, my breakfast was one box of cereal from a selection pack with one cup of milk and a cup of fruit juice. Snack time was one digestive biscuit and another cup of juice and lunch was a hot dinner off the menu – either fish, chicken or vegetarian.

They allowed us to be vegetarian at Huntercombe – and so of course all the girls were and I joined in too. It gave us something else to be in control of.

My first lunch there was fried veggie sausages with fried

parmentier potatoes and spinach creamed in butter with nutmeg. It was horrific for me – so many calories and so much fat. When I picked the spinach off my plate there was a disgusting yellow puddle of melted butter where it had been sitting.

At the first opportunity I shoved one of the sausages up my sleeve. There were eight of us at the table, all trying to get away with similar tricks and the nurses couldn't look at all of us all the time. So next a few potatoes went down my knickers. They were scalding hot, but I was desperate to get rid of them.

I managed to hide one and a half sausages and quite a bit of potato but what I hadn't reckoned on was the 45-minute time limit at Huntercombe for every meal. That meant you had to finish your main course, fruit, yoghurt and juice in the time otherwise you'd have to eat the whole lot again.

Disaster.

My time was up and I still hadn't drunk the juice.

'You were told the rules, Nikki,' said Adam, my key nurse, plonking another plate of veggie sausages and potatoes in front of me. 'You're going to have to do it all again.'

'No way!' I yelled. 'I'm not eating all that again.'

I sat there furious, glaring at the full plate and refusing to even pick up my knife and fork. And I was still there at afternoon snack time at 3.30, when a piece of fruit and a juice were added to the pile of food in front of me.

Adam tried desperately to persuade me to eat but I wasn't having any of it.

Normally, when dinner came I would then have been expected to eat my lunch, snack *and* dinner all in one go.

I begged Adam, 'Please, can we just forget about lunch and snack and start afresh at dinner. Please?' Finally he agreed, but the other girls in Huntercombe were furious that I had been let off.

It was the same rule of getting your entire meal replaced if you left anything on the plate or if you hid food or ignored three warnings from a nurse about playing with food or separating items of food on the plate. Separating food, moving it around the plate and cutting it up into tiny pieces are all anorexic traits. Lots of anorexics don't like the idea of one type of food touching another. For instance, chicken must never touch vegetables, so they'll separate them. Then they'll eat the items in strict order, starting with the one lowest in calories. I was always getting into trouble for separating food and for pressing food down on my plate with a fork to squeeze all the oil out of it.

For my first couple of weeks at Huntercombe I was allowed to start off on fairly low-fat foods – I think it was probably just to get me used to being there. But after that I was put straight on to 2,500 calories a day. I'd got used to eating just 300, so that was a terrible shock.

Meals suddenly became things like pizza and chips. But chips were horrific for me. I hadn't eaten them in literally years and I couldn't handle it at all.

There were other nightmare dinners too. Bubble and squeak was horrendous because it was fried, and spaghetti soya (like spag Bol but veggie) always came in huge portions and was really filling. Macaroni cheese and the risotto were killers too, as they came drenched in cheese and butter. They were delicious but you could feel the calories melting into your body.

I'd always hide anything I could get away with but if I was spotted and had my meal replaced I'd go mad. I could feel anger building up inside me like the engines of a space rocket about to blast off. The anger would build and build in my chest and then I'd explode, shouting and lashing out at anyone who came near me.

I'd cry hysterically, screaming for my mum and to be allowed home. I'd fling myself around the room, hurl my chair and writhe around the floor, clawing at my skin and pulling clumps of hair out of my scalp.

It must have been horrible for people to watch. The anger would come pouring out of my body, leaving me shattered. At the same time I was fully aware that my fits were pretty good for burning up calories too!

I really think my mental torment did help me avoid putting on weight. I was always so anxious and stressed thinking about how to avoid the next meal, and how to get out of there, that it must have had an effect.

My fits were happening more and more frequently – most days and sometimes every mealtime. The other girls hated me for them.

'Just fucking get on and eat it, Nikki,' they would shout if I was refusing food and building up to an hysterical fit.

A characteristic of this eating disorder is the competitive urge to be the thinnest and most celebrated anorexic in a particular place. So the other girls were already jealous because I was the thinnest and the illest. I was top-dog anorexic.

Hannah was particularly jealous. She was an incredibly clued-up anorexic, just like me, and between us we must have known the calorie content of every food in the world.

I'd say to her things like, 'Hannah, how many calories

do you think were in that lentil cutlet?' She'd sigh deeply and say, 'Ohhh, what do you care, Nikki? You're *sooo* skinny already. I don't want to talk about it.'

Hannah could be really mean. She would always copy what I chose on the menu just to make sure I wasn't getting away with fewer calories than her. And if she ever saw me hiding food at mealtimes she wouldn't hesitate to tell a nurse. But I'd land her in it if I saw her hiding food too. It was every anorexic for herself.

I'm sure a lot of the nurses hated me. They were always having to tell me off and I was probably just too much trouble for them. Every mealtime I would be refusing to eat, yelling and getting hysterical and violent, so it must have been really hard work looking after me. In the end I think some of the nurses just stopped challenging me every time I hid food or refused to eat and they just let me get on with what I wanted – which was not eating.

I can't blame them. A lot of them were in their late teens or 20s and probably just wanted an easy life. They got paid the same amount whether they chased me around trying to make me eat all day or just didn't bother. And I'm sure it was much more enjoyable for them to spend their shift sitting with a compliant kid who was making progress than some shrieking nightmare like me.

I was foul to some of the agency nurses. I was so rude, telling them to fuck off at mealtimes and pushing food away. One day I was having a screaming fit about being made to eat something when one of the agency staff, Sharon, really lost her rag with me. She shoved me under the desk where she was working, pulled her chair in tight so I had no chance of escaping, then left me there for over an hour. I was trying to scratch and bite her legs but she just carried on typing away on the desk above my head.

Sometimes I think Carly was the only person at Huntercombe who liked me at all. She wasn't like the others. In fact she wasn't even properly anorexic. She was more obsessive-compulsive, although she had been dangerously thin when she was admitted. Her problem was that she couldn't eat anything which she thought might have been contaminated by someone's fingers. So she didn't even mind foods that were higher in calories so long as they came out of a sealed wrapper. She wouldn't eat a piece of fruit because anyone might have touched it but she would eat a chocolate bar if she opened it herself. And she would only eat a slice of bread if it came out a fresh bag that she had opened.

In the kitchen at Huntercombe there would be 12 cartons of juice or ten bottles of milk open at any one time, because Carly could only drink something she had just opened herself. She and I had had similar upbringings and as soon as we met it felt like we had loads in common. She'd been at stage school and I wanted to be an actress, so we would put on shows in the day room, singing songs from *Bugsy Malone* and *Starlight Express*. Carly loved doing it and I enjoyed it too – but for me the chief motivation was always that it was a way of moving around and exercising. The rest of the time the nurses would make me sit down so as not to use up calories.

Sometimes at night Carly and I would sneak into the grounds of the manor house and slip into the walled garden, looking for ghosts and trying to scare each other.

In the adolescent unit I had my own room and Carly was sharing with Debbie but she still spent every evening in my room until the nurses threw her out. Sometimes the nurses would let her bring cushions up from her bedroom and put them on my floor and stay for a sleepover. We'd be awake chatting for hours and could talk about anything – although never about our illness.

We terrorised the nurses and made up songs about them. 'More ag, more ag,' we'd shout at one called Morag every time she walked past.

After dinner Carly and I would often go and sit in the phone booth downstairs and ring our mums. In the evenings there was a receptionist on the front desk called Barbara who would sit and knit. One night, Carly and I thought it was hilarious to keep ringing the front desk from the phone booth, pretending we were Chinese and trying to get through to a takeaway. 'Harro,' we shouted down the phone. 'We want chicken noodles and egg flied lice, prease. You deriver?'

After about the fifth call Barbara must have realised what was going on, and she stormed round to the phone booth and yanked us out. 'I'm fed up with you two,' she shouted. 'I don't wanna be working 'ere, do I?'

We ran off laughing until our stomach muscles ached.

We'd have a great laugh in classes too. There were lessons every day, although I was too sick to concentrate on English or maths for very long. For a while the only thing I could focus on was art.

After my first fortnight at Huntercombe my weight had increased by about 1 kilo (2 lb), but from then on it hardly rose at all.

I'd become determined I would never ever go above 33 kilos (5 stone 2 lb) and so the closer I got to that figure the more difficult I became to control.

CHAPTER 16

I'LL NEVER HAVE TO EAT AGAIN

By the midsummer of 1997 – three months after arriving at Huntercombe – it was very clear I wasn't getting any better.

I remained adamant I would not go above 33 kilos and was exercising at every opportunity. Each night I would pace up and down my bedroom before doing a round of star-jumps and sit-ups. And if there were no nurses around I would run up and down the stairs over and over again. Once, I even managed to lock myself in a room with an exercise bike. I was in there for 15 minutes before a nurse found me and pulled me off it. I felt particularly victorious that day.

Even in the day room I stood up all the time, stamping from foot to foot. But all the girls in the unit would stand whenever they could to burn off calories. We must have looked so strange to people who came in.

I also used a relentless succession of scams to avoid food.

I hadn't been at Huntercombe very long when one day I

saw a member of staff returning to the kitchen, tapping her security code into a keypad and pushing open the door. The next time she went back to the kitchen I stood closely behind her and committed the security code to memory. What a brilliant bit of ammunition, I thought.

That night I waited until all the nurses were busy elsewhere, then I went up to the kitchen, typed in the code and I was in. I didn't really have any specific plan – it just felt that I was having one over on the system.

Inside the big kitchen, lined with cupboards and worktops, I began rummaging through boxes of food and inside the fridge. I took a couple of large, half-full cartons of milk out of the fridge and filled them up with water. That'll be a few less calories on our cereal in the morning, I thought. Another little victory.

A few weeks later I sneaked back into the kitchen and went through all the paperwork until I found my personalised diet sheet. Then I picked up a pen and drew a neat line through my afternoon snack. No more two-finger KitKats!

The next time the dietician checked my list she saw what I had done, so it was a very brief victory, but worthwhile all the same. From then on the dietician had to sign every single alteration made to anyone's diet sheet.

By now I was supposed to be on a 2,500-calorie diet but because of hiding food and exercising I still wasn't putting on much weight.

Every meal was a battle and the doctors wanted to take action before my condition deteriorated further. They decided there was only one solution – I'd have to go back to being tube-fed directly into my stomach.

'We're going to have to reopen your gastrostomy,' a

charge nurse called Kate told me one afternoon after I'd refused yet another lunch.

Just the mention of gastrostomy made me feel ill. 'I'll eat,' I said immediately. 'Please, anything but that.

'You can't talk your way out of this one,' Kate said firmly. 'You're having the op to put a tube back in whether you like it or not' – she paused – '*but* we promise we'll only actually use it at night if you refuse to eat during the day.'

The night before the operation I was so nervous I couldn't sleep. I was desperately tired but I couldn't close my eyes, I was too scared of the coming morning.

In the end I got Mum, who was there, to push me downstairs for a cigarette. I was still on about 20 a day at that point.

Once again there were huge risks in my having a general anaesthetic and such major surgery when my weight was so low. But if the alternative was death, the doctors believed it was a risk worth taking. As for me, I didn't care about the op, only about how much food they could pump down the tube.

In the morning I was transferred by ambulance to Great Ormond Street. It felt strange being back there again, almost like going home.

A few hours after my second gastrostomy operation in 18 months, I was back in Huntercombe. There the doctors gave me a choice – 3,000 calories a day if they used the tube, or a couple of hundred less if I ate proper food. To me that 200-calorie difference was enough to make me, eat proper food and so for the first couple of days I complied and ate their enormous meals during the day to avoid being tube-fed at night. I could feel the tube sticking out of my stomach and it remained a constant threat of what would happen if I refused to eat.

But the food was too much. One day, after a massive bubble and squeak, they served up profiteroles with cream. I can't do this any more, I thought, looking sadly at the mountain of choux pastry and chocolate. How could they expect someone like me to eat all that? Even someone with a huge appetite would find it intimidating.

I was also clashing with the nurses all the time and found it exhausting. They were trying to prevent me from walking anywhere to lose calories, so every time I stood up they'd say, 'Sit down, Nikki. What it is you want, we'll get it for you.'

My mood was very low. I was having big meal after big meal and not even being allowed to move around in between times. Imagine how you feel slumped in the chair after Christmas dinner. Well, it was like that every single day.

I knew I couldn't take any more – of the food or of any of it. I was sick and tired of everything. I didn't even get any joy from Mum and Dad's visits any more.

Once Dad came to see me and he said, 'Sit down, will you?' as I paced about the room.

'No,' I snapped. 'I won't. You can go home if you want me to sit down.'

Having him there meant nothing more to me than an excuse to be out of sight of a nurse and to be walking up and down using up calories.

I'd rather stand up and walk around than have a visit from him, I thought. I don't want to see him that much.

I knew Mum and Dad weren't going to take me out of there – I'd been told I wouldn't go home until I was at least

18. If they're not coming to take me back with them, I'd think, what's the point of their coming at all? I was angry at them for leaving me there and felt very alone.

It was during one of Dad's visits a couple of months earlier that I had slipped a bottle of paracetamol into my pocket one afternoon when he'd taken me to Sainsbury's to buy toiletries. I'd kept them in my bedside drawer as a kind of security measure in case things ever got really bad. And now they really were bad.

One night I climbed into bed with the bottle and sat staring at it. I knew exactly what I was going to do. I just can't be bothered with any of this any more, I thought. I can't face the food. I'm going to be stuck in here – or somewhere pretty similar – for years and I hate Mum and Dad for letting me go through it.

The first time I'd taken a paracetamol overdose, at Great Ormond Street, was to show everyone how angry I was they hadn't let me home for Christmas. That was a 'this'll teach them' protest. But this time, this was it – I wanted to die. I'd run out of steam, I'd run out of energy for fighting and I wasn't winning any more. They'd beaten me with their tubes and their drugs and their power. They were going to feed me whatever, so what was the point of carrying on?

I wasn't scared or worried or tearful. It just seemed the logical thing to do. There really wasn't anything worth living for. I just wanted the whole nightmare to be over.

My bedroom door was wide open as I wasn't allowed to close it any more in case I was exercising, but I was still able to swallow the pills without anyone noticing. I got out of bed and went nearer the door so I could hear if anyone was coming. The first pill tasted sour in my mouth as I jerked my head back and swallowed it down. The second was easier and by the third I was used to the metallic flavour on my tongue.

I didn't have any water, so it became harder and harder to swallow each pill as the moisture in my mouth dried up. But nothing was going to stop me and I kept on swallowing them, sometimes ramming two down at the same time, sometimes gagging as a pill stuck to the back of my throat. Then I started to retch with the effort of getting them down. A couple of times one came straight back up again but even that didn't stop me. I just swallowed it again.

I didn't give Mum and Dad a single thought. I didn't give a shit about them.

Pill followed pill followed pill. And I felt glad. Just another couple of hours and this would all be over. No more calories, no more screaming, no more injections, no more hospitals.

I remember getting to 25 and thinking that was probably enough.

Then I climbed back into bed and closed my eyes. This is it then, I thought. This is the end of it. I've finally got what I want. I can go to sleep and I'll never have to eat again. I'll never have to put on any more weight.

Then I slipped into unconsciousness.

But it wasn't to be that simple. Two hours later I came round, feeling more sick than I'd ever felt before. I managed to swing my legs off the bed and staggered down the corridor to the toilet, where I was violently sick. I was roaring sick over and over again until I was bringing up acid-green stomach juices. I lay on the floor of the toilet for hours, too weak to move.

Eventually a nurse came in and found me and asked what was the matter. I couldn't even answer and they assumed it was an extreme tummy bug and took me back to bed.

I lay there totally gutted that I had failed. I was crying, desperate and furious. The pills had been my last resort and they hadn't worked.

The next day they said there was no point in giving me any food because I was still being sick, so I stayed in bed all morning, sipping Diet Coke because I felt so thirsty.

When they called Mum she guessed immediately that I had overdosed. She rushed to the hospital and, without questioning me first, went straight to the nurses and told them what she feared.

'It's impossible – she can't have done,' said the charge nurse, Pauline. 'She has been on close supervision, so there's no way she could have got hold of any tablets.'

But Mum knew me better than anyone. And she knew the look of utter hopelessness in my eyes. She came and sat with me but I couldn't speak to her or even look at her. I was just so traumatised that I'd failed.

What I didn't realise, though, was that I was still in grave danger of dying from liver failure, which can happen up to two days after an overdose. A paracetamol overdose is particularly dangerous in anorexic cases because of the effect that continual starvation has already had on the liver.

After sitting with me for a while, stroking my head and holding my hand, Mum went back downstairs to the nurse. 'I'm telling you my daughter has overdosed,' she said firmly. 'And if you don't help her and anything happens to her I will be blaming you.'

Still nothing happened – and I didn't admit a thing –

until Mum finally made the doctors give me a blood test a couple of days later. The results immediately showed a high dosage of paracetamol in my system. All of a sudden it turned into panic stations and I was immediately wheeled into an ambulance and taken to A&E at nearby Wexham Park Hospital.

There I waited an hour and a half to be assessed. Mum was terrified I could be dying in front of her eyes and still no one was doing anything to help.

'Please, please, will you get her on a ward?' Mum begged one of the nurses.

The unit was heaving with people and the nurse just looked at Mum with irritation and said brusquely, 'I'm sorry, but your daughter has put herself here. She can wait. We've got sick patients who haven't chosen to be here and they are our priority.'

We waited some more and finally I was put on a ward, assessed and placed on a drip.

By then I was feeling a bit better. I hadn't had to eat a thing for three days, so that alone had made me happier. But I was still angry I hadn't succeeded with the overdose.

After a couple of days' observation I was free to return to Huntercombe. But first I asked to speak to my specialist, Dr Lask, on the phone as he was still overseeing my treatment.

'I just can't do it, Dr Lask,' I said. 'I just can't face all that food you are giving me.' I really liked and respected Dr Lask. I felt he listened to what I was saying.

'I can only come back to Huntercombe if I can go back to 1,000 calories a day.'

He agreed.

So one week after the overdose I was back in

Huntercombe, my weight down to 28.3 kilos (4 stone 6 lb) as I hadn't been eating at Wexham Park.

I was put on 1,000 calories a day and I got away with murder with the nurses. They were all terrified that if they confronted me about anything I'd try to top myself again. It was all cool by me.

I was also allowed to negotiate my diet sheet with Yvonne, the dietician. She was lovely but she could be a bit of a soft touch and let me get away with a lot. On my sheet it said I had to have two digestives as my bedtime snack but I came up with a far better idea. 'Yvonne, I really want to try and have chocolate again,' I said one day. 'So maybe I could have one Jaffa Cake at night instead of the digestives.'

And she agreed! So, instead of two 78-calorie digestives, I was having one 45-calorie Jaffa Cake. Result!

Within days all the anorexics had suddenly developed a passion for Jaffa Cakes. And I had a great trick of holding one next to my hot night-time drink so that all the chocolate melted off on to the side of the mug.

I was constantly wiping chocolate, grease, cream or anything else I didn't want on to cups, plates, clothes or even my hair. My tops were always stained and dirty – but I didn't care, so long as I'd avoided some calories.

Back in Huntercombe my condition only deteriorated, though, as I again refused to eat.

My fragile mental state was even more precarious. I was having more and more temper fits. If the nurses tried to make me eat or I felt anything was getting out of control, I would start shouting, screaming and hyperventilating. I would flail around until my body became rigid and my back arched right back. It's a condition called opisthotonos, which I've since learned can be caused by a depressed brain function or is in some cases a side effect of a large amount of medication.

They injected me with a sedative a couple of times at Huntercombe but it wasn't as common as at Great Ormond Street.

The only person who could calm me down when I was having a fit was Carly. The nurses would shout at me, 'Come on, snap out of this! Get out of this, Nikki.' But Carly would wrap her arms tight around me and keep cuddling me and soothing me as I sobbed and screamed.

I'd still be trying to smash my head and my body against walls and the floor but she would hold me and protect my head. I really didn't care if I knocked myself unconscious or even killed myself – ever since the last overdose I'd had no fear of dying.

But whatever I did, Carly never let go of me. She would stroke my hair until eventually exhaustion overwhelmed me and I calmed down. I guess all I really wanted was to feel cuddled and loved, and that is what she did.

Other days I would go out into the grounds to the 'screaming tree', which was where kids could go to get their anger out. I'd stand there for hours screaming into the wind, trying to force out of my body this ball of fury which was dominating my life.

Sometimes I'd feel as though I was going to explode with the poison that was swilling around inside me. Most of the time I felt anxious, agitated and fat. Sleep gave some relief but often I would toss and turn for hours, locked in my misery.

I'd become too sick to even consider getting better. I could hardly think about the next five minutes, let alone the future and what I wanted from it. I couldn't imagine any other existence than the one I was living at that moment. Maybe I'd become institutionalised within my own anorexia. Certainly I'd known nothing else and thought of little else for the past seven years.

In my head I was just stuck where I was and nothing could shift me.

At that point I was on all sorts of drugs, including Prozac. After a while I was put on a different anti-depressant, Seroxat, as Prozac was making me twitch. Then there were the sedative pills at night to keep me calm and help me sleep – but also to prevent me getting out of bed and exercising.

One evening we all had a Chinese takeaway for dinner. Supposedly it was a treat but for me it was horrific. It was stir-fried vegetables, wallowing in grease – which was, and still is, my worst food fear. As I looked at the greasy pool of food on my plate I thought, Just eat it and then you can run away. You can exercise off the fat and then you'll never have to eat anything like this again. That thought was the only thing that got me through that awful meal.

Afterwards I waited until the front-desk receptionist went home at nine o'clock, then slipped out of the main doors. Huntercombe isn't a locked unit and it was so easy. We were allowed lunchtime strolls, so I knew exactly where I was going. I ran down the lane that led to the main road, then jogged straight to Taplow railway station.

It was pitch-dark but quite a warm night. I waited for 20 minutes on the platform, then jumped on a train to Paddington. There I changed on to the tube, all the time dodging ticket collectors and any commuters staring at my emaciated frame in concern. I jumped off the train at

Northwood Hills and ran all the way home. It felt so good to be back.

I banged on our front door and waited breathlessly. I thought Mum would be shocked to see me, but surely she'd be glad too – she'd throw her arms around me then we'd snuggle up on the sofa in front of the telly. Wouldn't we?

When Mum opened the door she didn't look at all shocked – just angry. Huntercombe had already called her to say I was missing.

'You're not staying, Nikki,' she said. 'You've got to go straight back.'

'But I want to come home!' I yelled. 'I'm not going back.'

Ten minutes later, though, Mum had started the car and was bundling me into the back with Tony's help. It took both of them to haul me in there and slam the door shut on my kicking and screaming.

And then back we went. I hadn't even seen my bedroom. Hadn't even had a night snuggled under my own Forever Friends duvet. Instead it was hell once again for me.

I'd probably only been gone about three hours when Mum guided me back into the massive entrance hall at Huntercombe, the ceiling murals gazing down on me as I stood there beaten and exhausted. At least I've missed evening snack, I thought dismally. That's some calories avoided.

Soon afterwards, in January 1998, Mum and Dad were called to Huntercombe for another big meeting about my future.

My weight was at 32.4 kilos (5 stone 1 lb), which meant that in the eight months I had been there, I had put on just 4.7 kilos (10½ lb). Dr Lask had reached the point where he had to accept Huntercombe wasn't working for me. I sat in the dining room and waited to be called down to join everyone in the main office. Although I had no idea what they were discussing, I knew instinctively it wasn't going to be good news for me.

Finally one of the nurses called me into the meeting. She suggested Carly go with me – they must have known I was likely to have a major fit and Carly would be the only one able to calm me down.

Carly and I walked into the grand, wood-panelled office with huge sash windows looking over neatly mowed lawns. Mum, Dad, Dr Lask, a man from the Social Services' funding department and Dr Mark Tattersall and Dr Lakintosch from Huntercombe were all sitting round in a large circle.

Carly shot me a reassuring smile as we sat down and Dr Tattersall began talking.

'Now, Nikki,' he said. 'We've spent a very long time discussing the best way to help you get better and we've come to the conclusion that you could really benefit from some time at Rhodes Farm. It's an excellent place with all the facilities to really help you.'

Well, I think he said that last bit, but I didn't really hear much after the words 'Rhodes Farm'. The two words pulsated in my head – it was every anorexic's nightmare come true.

I didn't need any explanation of what Rhodes Farm was like – everyone on the anorexic circuit knew all about it. It was the stuff of horror stories told in hushed voices late at night: deep-fried fish in batter, cheese sandwiches, cream with everything and mayonnaise shoved up your nose through a tube if you didn't comply.

Nina and Debbie had both been at Rhodes Farm and their stories of plate after plate of huge-calorie meals had left girls in terror of the place. And there was no healthy-eating regime at there at all. You would get one apple a day and everything else was microwaved meals already engorged with calories and then laden with extra cheese. Just mentioning the name sent a shudder of fear through the girls at Huntercombe.

'No,' I said quite simply. 'No, I'm not going. Not me. I'm doing OK here, I don't need to move.'

Rhodes Farm was for other girls, for losers who'd get beaten by the system. It wasn't for me – I was too good at getting away with stuff, with winning. Going to Rhodes Farm meant no chance of winning any more. My battle would be over. And that was terrifying.

'I'm afraid there is no choice, Nikki. You have to go,' said Dr Tattersall.

'But I'm not going there – I'm really not,' I kept repeating, aware of the terror in my voice as it became clear their minds were made up. I could feel, too, that familiar sense of anger building up inside me and I knew I was going to flip.

I sprang out of the chair and darted for the door but Mum jumped up and stood in my way. I lashed out at her with my arms, then spun around and made for the partly open window. No one was quick enough to stop me as I flung myself through the gap and jumped four feet down to the garden. Then I ran until my legs buckled and I went sprawling.

In moments Carly was with me, holding me as I cried, and then I threw myself back, slamming my head into the ground and clawing wildly at myself.

'No, no, no. I'm not going!' I kept screaming.

I went totally mental and this time there was nothing even Carly could say to help me.

They were going to send me to Rhodes Farm. After all those years of fighting, they had beaten me.

CHAPTER 17

RHODES FARM

'Right, Nikki, listen and I'll explain. Monday it's a four-finger KitKat, Tuesday is a Toffee Crisp and Wednesday is a Lion Bar.'

It was my last night at Huntercombe and Debbie was talking me through the feeding regime I would face on my arrival at Rhodes Farm the following morning. 'Thursday is a Picnic and Friday it's a Caramel,' she continued. 'You have to eat a chocolate bar every single day.'

I was lying on cushions between Debbie and Carly's beds. As a special treat before leaving I'd been allowed a sleepover in their room. Although I'd never been particularly good friends with Debbie I needed her that night, and she and I lay awake for hours as I pumped her for information about life at Rhodes Farm.

Poor old Carly, my best mate, who for months had held me when I cried and been the only person who could make me laugh when everything seemed so bleak. That night she didn't get a look-in. In the end she fell asleep, leaving me and Debbie dissecting every detail of the Rhodes Farm regime. Debbie had spent several months there and, like all its other patients, she had piled weight on during her stay. It was only afterwards that she had lost it again and had to be admitted to Huntercombe.

'But there must be some way I can beat the system, Debbie,' I said for the hundredth time.

'I've told you, Nikki,' she replied. 'There isn't.'

When Debbie finally fell asleep I cried into my pillow, terrified of what was going to happen. My only hope was that I wasn't just any other silly anorexic off the street, but I was the best anorexic out there and if anyone could beat Rhodes Farm I could.

The next morning I said goodbye to Carly. She'd been such a good friend to me and I loved her. But at that point I was so stuck in my illness that all I could think about was what was waiting for me at Rhodes Farm.

I climbed into the back of Mum's car and we set off for London. Soon we reached the western suburbs and the traffic grew thicker. This is it then, I thought. I'm just going to have to give myself over and let them get on with whatever it is they want to do to me.

I didn't have to wait long to find out exactly what that was. Within a couple of hours of arriving at Rhodes Farm I was sitting in front of a mammoth plate of chicken Kiev and chips, followed by a large KitKat.

From the outside, Rhodes Farm Clinic, in Mill Hill, north-west London, looks like a large, detached family house. Inside too it was like a proper home, with a cosy blue-tiled kitchen complete with long dining table and Welsh dresser. There were lounges with sofas you could sink deep into and floral curtains at the windows. Upstairs it was a rabbit warren of one-, two-, three- and four-person bedrooms, each decorated in a different theme with matching duvet covers and curtains.

Rhodes Farm had been the home of Dr Dee Dawson when she first started taking in teenagers with eating disorders back in 1991. But by the time I arrived it had been turned over entirely to caring for up to 32 kids at any one time.

Mum and I stood on the front step and rang the doorbell. After a couple of minutes it was flung open and there stood Helen, one of my nurses from Great Ormond Street. She didn't even need to say hello for me to hear her voice in my head again. 'Neeekkeeee, I reeeally want you to eat that bisceeeeet,' she had used to say to me time after time in her thick Geordie accent. Oh great, this is all I need, I thought as I summoned up all my energy to flash her a forced smile and step into the main hall.

As soon as I arrived I was weighed and measured and then Mum and I were shown into the garden for a meeting with one of the nurses, who spelled out exactly what was going to happen to me.

Rhodes Farm has an extremely strict policy whereby all patients must put on 1 kilo (2 lb) every week of their stay – not more and certainly not less. The clinic's success rate with this is remarkable and they boast that no child remains in their care not putting on weight. I'd spent months and months in various different units never putting on weight, and I was terrified about how they could be so sure they would achieve it with me.

Under the 1-kilo-a-week scheme, everyone who goes into Rhodes Farm is immediately given the date they will be discharged at their target weight. I went in on 9 January

1998 weighing 31.3 kilos (4 stone 13 lb) and was given a discharge date of 8 May, at which point, they calculated, I would be 45 kilos (7 stone 1lb). But when they revealed this target to me, I went mad. 'There's no way I'm going up to 45 kilos,' I stormed. 'I won't do it.' I flew into a tantrum and threw myself around the garden for the best part of an hour, screaming and thrashing my arms around.

I smashed Mum in the face, I was so mad at her for bringing me there, and the following day she had a terrible black eye.

What I didn't know then was that my every move was falling under the scrutiny of Dee Dawson, who was staring out of the kitchen window at my antics as the other girls quietly ate their lunch. 'It would appear,' she said to the girls in her very correct and considered manner, 'that the child from hell has arrived.'

When I finally calmed down enough to go inside, Dee came over and slowly looked me up and down, before saying, 'What a strange little thing you are.' She was probably right as what she must have seen that day in front of her was a scrawny little creature with tear stains down her face, pink hair, umpteen rings through her nose and ears and purple nail varnish.

Dee, by contrast, was a strong-looking woman in her 50s, her suit and brown bobbed hair reinforcing her no-nonsense appearance.

Standing face to face, maybe at that moment we both met our nemesis. We were poles apart but in some ways very similar, both being determined to succeed. This was going to be my greatest battle yet.

'No nonsense' pretty much summed up the philosophy of Rhodes Farm. The main focus was on feeding up dangerously ill girls so that they could enjoy some of the activities on offer there – dance, drama, trips to the theatre, sport – and then begin to actively engage with individual, group and family therapy.

Dee felt other institutions placed too much emphasis on therapy in the early stages and gave girls too much choice and involvement in meal planning. At Rhodes it was 'like it or lump it'.

Mum kissed me goodbye and Dee took me to the dining room, where the other kids were finishing their lunch.

Everyone in the room looked at me. I could see them assessing my weight, looking for the jagged edges of my bones jutting through my jeans and T-shirt. They'd heard about me already – how I'd been kicking around the anorexic circuit for seven years with no one yet able to sort me out.

I'm not sure what they were expecting me to do when I took my place in the empty chair at the table, but they weren't going to get any dramas. Not that day, anyway.

Instead I picked up my knife and fork and calmly ate the chicken Kiev and chips placed in front of me.

All new arrivals at Rhodes Farm are on 1,500 calories a day for the first three days, which I could just about cope with. But then my daily allowance was upped to 2,000 and after a week to 2,500 until it finally hit 3,700 because I had so much weight to gain. Not even the stories I'd been told by former Rhodes Farm patients could have prepared me for day after day of 3,700 calories.

At Huntercombe we had eaten generally very healthily from a menu devised individually for each patient by a qualified dietician. But at Rhodes Farm all you had was a number – your calorie intake for the day. And they didn't care if the food was healthy or unhealthy, as long as we got it down us.

In fact I thought at the time that I was on loads more than 3,700 calories a day because the portions were so huge. For breakfast I had 55 grams (2 oz) of high-calorie triple-choc muesli or maple pecan from Marks & Spencer mixed with 90 grams (3 oz) of Frosties, Golden Grahams or another sugary cereal soaked up with 0.15 litres (¼ pint) of full-cream milk – every morning. Thick globules of cream would float on top of the cereal. Disgusting. The milk alone was 68 calories but they didn't even count that. Or the 50 calories in my fruit juice.

Then to finish breakfast there was a 200-calorie muffin with so much butter on it that it would slide down my chin and arms as I ate it.

Lunches and dinners were often chicken Kiev and rice or similar, which they loved because the rice was good at mopping up the grease. They'd put maybe one carrot and a tomato on the plate but that was just to make it look pretty.

For pudding it would be something like a steamed sponge pudding with two scoops of ice cream. The pudding was 350 calories and the ice cream was supposed to be 150 but one day I had such a huge scoop – they'd put at least 300 calories of ice cream alone on my plate – that I called Dee in to complain. She went mad at the nurses. 'Who served this up?' she said. 'We'll never be able to calculate the girl's weight if we are confusing the portions like this. Take half that ice cream off her plate.'

After every meal I could hardly move, I felt so full. I was lethargic and uncomfortable all the time.

Then we'd go into class but we would only just have sat

down and started on our work when it was 'extras time'. They didn't even bother calling it snack time at Rhodes Farm. 'Extras' simply meant extra calories. Four boxes were laid out, labelled to show their contents: 50-calorie biscuits, 250-calorie biscuits, 300-calorie biscuits and king-size Mars Bars (450 calories). You had to select the right combination to meet your quota for the day. My 'extras' had to total 500 calories, so that was a king-size Mars and a 50-cal biscuit. And that was only an hour and a half after I'd finished an almighty great breakfast. For the first couple of weeks I complied, though eating those portions was agony.

I had a few mealtime tantrums but the staff weren't interested in my histrionics – they just told me to sit down and eat. A couple of times I was sedated with an injection but as the weeks rolled on even I realised that tantrums weren't getting me out of anything at Rhodes Farm.

Also, I think something in my mind had switched and deep down I was ready to cooperate and it was just habit which prevented me from doing so. Because for the first time in five years someone had offered me the chance to go home. To go back to my old bedroom, see my old friends and have a normal life again. Oh my God, I thought one morning. I could actually be going home in just 17 weeks' time.

There were two kitchens at Rhodes Farm. The brown kitchen was for the very severely anorexic kids and the blue kitchen was for those who were on the road to recovery and so were allowed to prepare their own food. In the brown kitchen sat the three anorexic 'pros', Janice, Sara and me. We would all sit in a line at the dinner table, Janice at the top because she had been there longest, then Sara and then me. I hadn't been there very long at all but my reputation as a 'special anorexic' won me a good position.

The meals would be handed by a member of staff to Janice, who would then hand them down the line. Janice, being first, would get first choice of whichever plate she thought looked smaller or lower in calories. Next it would be Sara's go, then mine. It was all-out war between the three of us as we were all so desperate to get the smallest portion, even though in reality there was probably almost no difference between them.

As each day passed I felt more and more sick at the thought of how much food they were going to serve up. I started trying to hide food at mealtimes and I got away with it for a few meals, but then one day Rachel, a really strict nurse, spotted me.

You could never get away with anything for very long at Rhodes Farm. They knew every trick in the book and watched you like hawks at dinner in case you were hiding or rubbing grease into your hair or clothes. Then there were regular room searches and spot checks on weight.

'OK – it's a cheese sandwich for you, Nikki,' said Rachel as she made me empty the food I'd just stashed down my knickers. They were the words everyone dreaded at Rhodes Farm. Cheese sandwiches were the punishment meals for breaking the rules. Each sandwich was about 500 calories, with chunky cubes of cheese put between two slices of bread lathered in butter so thick you could carve your name in it.

But if you refused the sandwich or spat it out you'd go on to a nasal tube feed. And this wasn't any namby-pamby milk feed like I'd had at Great Ormond Street. At Rhodes

Farm they liquidised a mixture of mayonnaise, double cream and Mars Bars, then squirted it up your nose. It seemed utterly barbaric. I couldn't believe they would do that to people – but they did.

What I didn't realise then, though, was that they rarely tubed people at Rhodes Farm and kept it for the absolute last-resort cases. Because in many ways tubing makes it too easy for anorexics – it gives them the option of totally retreating from food, which is what had happened to me at Great Ormond Street. By using the gastrostomy for more than 14 months I was able to remove myself from any interaction with food at all. I didn't need to get better, I could just plod along, taking in the calories they pumped into me. That's why they avoided the tube wherever possible at Rhodes Farm. Instead their philosophy was 'just get on and eat it'.

It was only now that I was able to see how most of the units I'd been in up until this time had pussyfooted around me. I'd been allowed to select meals and persisted in my tantrums. But at Rhodes Farm I wasn't being asked, persuaded or bullied into feeding. I was simply being told to do it. And I did.

There was no time or attention for people who messed around or wanted to hog the limelight. And, more than anything, there was the idea that if you did follow the programme you would go home – and soon. That was an amazing thought for me after so long away.

That's not to say I didn't continue to fight the system. It was still to be a while before I could let my guard down and give in. Meanwhile I continued to leave the dinner table with as much food still crammed in my mouth as I could squeeze in without looking like a hamster. As soon as I was out of the room I spat the entire mouthful into any bin or toilet. But when a member of staff spotted me doing it one day, it was cheese sandwich time again.

I was also exercising at any opportunity I could find. Every lunchtime we were allowed out for an hour's walk, the idea being that a bit of fresh air would make us feel better. But as soon as I was out of eyesight of the building I would break into a brisk run, although that was risky because members of staff would often come out checking on us in their cars. In addition I was exercising every night that I could get away with it in my bedroom.

But my best trick was picking up my plate at the end of the meal and taking it over to the sink, where I would pretend to wash it up. Then, with my back to the room, I'd throw up my entire lunch into the sink and ram it down the plug hole with my fingers. I'd learned to do it totally silently so no one noticed a thing.

I could puke up a 1,000-calorie lunch in less than a minute. First up would be the ice cream, which would reappear like foam, and then the main course. When I started to get an acidic residue swilling around my mouth and teeth I knew I'd got the lot up. Then I'd feel good again – nice and empty.

A lot of trust was placed in us, but the staff were able to monitor exactly what we were up to through the weekly weigh-ins, at which we were supposed to have gained a kilo each time. If a fortnight went past and you hadn't hit your target, all your privileges, including the lunchtime walk, were taken away and you were placed on supervision.

Once I'd started throwing up, hiding and spitting out food, my weight soon failed to make the weekly target and

I was put on supervision. At first I was supervised for one hour after meals to ensure I wasn't being sick. This meant that for the hour after a meal I'd have to sit with all the other kids on supervision in the brown kitchen, unable to go out of sight of members of staff for even a moment. But, the minute my hour's supervision was up, I'd still run off and be sick.

But when my weight still didn't increase it became two hours post-meal supervision, then three and four. Even after four hours of post-meal supervision I'd still go off at night and puke up anything that might be left in my stomach. By that point I was only really bringing up stomach juices but I still did it. My teeth are destroyed now by the amount of acid I regurgitated.

Around that time Janice, Sara and I went down to Argos one lunch break for our walk and bought a pair of electronic scales. It meant we could calculate our weight perfectly before our official twice-weekly weigh-ins, so we knew how much we needed to waterload if necessary. Sometimes I'd drink 5 litres (9 pints) of water, which weighs around 5 kilos (11 lb), before a weigh-in to ensure I hit my target.

I also had another brilliant scam for adding a bit to my weight. One of the other girls had come up with the idea of sewing fishing weights into her hair scrunchy, so one weekend I went into a fishing tackle shop and bought myself some too. I cut a neat slit in the scrunchy, slipped the weights in, then sewed it up again. It may have added only half a kilo or so, but it all helped.

We hid the scales in a boiler cupboard beside the fire escape and only referred to them by the codeword 'hairdryer'. So Sara might say to me, 'Can I borrow your hairdryer?' and I'd reply, 'Janice is using it at the moment but you can be next.' It was a brilliant way of staying ahead of the game and the 'hairdryer' scam survived for a couple of years after I left Rhodes Farm before it was discovered.

There was one member of staff called Tony and I'm sure he knew something was going on but he didn't know what. On weigh-in days he'd always say to me, 'Isn't it amazing, Nikki, how your weight is always bang on target every week?'

'What do you mean?' I'd say in mock horror.

'Oh nothing,' he'd reply. 'It just seems quite incredible, that's all.'

Because I was able to stay on my target week after week, I was allowed evenings out with my parents and even some weekends at home. For my first 'meal out' Dad took me to a Beefeater but he'd been given strict instructions about what I had to eat – something with chips for a main course and then the pudding had to include pastry and cream. A sorbet or mousse was out of the question.

Afterwards, though, I got Dad to give me a game of badminton at a gym in London. He loves sport and I just loved the chance to exercise.

Staff at Rhodes Farm must have become increasingly suspicious that I was manipulating my weight on weigh-in days because late one night my little scam came to a sudden end. I'd been fast asleep when one of the nurses knocked sharply on my door and walked in. I opened my eyes slowly, blinking as the brightness from the corridor pricked my eyes.

'Hello, Nikki,' the nurse chirped as if she'd just popped in for a chat. 'I'm just going to take you downstairs to weigh you.'

When they put me on the scales I was 4 kilos (9 lb) lighter than they had thought. After that I was back on those enormous meals, being watched so closely now that there wasn't a moment for me to exercise or vomit any more. I felt full to bursting with their disgusting food and it was unbearable. I felt I hadn't got any other choice – I had to run away. I waited for the perfect opportunity when I could slip away unnoticed.

It came shortly afterwards, on a Sunday morning. There was no one around, so I didn't pause for a moment but darted straight down the stairs and out of the front door without looking back. It was a chilly spring day and I was wearing a thin cotton purple dress and flip-flops, so I was soon absolutely freezing.

I ran to the tube station, desperately wondering where to go next. The only person I knew who lived anywhere nearby was Nina, my old friend from Great Ormond Street, who was back home in North London. I ran into a phone box and dialled her number. 'Nina, I've run away,' I told her. 'I'm coming round.'

My hands were numb with cold and my teeth were chattering by the time I knocked on her door. I'd been imagining us curled up on Nina's bed, giggling and chatting the way we had at Great Ormond Street. But one look at her face as she opened the door told me it wasn't going to be like that.

'Come in for a minute, but I'm sorry, Nikki, you can't stay,' she said immediately. 'My Mum knows you're here and she's ringing Rhodes Farm. You're going to have to go back.'

We went into Nina's bedroom and she dug out a pair of her trainers for me to put on my freezing feet as I warmed my hands on a radiator. I could see her mum hovering in the hallway. I knew she already hated me, seeing me as a 'bad influence' on Nina.

Five minutes later I was back on the street again. I took the tube to Camden Town and wandered around for hours. It was so cold that my bones were aching and I couldn't stop crying.

After a couple of hours I looked through the steamed-up window of a café. Inside it looked warm and welcoming, so I popped in and asked to use their toilet and begged a cup of hot water. I sat at a table, cradling the mug in my hands and trying to get just a little bit of warmth back into my body.

I didn't know it then but when Dad got the call from Rhodes Farm saying that I was missing he thought I might go to Camden and spent hours driving around the streets there. He even went into the same café just five minutes after I'd left it.

I carried on wandering about aimlessly. Then I rang Mum's sister, Auntie Rita, and asked if I could come round, but she said no. So I carried on walking, getting colder and colder until my hands were turning blue and I felt more lonely than I could remember. I knew it was pointless, I had to go home. I caught a tube and was soon at Mum's doorstep, but I'd barely got inside the door before she had turned me round and bundled me back in the car for the return journey to Rhodes Farm.

There I was presented with a snack and told I'd have to wear my pyjamas for the next three days for running away. And I was put straight on total supervision, or 'total' as we called it. People in prison probably get more freedom than we did when punished in this way. All the girls on 'total' would have to sit in the brown kitchen all day long so they could be observed every minute by staff. We'd do schoolwork during the day, then watch television in the evening. And that was it.

The only time you were allowed out of that room was to go to the loo or take a shower. Even in the toilet a member of staff would come into the cubicle with you, shut the door and stand there with their back to you as you had a wee or a poo. It must have been horrible for them.

At night they would roll out lightweight mattresses on the floor of the kitchen and we would sleep on these next to one another. The lights would be kept on all night and a staff member would stay awake in an armchair watching us in case anyone tried any tricks.

I remained on 'total' for months and all that time my weight could only go up because there was just no chance of getting away with any of my dodges.

Running away, though, had reminded me what it was like outside of institutions, and gradually an idea was taking shape in my mind. I wanted to get out of there and places like it. I wanted to live a normal life, surrounded by normal people. I started wondering what Lena looked like now and if she and my other friends had boyfriends or were going out to discos. I'd like to go to discos, I thought. I'd like to have a boyfriend. I'd like to have a life.

For years at Great Ormond Street, Sedgemoor and Huntercombe going home had never really been an option and so my only means of having any control over my life had been to starve myself. But at Rhodes Farm they'd told me that very soon I would be back in the big, wide world again, like a normal person. And I craved that desperately.

But the amount of food being served up was unbearable.

I felt bloated and sick all the time. As the weeks passed I felt I no longer needed help from Rhodes Farm. Because I didn't want to starve myself to death any more, I could cope on my own now.

And because I was in a hurry to get on with living, I was determined to run away again.

CHAPTER 18

I WANT TO LIVE

I eased myself through the tiny gap in the window of the telephone room and jumped down silently into the garden.

I'd done it. I'd escaped from Rhodes Farm – again. With a bit of planning it hadn't even been that difficult. When I was on 'total' the only time I had a moment to myself all week was during my Thursday evening phone call to Mum. So I persuaded Sara to come down to the telephone room while I was there, bringing with her my trainers and a jacket. Then, cutting short my conversation with Mum before the nurse was due to escort me back upstairs to the brown kitchen, I jumped out of the window and was away.

It was already dark outside and a chilly evening but I started running and headed for the end of the tree-lined garden. I knew from our lunchtime walks exactly which way I needed to go to get to the tube station without being spotted.

Rhodes Farm was next to a church and I had to run through the graveyard if I was going to keep away from the road. It was pitch-dark and really spooky and I kept tripping over every bit of uneven ground, but all I could think was that I had to keep going.

From the graveyard, I had to jog through a tunnel before I emerged on to Mill Hill Broadway, from where it was just a couple of hundred yards to the train station. I slipped through the ticket barrier when no one was noticing, then ran down to the platform and on to the first train that pulled in.

I'd already decided where I was going – Taunton. I knew I couldn't go home as Mum would take me straight back to Rhodes. And I couldn't think of anywhere else to go. Besides, I'd quite enjoyed my time at Sedgemoor and liked the idea of being a long way from London.

Once I was on the train at Paddington I went into the toilet and lay on the floor the whole way to avoid the ticket collector. It was filthy and stank but I didn't dare go outside in case I was caught and made to get off the train.

It was about one o'clock in the morning when the train finally pulled in at Taunton. I came out of the station and walked down to the centre of the town. I was still wearing the short black cotton flowery skirt and thin coat I'd had on when I left Rhodes Farm and it was perishing cold.

Now I was in Taunton I realised I had absolutely no idea where I was going next. I walked along a deserted street, rehearsing in my mind what I'd say if anyone asked me what I was doing. I'd decided to tell them I'd had an argument with my mum and run away from home, simple as that. Hopefully they wouldn't ask any further questions.

After half an hour I realised I was just going to have to find somewhere to sleep until the morning. I looked around and saw the recessed doorway of an estate agent. I found a box and wrapped it around me, like I'd seen homeless people do. I knew I'd rather sleep on that than the filthy ground, and I told myself it would soon be morning anyway. I lay still and clamped my eyes shut but it was too cold to sleep. My body was aching with the biting cold and I felt utterly miserable.

Every minute seemed like an hour. I don't think I can do this, I thought. But I didn't know what else to do. I stared at my watch, following the minute hand with my eyes as it dragged itself around. Please, morning, hurry up and come.

I had a little money to buy food with later and I started to feel confident I could look after myself now. I'd been more compliant at Rhodes and knew how much I could eat to be healthy, so I felt I was never going to get really ill again. Meanwhile, if I could just get through this one night, everything would be OK.

But I'd been lying there for about an hour, every fibre of my body crying out from the cold, when I realised I just couldn't do it after all. A couple of minutes later I looked up and saw a bloke walking past. He looked quite respectable with his smart suit and neat hair, so I called out quietly, 'Excuse me.' It took him a couple of seconds to focus on me and I could tell he'd had a couple of drinks.

He looked me over slowly and I knew exactly what he was seeing – a skinny little girl with pink hair who was a long way from home and way out of her depth.

'Oh my God, what are you doing out at this hour?' he said.

I already had my well-rehearsed answer: 'I've had a row with my mum and I've run away from home. Do you know if there any hostels or anything around here I can stay at, because I've got nowhere to go?'

He stared at me for a while, obviously taking in the situation, and then said slowly, 'I want you to call your mum now. I want you to ring her and tell her that you're OK.'

It was before everyone had mobile phones, so we walked in awkward silence to the nearest phone box. He stood outside while I dialled the number. It rang just once before Mum picked up, so I knew she'd already been told I'd run away. 'Where are you, Nikki?' she said, the panic clear in her voice.

'I can't tell you, Mum,' I said. 'I just want you to know I'm OK.'

Before she had the chance to say anything else, I put down the phone, pushed open the heavy door and stepped outside.

What I didn't realise was that Mum had recognised the code that flashed up on her handset as the one for Taunton. She assumed I'd gone back to Sedgemoor, so that put her mind at rest a little bit.

Outside the phone box the man looked me up and down again. 'Right, come back to my hotel and you can stay there the night. There are two single beds in the room and you can have one of them.'

He could have been a rapist or an axe murderer but that didn't occur to me then. I was just desperate to be somewhere warm.

We walked further down the street to his hotel, through the deserted reception and up to his room.

'You take a shower and relax while I pop downstairs for a bit,' he said.

I had the most gorgeous long, hot shower and towelled myself dry before putting my clothes back on and climbing into bed.

Amazing, I thought. A free night in a hotel and no one here to make me eat. This is living it up!

I hadn't even closed my eyes when there was a sharp knock on the door. I climbed out of bed and opened it to find a policeman and a policewoman staring at me. 'Hello, we'd like to take you down to the police station,' they said.

My heart sank. It really had been too good to be true. My kind stranger must have gone straight downstairs and shopped me to the police. I can understand now why he did it, but at the time I was gutted.

It was 3am when we arrived at the police station. The policeman pointed me to a chair, then sat down opposite me.

'OK, love, you've got two hours and then at five o'clock we're going to sling you in a children's home, so why don't you just tell us where you're from and you can be on your way home?'

Hallelujah! I thought. A children's home is exactly where I want to be – I'll be able to eat what I want, no one hassling me. Don't wait till five, do it now.

But I didn't say that. I just sat there sullenly, kicking my feet backwards and forwards.

'Come on, then,' he said, pushing my chair leg with his foot. 'Where are you from?'

I gave him the same old bullshit about having an argument with my mum and running away from home. But I wouldn't tell him my name or where I was from.

'Skinny little cow, aren't you?' he went on. 'When did you last eat? And why aren't you wearing more clothes for the time of year?'

By this point I hated him and had made up my mind I wasn't telling him another thing.

Come on, five o'clock, I kept thinking. I really want to go to sleep now – I'm so tired.

At 5am they pushed me into a police car and took me to a children's home on the outskirts of the town.

The home was like a big family house. It was a bit shabby but warm and had a friendly feeling about it. A kind-looking woman helped me upstairs to a room with clean sheets and a rough but chunky blanket on the bed. What a result, I thought. I could stay here for years. I guess other kids would have been horrified by living somewhere like that but I'd been in and out of institutions for the past seven years and this seemed like a nice one.

I told them the same dodgy story about running away from home, and even if they didn't believe me they didn't give me a hard time about it. Then they gave me £50 to go into the town to buy some warmer clothes with some of the other girls who lived there. The girls were really nice and we chatted all the way there and back, but I was careful not to give too much information away to them either.

In the evening we sat around watching films and having a laugh. Some of the kids were total nutcases but I was used to that. I'd grown up with nutcases.

I stayed there for five nights. And I ate. I'd already made the decision at Rhodes Farm that I would eat because I wanted to live.

I called Mum a few times from the children's home. I

told her where I was and what was going on but said I still didn't feel ready to come back, not yet.

Then one afternoon I called her again.

'Hi, Mum,' I said. 'I want to come home – I want to get better.'

I could tell by the silence that followed that Mum wasn't sure whether it was another of my con tricks or if this time I was serious.

'But I don't want to go back to Rhodes,' I continued. 'I can do it on my own now.'

Mum offered to come straight down to collect me but said I had to go back to Rhodes Farm. We couldn't agree but the next day she turned up anyway.

We had a long wait before our train back to London, so we went into Debenhams department store for lunch. We sat at a table and I said, 'Mum, I'm going to prove to you that I am going to eat – that I can eat and that I am coming home for good. I'm going to do this if you promise not to take me back to Rhodes.'

I chose one of those little picnic boxes they have for children and I ate the lot – no fuss, no bother. Mum couldn't believe it. She didn't dare believe that our nightmare might be coming to an end. We spent the train journey home talking and laughing like the old days.

Mum had changed a lot too and it was good. For years she had been having counselling at the different units treating me but then she had met a therapist who helped her turn everything around. She taught Mum to be true to herself and to stop pleasing other people all the time and showed her she could be a good mother *and* look after herself.

I think when Mum really started to believe that, it was

the point she was transformed from a quivering mess into someone strong enough to keep her daughter alive.

So she had got a job as a radiographer's assistant. I hadn't liked it at first as it meant she wouldn't be there to attend to my every beck and call any more. But I got used to it.

And she had become firmer with me too. She was able to look at things more dispassionately and less emotionally. Sometimes she'd even get tough with me. 'For God's sake, Nikki. Just stop this behaviour,' she'd say when I started one of my fits.

She had kitted herself out with a whole new wardrobe – slinky dresses, high heels and pretty underwear. For the first time in ages she paid attention to the way she looked.

Maybe seeing Mum get stronger during the time I'd been at Huntercombe and Rhodes Farm made me feel safer deep down. Maybe it took away so much of the uncertainty in my life and had helped me on my road to recovery.

Back home from Somerset, Mum cooked me a plain piece of cod and some new potatoes, followed by a yoghurt and a piece of fruit. I ate the lot.

After dinner we sat down with Tony and watched telly. I felt normal. After all those years I was doing what normal people did on a Tuesday evening. And it was great.

For a week I lived at Tolcarne Drive and loved it; sleeping in my bedroom, going shopping with Mum, hanging out with Natalie and seeing my old school friends.

I'd begged Mum not to tell Rhodes Farm that she had seen me if they called, and she agreed. She wanted me home too.

One afternoon I went round to Carly's house as she was

221

back home and only living 20 minutes' walk away. Then the phone rang – it was Mum and she needed to speak to me urgently.

'You've got to come home straight away,' she said. 'I'm taking you back to Rhodes Farm.'

I felt like I had been kicked in the belly. 'No, Mum, no,' I begged down the phone. 'You promised, you promised.'

'I've got no choice, Nikki,' Mum said, her voice desperate. 'Social Services have been on the phone. They must have worked out you were home, and they've said if I don't take you back now they will take you away and section you. If they do that you could be locked up until you're 18.'

Mum was crying and I could tell there was going to be no way out of this one.

Within five minutes she was outside waiting to pick me up. I hugged Carly goodbye, dreading my return to Rhodes Farm.

Back there I was put straight on three days in pyjamas and total supervision again.

I've just got to get the hell out of here as quickly as possible, was all I could think.

I'd been out of there for a fortnight and it had really made me realise for the first time how much I was missing the outside world. I was now certain I wanted a life outside of hospitals and eating-disorders units. They say that if you spend years and years in prison you don't see a way out, you don't even want to get out because it has become your life. That is what had happened to me even before I went to Rhodes Farm. I was so institutionalised that for years I couldn't even think about going home – I didn't even know about the outside world any more. But the thought of being able to go home opened up a whole world of new possibilities for me.

However, while I'd been away my weight had fallen way below my target, so I had loads of catching up to do. I started bingeing in a bid to get my weight up so that I'd be discharged as quickly as possible.

I'd steal bottles of full-cream milk from the fridge and neck the whole lot while I was in the shower if I had a moment unsupervised.

Then one night we were allowed into the video room to watch a film as a special treat. On the way down I sneaked into the pantry and stole a loaf of bread. Once the film started I sat behind a sofa and ate the lot.

And one morning I stole some jam from the breakfast table and that night scooped great handfuls straight from the jar into my mouth.

I even got Mum to send me chocolate bars through the post. And she did it, because she thought it was great that I was eating. One evening I ate nine chocolate bars – 350 calories each! I couldn't sleep that night I felt so sick, but I kept them all down. I didn't even feel guilt about eating so much any more, I just wanted out. I wanted to make a go of life.

As my weight increased I was finally taken off 'total' and moved into the blue kitchen, where you could prepare your own food and sit without supervision. I was even allowed out to do work experience looking after children at a nursery in the hope it would help me get a job when I went home. I loved it, and I loved being part of the outside world – although it was still a pretty scary concept to grasp.

I admit I still waterloaded before weigh-ins to be on the

safe side but apart from that I'd given up fighting. For the first time in eight years I handed myself over to the system and let them do what they wanted with me. And it was an incredible relief. I suddenly felt tired, utterly exhausted. For weeks, whenever I could I'd go and lie down on one of the sofas and sleep and sleep. It was as if the effort of all those years of battling had finally caught up with me and I was shattered.

I still didn't want to be 45 kilos and I was certain I would lose some of it when I got out of Rhodes Farm, but I was never again going to starve myself almost to death. I wanted to live too much for that.

On my last weigh-in on my last day at Rhodes Farm, on 19 June 1998, I was 46.7 kilos (7 stone 5 lb). It was the first time my weight had been within a normal range for years.

'I won't be back,' I said to Dee as I packed my bag that last morning.

'I hope not,' she said. 'But we will always be here for you if you need us.'

CHAPTER 19

A NEW STRUGGLE

Some of the institutions I had been in had been frightening, harsh and lonely. But living in the real world again was the hardest thing I'd had to face yet. Because, however bad it had been in a hospital or a specialist unit, at least I had felt secure there, safe from the challenges and disappointments of the outside world.

Now it was time to face reality.

I'd made the decision I wanted to get better, but that was just the start of the battle. Returning home to Tolcarne Drive that summer of 1998, I felt like a freak, a leper. I'd been away from normal life for most of the past eight years and had no idea how to behave, no dress sense, no social skills, no qualifications – nothing. I had missed the vital transition from childhood to adulthood.

Now I was 16 I didn't have to go to school any more, so I started looking for a job. I tried loads of places but nowhere was interested in me. Even McDonald's wouldn't have me because I hadn't got a single GCSE after missing out on so much education.

I must have looked a total mess too. At that point I was a little plump by my standards and my hair was all frizzy and short like a baby's because I'd destroyed it with so much dye. I had no idea about make-up or what was cool or fashionable and was still wandering around in dungarees and Dr Martens when other girls my age were looking glamorous and trendy.

Natalie was away at Manchester Met University studying drama, so I was stuck at home with Mum and Tony. When Nat came home for holidays she would take me out with her mates but I was totally socially inept. I had missed out on so much growing up I had no idea what to say to people, and for years the only thing I had discussed with anyone was calories.

One of my first 'normal' nights out was for a drink with Natalie and a big group of her friends. We were in a beer garden and Nat was drinking a pint of lager. 'Oh, I feel a bit pissed,' she giggled.

'That's because Prozac doubles everything,' I said matter-of-factly. There was a moment of total silence. I looked at the shock and embarrassment on Nat's friends' faces and it slowly dawned on me that taking Prozac for depression was probably the sort of thing people in the outside world preferred to keep private. Everywhere I'd been for the past ten years almost everyone had been on Prozac or some kind of drug, and I didn't realise it was such a big deal.

Natalie glared at me while everyone else around the table all started chattering at once to fill the silence.

I was like that all the time, embarrassing poor old Natalie. Despite that, she stuck by me, letting me hang around whenever she was at home. When she was back at uni, though, it was horribly quiet. Old friends from school had moved on and obviously thought it was very uncool to be seen hanging around with a weirdo like me. I had no social life apart from a Christian friend of Natalie's called Sian who used to invite me out occasionally, on the condition I embrace the Christian way of life, but that didn't interest me at all.

And I wasn't happy about the way I looked either. Although I'd made the decision not to starve myself ultra-skinny again, I still felt too big at just 44.5 kilos (7 stone). One day I went shopping with Mum and cried the entire time because everything I tried on looked so bad on me.

I joined a gym and spent my days exercising – it was the only thing I knew how to do. I'd walk to the gym in the morning, train, walk home again, then watch telly all evening with Mum and Tony. And that was my life.

But I was just about in control of my eating, and I was determined not to get really ill again. I wasn't out of the woods by any means, though. I was drinking high-calorie drinks rather than risk eating anything with fat in it. I couldn't even bring myself to touch fat.

I could tell Mum was terrified that with all the knocks I was getting I was about to relapse again. All those years I'd been lying dying in hospital, she had always said, 'You've got to fight, you've got to get well, because there's a world out there for you – a life.' But then here I was out in the world and there was no life at all – no job, no friends, nothing.

I'd been home about five months when Dad got me a job through a friend of his, serving breakfast to the homeless at Watford YMCA for £3 an hour. The homeless were only allowed one slice of toast each but they used to try to distract me so they could nick another couple. Imagine anyone trying to pull that stunt on me – the expert at food cheating in communal dining halls!

I'd get up at six to be there for seven, then work a four-hour shift. But it was really hard because by then I'd developed a phobia about eating in front of anyone. I just couldn't do it and I would get starving hungry waiting for my shift to end before I could eat. After a couple of months I gave up the job.

My fear of eating in public was so bad that when I went shopping I'd take a sandwich with me and go into a public toilet and eat it. I had it in my head that everyone would be staring at me if they could see me eating, so I wouldn't do it.

After Rhodes Farm I also developed other obsessive-compulsive behaviour. It was a new thing to focus on rather than just calories. I became obsessed with cleanliness and hygiene. Experts would have described my fear of germs as morbid. When Mum set the table for dinner I would have to wash my knife, fork and plate three times before I could use them. Everything became a ritual, a routine. I guess it was another way of feeling in control in my life now that I'd stopped starving myself.

If Mum ever put my dinner on a plate I hadn't just washed I would go mental, shouting and screaming like the old days. I was the same about bad smells. I felt they were getting into my body and polluting me.

Then I got a place at Stanmore College to study for a Business & Technology Education Council qualification in the performing arts. But from my first day there I locked myself in a toilet cubicle to eat my lunch. I was marking myself out as different and as a teenage girl that is always dangerous.

Within a week the bullying had started. At first I was aware of the other girls staring at my body and whispering. Then they would snigger at the way I looked and the clothes I wore.

I only made matters worse when I started falling asleep in lectures. Because I wasn't sleeping well at night I always felt exhausted during the day. That only gave the other girls in my class something else to laugh at me about.

One day we were doing a performance and the girls said we all had to wear hotpants. I didn't have any with me so I went all the way home on the bus in my lunch break to get them. Then, when we all went on stage, everyone apart from me was wearing leggings. They just wanted me to feel different and uncomfortable – and they succeeded.

I became really miserable and dealt with it the only way I knew how – by cutting down on what I was eating. Looking back, at this point I should have asked Rhodes Farm for help again but I was terrified that as a returner they'd put me straight on 4,500 calories a day. They do a scheme there where you can return for weekends if you've lost just a little weight but I had refused to do that in the first few months after leaving and now my weight was falling fast and I was too scared to go back full time.

Within weeks I was living on sandwiches made from fat-free crumpets and fat-free soya cheese and Lucozade tablets. I wouldn't eat anything containing fat.

After the first term I couldn't face going back to college, so I packed it in.

Then I got a job as a waitress at a private health club in

Northwood. I loved the work at the Riverside Club, but soon I started to feel excluded again by the other members of staff. I think I must have just been a bit too weird, with my skinniness and my secret eating and my social inadequacies, for them to be comfortable with. I made myself an easy victim for people, although I didn't realise it then.

My only friend there was a guy called David, who I'd known since I was ten, from the church youth club, and we had such a laugh together. We'd chase each other down the corridors, waving mops at each other. Once we were in the men's toilets and I'd climbed up on a sink trying to get him with my mop when our manager walked in. That took some explaining!

The first Christmas I worked at the Riverside the staff party was at a nightclub in Watford called Destiny. I was so excited because I'd never been to a nightclub before. Mum and I spent hours traipsing around the shops looking for the perfect thing to wear before I found a little black Lycra dress and some black and white platform shoes.

I really fancied one of the chefs, and that night he and I got chatting. He knew I fancied him and I was just bowled over that he was showing me any attention at all.

He came home with me that night and stayed over. Mum was cool about it. I think she was just happy I was doing normal teenage things.

But pretty soon it was apparent things were very one-sided. I wanted to go on dates, to the cinema and nice restaurants. He just wanted to come round late at night after he'd finished work or been out with his mates. It was obvious he was using me. In the end I think he felt guilty about it and after about a month it fizzled out. That hit me really hard and I fell into a dark depression again. I'd spend hours lying face down on my bed crying. I'd lost the man I liked, I had no friends, I was a freak of society and couldn't see any future.

I'd worked so hard to get out of hospital and it was all for nothing. Everything in the outside world was so unreliable and scary. I didn't belong here.

Even in my misery I was aware I was entering a dangerous phase. I was beginning to think, I can block out all this misery now if I stop thinking about it and focus on not eating, because I'm good at that.

I knew I needed to go somewhere I'd feel safe and where I belonged – hospital.

Hospital was where I'd grown up, so I suppose it was just like other people wanting to go home when they're going through a rough patch.

I dismissed the idea of Rhodes Farm because I knew it would be mammoth amounts of calories and fat. So instead I rang Dr Lask and on 13 January 1999 I checked myself back into Huntercombe.

I'd lost 9 kilos (1 stone 6 lb) in the seven months since I'd left Rhodes Farm and was down to 36 kilos (5 stone 9 lb) and suffering from dehydration. I knew that at Huntercombe they would let me do things my way and I was keen to make it work. The dietician helped me draw up a meal plan and I stuck to it.

I requested therapy with one particular counsellor who was young and cool and they agreed. He was fun but gave me good advice on how to cope in situations I found stressful in the outside world and it really helped.

But it was while I was back there that my obsession with cleanliness really took hold. I started washing my plates and cutlery excessively and if anyone looked at me while I was washing a plate I'd have to wash it all over again. I wouldn't allow anyone to touch anything I ate or anything I ate my dinner off.

After staying at Huntercombe for just over three months I left weighing 39.2 kilos (6 stone 2 lb) and feeling ready to go home and back to my job at the Riverside Club.

I was still having to nip to the toilet to eat a sandwich halfway through my shift and I survived on cups of peppermint tea with four sugars, but I was better than before.

I avoided the chef and got on with my work. But then some of the girls I'd been friends with at school got jobs there. I was still too freaky and immature for them to hang around with and they did everything they could to make my life a misery. They'd go to nightclubs in Watford but say there was no way I'd get in because I looked so young. Eventually, though, they agreed I could go out with them one Saturday night.

Beforehand I spent days agonising over what I should wear. I remembered them showing me pictures of when they'd gone out while I was at Huntercombe and one of them was wearing a grey suit. That must be fashionable – I'll get one of those, I thought. On the day we were going out I went to Mark One and found a virtually identical suit. Later, after I'd spent two hours doing my hair and make-up, I got Mum to drop me at Northwood Hills station to meet the girls.

As I stepped out of the car I saw two of the girls – I'll call them Jill and Karen – staring at me, obviously trying to stifle giggles.

'Why are you dressed like that, Nikki?' one of them

asked. 'We're only going round to Karen's house to watch a video.'

I was mortified.

When we got to Karen's we passed round a bottle of vodka. They were saying, 'Go on, Nikki, neck it – get drunk and let yourself go.'

I was so naive that I did just that. Soon I was completely out of it and they had to almost carry me back home. On the way I collapsed on the street. All I remember is them falling about laughing as I lay there. They called an ambulance to check I wasn't dying and paramedics came and looked me over.

I was OK but once again I felt totally humiliated.

Not long after that I was desperate to go up to Leicester Square to see the crowds and the fireworks on the eve of the Millennium. I'd heard that the girls at work were all going, so I dashed up to one of them, and asked, 'Can I come with you for New Year's Eve?'

'Er, we don't know what we are doing yet,' she said.

Then I rang Jill and she didn't seem to know either.

Then I rang Karen and it was the same again.

Finally our mutual friend David had to tell me the truth: 'Sorry, Nikki, but I don't think they want you to go with them.' I was devastated.

I was really struggling with life on the outside and not attending my outpatient counselling sessions at Huntercombe as often as I should have done. My eating and exercising were both under control – but only just.

As well as being so socially immature and out of touch I also looked much younger than other girls. I may have been approaching 18, but I was still living inside the body of a young boy – no breasts and still no periods. So I decided to have a boob job. I knew it was too late for them to ever come naturally now because of the damage anorexia had done to my body. I went on an NHS waiting list before undergoing the operation to boost me from a pancake-flat AA to a more shapely B cup.

The operation was a bit of a disaster. They put far too much drainage tube inside me and my body rejected it. I had to stay in for six nights while they sorted it out. It really hurt but when the swelling eventually went down I was delighted.

I bought loads of new clothes and a fortnight after the op Lena agreed to take me out to celebrate my birthday. I was 18 and finally felt like a woman. For the first time I felt confident about the way I looked. My new boobs also won me kudos and respect from the girls at work.

In my spare time I had started doing dance classes at Pineapple Dance Studios in Covent Garden. Then I decided I wanted to do it full-time and enrolled on a course at the Gypsy Booth School of Ballet and Theatre Arts near Watford. It was clear that I had a degree of natural talent – like at gymnastics all those years earlier – and I was soon keeping up with girls who had been doing ballet since they were kids. I wasn't the best, but I was good at it – and that made me feel good.

And for the first time I made friends who made me feel comfortable and who I enjoyed going out with. That group of friends saved me. We'd go out most evenings and even went on holiday for two weeks to Ibiza.

For a year everything was brilliant but then history started repeating itself.

There were more exams and more shows at Gypsy

Booth and I could feel pressure mounting on me. There was also a lot of competition for places at the big dance schools we hoped to get into after finishing our course. I dreamed of going to Laine Theatre Arts, in Epsom, one of the best schools in the country, but competition was fierce and that panicked me.

Meanwhile some of my friends were leaving and going to various colleges. Everything felt uncertain and difficult again and I tried to regain control the only way I knew how – by losing weight.

I realised that I was no longer dancing because I enjoyed it but because it was exercise and that, for me, was wrong. I would arrive at the college in the morning and do body conditioning for an hour, then ballet, then contemporary, then jazz, and stay until nine at night.

At the same time I was eating less and less. Gypsy Booth, who ran the school, called me over one afternoon. 'Nikki, I'm really sorry but I'm going to have to pull you out of some of the dances for the Christmas show,' she said. 'You're too weak.'

I told Gypsy I had an overactive thyroid and I was waiting for the doctor to sort it out but I don't think I fooled her for a moment. For some time I'd known I wasn't doing the jumps properly because I was so weak but I'd been trying to ignore it.

I was distraught at being dropped from the dances and that just made me more stressed. So I ate even less. And as the weight dropped off me and I spent day after day looking at myself in front of a dance mirror in a leotard, I got to like what I saw and wanted to get even thinner. I had tumbled back into that old vicious circle.

Mum was desperately worried too.

I knew perfectly well what was happening – I could tell from the haunted look in my own face. And I knew I had to do something if I wanted to avoid going back into hospital. I tried making myself eat things like Twix bars but then I'd be so racked with guilt afterwards that I'd make myself exercise like a freak again.

By the beginning of 2001 I was in a bad state and my weight had slid to 34.5 kilos (5 stone 6 lb). Then one afternoon Gypsy sat me down and said, 'I'm sorry, Nikki, but I'm going to have to bar you from the school until you put some weight on. If anything happened and you had an accident because you are so weak, it would be my fault, and I can't have that on my conscience.'

I was devastated. I'd been planning to make dancing my career and now the dream was being ripped away from me. I admitted to myself that I had to go back into hospital – I was too far down the road to pull myself back on my own. But now I was an adult there were more problems than ever securing funding from the local authority to get me a place in an eating-disorders unit.

My GP tried everywhere to get me help. By April the situation was critical and I lost a further 2 kilos (4½ lb) in four weeks. But, with the restrictions on funding, even Dr Lask and Huntercombe were unable to do anything. I was getting more and more angry and miserable that no one seemed to want to help me and my weight dropped further. I spent my days charging round the local streets, burning off calories. I'd gone past the point of being able to help myself.

Then in June they admitted me to the Adult Psychiatric Unit at Hillingdon Hospital. It was to be my first experience living with adults with severe mental problems and it was utterly terrifying.

CHAPTER 20

NEVER
GOING
BACK

At night, men would trail their bodies up and down the corridor outside my room. Sometimes they'd bang their heads on the wall in frustration, as if trying to rid themselves of whatever demons writhed inside. Other times they would rattle my door handle, terrifying me as I lay, hiding under my duvet.

Schizophrenics, alcoholics and the homeless, unloved and unwanted, had washed up in the psychiatric unit, their minds disconnected and floating free of the outside world. I hated it and couldn't face leaving my room to be brought so close to the brutal sadness of others' tragedies.

Day after day I sat in my room and watched television. If I even went to the loo I had to take my valuables with me so they didn't get nicked.

Being in that place didn't help me one bit. It didn't make me eat – I was just given my meals and left alone, so it was little different from being at home. I'd been there about a week when one evening I was in the day room watching telly when I became conscious of an old man sitting in the chair opposite, staring at me. When I looked over at him, I glanced down and thought I was going to be sick. His eyes focused on me, he was masturbating.

I ran straight out of the room and to the phone, where I rang Mum's number, my hands shaking.

'You've got to get me out of here!' I screamed. 'Now.'

Mum was there within half an hour and as we accelerated away from Hillingdon Hospital I was shuddering with relief.

Almost immediately I was found a bed in the Eating Disorders Unit at the Bethlem Royal Hospital in Beckenham, Kent. The world's first psychiatric hospital, it is famous for being known originally as 'the Bedlam' and giving that frightening word to the English language. Nowadays it has staff expert in treating adult eating disorders. But the regime was horribly tough.

When I arrived I weighed in at 32.8 kilos (5 stone 2 lb) and was 155 centimetres (5 feet 1 inch) tall. And although I was a voluntary patient there was no messing around. If I didn't eat what they served up to make me put on weight, I'd be instantly tubed.

The meals were terrifying, and you had to eat it all, every time. For breakfast it was a cup of tea with two sugars, three Weetabix with 0.15 litres (¼ pint) of full-cream milk, then beans on toast plus two extra slices of buttered toast and orange juice.

Ten o'clock was snack time – a mug of full-cream milk with two sugars or a Nesquik milkshake and two digestive biscuits.

For lunch you were allowed to choose from a menu but

it was usually something like quiche and veg, followed by chocolate sponge with chocolate sauce.

The afternoon snack was a cup of milk and a doughnut. Dinner would be similar to lunch.

There was a 45-minute time limit for finishing every meal and if you refused food outright, or even just messed around with it, they would use the replacing rule that was so familiar to me.

The nurses didn't take any nonsense. Once, I said, 'Please, I really can't drink that milk with all that cream in it.'

'Deal with it,' the nurse snapped back.

They wouldn't even let me know how much I weighed, making me stand backwards on the scales so I couldn't see the reading.

There was no camaraderie between the patients either. Everyone was out for themselves and anorexic competitiveness and bitchiness was at its worst.

It was shocking to see how sick some of the adults were. There were women with really high-powered jobs being sick in paper bags and ex-junkies wandering around. Then there were other women in their 40s with kids, sitting sobbing as the nurses just walked past them. Other women had been banged up in there for years.

The whole place was vile but something there must have worked for me because I complied. There were no tantrums and I ate everything put in front of me.

The whole experience showed me how horrific those adult units are and made me determined not to spend the rest of my life yo-yoing in and out of them. I knew that mentally I'd left all that shit behind me and this was just a temporary relapse. I'd grown out of all this – I didn't need it any more.

And I hated being away from friends and family more than ever. I'd fought so hard to build myself a life in the outside world and I was in danger of losing it all over again.

But lurking at the back of my mind was another huge reason to comply. I knew that if I refused or acted up, they had the option of sectioning me – legally holding me against my will. And if they did that I'd be locked up in there for a minimum of six months and possibly for ever.

After two weeks at the Bethlem Royal I was eating sensibly again. I'd just needed a kick in the right direction. But I couldn't bear another moment in there and after the second ward rounds, I announced that I was discharging myself.

I knew I had made good progress, so they no longer had grounds for sectioning me, and on 9 July, a fortnight after I'd arrived, I walked out of the door.

As I sat in the back seat of a cab on the way home, I swore to myself: I am *never* going back into one of those places again.

And until now – touch wood – I haven't.

Back home I made some tough decisions. As much as I loved dancing I knew that for me it was too dangerous to pursue professionally, so I reduced it to a couple of evening classes and made it into a hobby instead.

Then I enrolled at college in Harrow to study for an NVQ in beauty therapy. I'd always loved beauty products and make-up and the course seemed perfect for me. At the same time I got a part-time job working on the Clarins counter at John Lewis in Watford.

I loved doing my NVQ – it felt like I was making up for all the school time I had missed out on. When I finished college I was able to make the Clarins job full-time. But I was always getting into trouble and had five disciplinaries against me for chatting on the phone at work, chewing gum, wearing the wrong shoes and even sleeping in the beauty room and putting on fake tan while on duty! At the same time I had the highest sales in the region, so they kept me.

I came pretty close to marriage around this time, when I met my first true love, Chris Jakes, at a John Lewis Christmas party. He was really good-looking but most importantly he was incredibly caring and warm. He was out that night with his colleagues from a different firm. Within days I had fallen for him.

A fortnight after we met he went on holiday with his family to Dubai for Christmas. I rang his Mum and said, 'I'm going to fly over to see him.' And I did.

A lot of people will think that is just bonkers but it was love. For six months I didn't tell Chris anything about my childhood or my anorexia – I needed him to think I was normal. But when I finally told him my whole story he couldn't have been more supportive.

But then I started feeling he was being too nice and I felt a bit suffocated. He wanted to marry me but I wasn't sure about that kind of commitment. I realised I was treating him like shit and he was letting me get away with it.

When I ended our relationship I broke his heart and I feel bad about that because he is such a nice guy. But we're still good mates now.

Eventually I got the push from John Lewis for being just too naughty but Clarins still wanted me, so they moved me to Debenhams and I loved it there too.

The only difficult area in my life was Mum's new boyfriend, Rory. She had split up with Tony soon after I came out of Rhodes Farm. Apparently they'd been growing apart for a while and it can't have been easy for him coping with me and Natalie. We'd both been pretty mean to Tony at times but deep down we were really fond of him and the separation came as a shock.

This new bloke, from Mum's work, was just awful. He was only 27 and I felt that he hated me and Natalie. Things got a bit tense at home and I went to live with Dad for a while. But then we had a fall-out and he kicked me out. It was a bit complicated really because Natalie was then working locally as a home carer and had been living with Dad when I turned up one day with all my bags in the back of a cab. There was no room for all of us, so Nat moved back to Mum's.

But after Dad kicked me out I couldn't turf Natalie out of a room again by moving back to Mum's and we were getting on so badly again I knew we wouldn't survive long under the same roof. One night we had a massive row after my friend wouldn't get off Natalie's computer and it ended up with us physically fighting. I was pulling her hair, then she kicked me and broke a rib.

My bones are very fragile because of my osteoporosis caused by anorexia but it didn't stop me getting into scraps with Natalie.

There was still so much anger and jealousy between both of us and the merest incident brought it all tumbling out. Natalie was still mad that Mum had dedicated so much time and attention to me when I was ill and I was mad at her that she'd been at home with Mum.

So all in all we decided it was best for me to find my own place and I went on the council list for accommodation. They found me a room in a hostel-type block with communal shower and kitchen areas. I was there for a year and a half and it was awful.

The shared areas were filthy. Sometimes I'd walk in the bathroom and there would be bloody sanitary towels stuffed behind the radiator and used razor blades lying on the floor. Some of the children even pooed in the back garden.

At one point the whole place became infested with cockroaches – they were there for three days before the pest-control team turned up.

One night someone tried to force their way into my room. Terrified, I just lay there rigid under my duvet. Another time I had to lie and listen as a guy beat up his wife. I could her head being banged against the wall. I was frozen with fear.

With all my OCD issues it was a nightmare and I ended up cooking most of my meals and taking showers at Mum's flat.

I signed on with an employment agency which got me work on beauty counters in all sort of different stores, including House of Fraser and Harrods. Working in the West End was brilliant – I loved the buzz of it.

Then I rented my own flat really near to Mum's and Carly moved in with me. We were both in control of our eating and things couldn't have been better.

CHAPTER 21

BIG BROTHER

I'd already applied to *Big Brother* once but hadn't been selected. On my application form I'd told them the whole grim story of my illness and the years away from home and they probably read it and dropped it like a hot potato.

So when I decided to apply again for the 2006 series I knew this time I had to hide everything about my anorexia if I was to stand any chance of getting selected. Open auditions were being held in Wembley towards the end of 2005 and I persuaded Carly to come along with me for moral support.

By the time we arrived, it was already mid-afternoon. We joined a queue which seemed to stretch for miles and waited our turn. I was supposed to be meeting another friend at five o'clock. She was dating a footballer and we were going up to Sheffield for the weekend to see him and his mate, who I really fancied.

As it got closer and closer to five o'clock and then

passed it, my friend kept ringing me, increasingly frantic that I hadn't shown up.

'I think I'd better just go,' I said to Carly. 'This guy in Sheffield is really fit and I'll never get chosen for *Big Brother* anyway.'

Another five minutes went by and my friend kept on ringing my mobile.

'That's it, I'm going,' I told Carly. 'I can't keep her waiting any longer.' And at that exact moment I was called in front of the judging panel.

'Right, you've got one minute to say why you should go into the *Big Brother* house,' a producer shouted in my direction.

And then my phone rang again. It was my friend going mad that I still hadn't shown up. So I spent the first 30 seconds of my precious minute on the phone to her, telling her to calm down and go without me.

By the time I came off the phone, all I had time to say was, 'My name's Nikki, I love *Big Brother*, I've watched every single episode.'

A woman from the production team stamped my hand and said, 'You're through.' I nearly collapsed!

Months later the Producer called to say he'd decided I was through to the next round from the first moment I opened my mouth.

Next I had a minute in a mock diary room in which I had to talk about myself. I remember saying, 'I want to be rich and I want to never have to work again as I hate work and being told what to do.'

That night I went home so excited. Deep down I had a feeling I was going to be accepted.

For weeks after that nothing happened at all. Then

finally I got a phone call from Endemol, the production company which makes *Big Brother*, asking me to come and see them. At the meeting they asked me what kind of things I enjoyed doing and all about my family and my job. But any questions about my childhood I neatly avoided – or simply lied.

The audition process went on for six months. I had home visits, medical checks, reference checks and psychiatric checks. Luckily I was an old hand at telling psychiatrists what they wanted to hear.

As for the home visit, they came round when Mum was on holiday and so they just met Carly at my flat instead, and she already knew not to mention anything about anorexia.

I hadn't told anyone in the world apart from Mum and Carly that I'd applied for *Big Brother*, I wanted this to be my secret.

As well as face-to-face interviews there were endless phone calls asking me more questions about myself, but whatever they asked I never let anything slip about my anorexia. I was a reasonable weight at the time, so there was no reason why they would have guessed.

The night before my twenty-third birthday I went on a big night out with a group of friends. Somehow we got separated and I lost them. They had my door keys, so when I got home to my flat in the early hours I couldn't get in and had to go round to Mum's.

The next day I was tired, hung-over and still in my clothes from the night before when my phone rang.

'Hi, Nikki,' said the woman on the other end. 'I'm Claire O'Donohue, Executive Producer at *Big Brother*.'

By then I knew enough about how things worked when

I heard the words 'Executive Producer'. I certainly knew one of those wouldn't be bothering to ring me if it was just another umpteen questions about my favourite colours and star sign. I sat down slowly on the edge of the chair, my hands beginning to tremble.

'I'm delighted to tell you,' she went on, 'you've been selected as a housemate.'

I screamed. It was the best news I'd ever had – ever.

'What, do you mean an actual housemate? Not just a standby?' I asked when I finally came back to my senses.

'Yes, an actual housemate,' she laughed. 'We need you to meet a chaperone at Sloane Square station at eight o'clock on Monday morning. And bring plenty of clothes – you'll be away from home for a while.'

When I put the phone down I could feel charges of electricity pulsing through my body. Mum and I hugged and screamed and hugged some more. At last I was going to achieve something special after all the awful things I'd been through. And something that would stick two fingers up at all the people who'd made fun of me in the past and thought I'd never amount to anything.

I also hoped it would help me challenge some of my demons, particularly my OCD problems. By throwing myself into an incredibly difficult situation I might emerge stronger.

In the heat of all that excitement and hope, I was thinking, This is the moment my life changes. And it was.

That evening Mum and I were due to meet all my friends for a curry. They were all late as they hadn't been home since the previous evening. Mum and I sat in the restaurant waiting for them, squeezing each other's leg in excitement, barely able to believe the adventure I was embarking upon.

That was a Friday, which meant I had just two days to prepare to meet the chaperone who would be minding me for the fortnight until filming began. I spent the whole weekend shopping, looking for an entire new wardrobe to take with me into the house – including my arrival and eviction outfits.

On the Sunday evening Mum came round to my flat to say goodbye.

'The next time you see me, Mum, I'll be coming down the stairs at the *Big Brother* house,' I said as we stood hugging in my hall. We were both crying.

Next morning I felt like a spy on a secret mission as I stood outside Sloane Square tube station looking for a woman called Anna Dunkley, a *Big Brother* researcher. When she came up to me and introduced herself, we got into a car and went straight to a nearby Holiday Inn, where we spent the rest of the day.

First there was a photo shoot for our official *Big Brother* pictures, then I had to fill in a mammoth questionnaire about everything you could imagine. What would my epitaph be? What was the most recent argument I'd had? The most upsetting moment I'd ever had? The happiest moment I'd ever had?

Then we spent the rest of the day eating, sleeping and just hanging around.

There was no phone in the room and Anna took my mobile from me too. The production team were terrified about the press finding out where we were, so security was paramount. And I wasn't allowed magazines, newspapers or even a television because they didn't want us to know anything about what was going on in the outside world.

I wasn't even permitted to step outside the room as other housemates were staying in the same hotel and we couldn't be allowed to meet before arriving in the house.

It all felt really weird, but I was used to weird environments and I'd spent years sitting around doing nothing in particular.

The next morning we got into Anna's car and headed south to Dover. We were off to Belgium. I guess it was a strange place to take me but if they were looking for somewhere remote where there was no chance I would bump into anyone I knew or be found by the press, then the Belgian countryside was the place.

Anna and I had a wicked time. We stayed in a really remote three-bedroom farmhouse which was part of an old castle. Cows were grazing in the fields outside but there was nothing else for miles all around.

We joined a gym and a video shop in the nearest town and hired videos every night as I wasn't allowed to watch television. We went to theme parks, hired bikes for the day and went shopping in Brussels and Bruges.

One day there was a carnival in the local town and we had a brilliant time watching everyone singing and dancing. And one night we went to see a band play there and we got really drunk on cherry beer.

It was one of the best holidays I'd ever had. Although it was like a girlie trip, I was still aware that at no time could I let my guard down to Anna, and I never let slip anything about my anorexia and childhood.

We took it in turns to cook and I ate quite well,

although after just a day my OCD became apparent when I kept having to wash my plate before every meal.

'Do you think you'll be OK in the house if you get like that,' Anna asked me seriously. 'Oh, I'll be fine,' I breezed. 'You'd be amazed what I could cope with.' She would have been amazed too!

I really missed Mum and was desperate to speak to her. Although I'd been away from home for most of my childhood and teens, I'd never gone a fortnight without speaking to her and it was killing me.

Sometimes I'd look at Anna's phone lying on the table while she was in the shower. A quick phone call to Mum wouldn't hurt, I'd think. *Big Brother* would never find out. But if anyone had discovered where I was then, I would be instantly thrown off the show and I wouldn't risk that, so I never picked up the phone.

As the ferry docked, after two weeks, at Dover and we drove off the ramp on to the terminal and headed to Elstree.

What I didn't realise was that my name had already been in the newspapers in Britain as someone thought to be going into the *Big Brother* house.

I'd left Mum with instructions to tell anyone who wondered where I was that I had gone on holiday to Tunisia. But it didn't fool everyone.

When Mum opened her paper one morning and saw my name printed there she nearly collapsed from shock. Then she had to lie her teeth off as she knew if she gave the game away I'd be pulled from the show.

Mum even lied to Dad and Natalie, saying I'd gone to Tunisia on a late holiday deal with some of my dancing friends.

Dad says he was never convinced because he'd known Mum long enough to know when she was lying. And he knew that going on *Big Brother* would be my dream come true. But Natalie believed her. I don't think she thought Mum would lie to her like that. Dad took Nat to one side and told her what he had guessed, but I think she chose to believe he had got it wrong. For her it was too horrific to contemplate that I might really be going on *Big Brother* and creating even more disruption for our family just as things were getting back on an even keel.

Back in London, Anna drove me to a Holiday Inn. There I had another medical check but it was pretty routine and they didn't pick up on any of my former problems. I saw the psychiatrist again too, but again I sailed through it. I had all my answers off pat.

The next morning I was woken up at 6am and driven to Elstree Studios, just north of London. There I was shown into a dressing room and told to change into a dressing gown while my suitcase was taken away to be delivered to the *Big Brother* house. The case was checked over and over again just to ensure I hadn't tried to smuggle in anything that was forbidden in the house.

Apart from clothes and toiletries, you could take in five photographs and I had included my favourite snaps of Mum, Dad, Natalie, Carly and another friend at the time. Those pictures were such a comfort to me on bad days inside the house.

That day before we entered the house was so strange. I was exhausted because I hadn't slept the night before and I lay down a couple of times to get a few minutes' rest but then my mind would start whirring again and I'd be unable to drift off.

The production crew were popping in and out all day too, filming segments for *Big Brother's Little Brother*.

As the hours rolled by before we would enter the house at 9pm, every second dragged. For the first time I sat there feeling utterly terrified about what I'd let myself in for.

I knew loads of stuff was likely to come out in the newspapers – all about my anorexia and ex-boyfriends. But that didn't really bother me. This was my chance to turn my life around. To seize it back after all that time stuck in the gutter and transform it into something amazing.

I had to have the stereo in my dressing room turned up really loud so that I couldn't hear any of the other housemates who were in other dressing rooms down the corridor. And if I even wanted to leave the dressing room to use the loo, I had to go with a member of staff and wear a plain white mask in case I bumped into any of the other housemates.

As the time crept closer to 9pm I was finally allowed out of the dressing room and into the limo which was going to drive me on the 30-second trip to the official entrance to the *Big Brother* house.

When the car drew to a halt, one of the *Big Brother* minders opened the door and I stepped out of the car to the loudest barrage of screaming and shouting I'd ever heard. 'Nikki, Nikki,' people all around me were yelling. I kept looking, thinking they must be people I knew, but they were total strangers. I couldn't work out how they knew my name as I hadn't realised Davina McCall had just announced my arrival as last housemate of the night.

It was so overwhelming seeing all those people looking

at me and screaming my name. I waved and stared, totally overcome by it all, and gradually I made my way up the red carpet to Davina, who took my hand and guided me up the stairs to the doors of the house.

For a couple of seconds I stood there, breathless with excitement, before the doors swung back and I stepped into my new life.

Then the doors slammed shut behind me. So here I was. Finally, inside the *Big Brother* house, being watched by eight million people from every imaginable angle.

A couple of minutes earlier, 15 miles away at home, Natalie had been curled up on the sofa watching a Jimmy McGovern drama on BBC1. Then the phone rang.

It was Natalie's godmother, Julie. 'Are you watching it?' she asked urgently.

'Watching what?' replied Natalie.

'Oh,' said Julie, suddenly realising Natalie had no idea what was unfolding. 'I think you should turn over to Channel 4 – your sister has just walked into the *Big Brother* house.'

Lunging across the room for the remote control, Natalie changed channels just in time to see me standing at the top of the stairs waving at the thousands of people who had gathered below. She said afterwards that all she felt at that moment was pure horror.

Natalie hated *Big Brother* anyway and loathed the idea of all the public scrutiny of our family which would inevitably follow my appearance.

But nothing could have been further from my mind. Inside the house I tiptoed down the stairs and into the kitchen, where all the other housemates were already standing chatting.

At first it was a horrible feeling, like arriving stone-cold sober at a party where you don't know anyone at all. I looked around the room and couldn't see anyone I fancied – or even anyone I could imagine being friends with.

But I guess everyone else must have been equally nervous because we all chatted manically for hours through a mixture of excitement and terror.

The most commonly asked question about *Big Brother* is, 'Are you aware of the cameras all the time?' For the first two or three hours I was and felt I had to be on my best behaviour, but after that I totally forgot about them for the rest of my stay. If you didn't forget about them and tried to think about everything you said and did in advance to make sure you always looked good, you'd go utterly demented.

And it didn't bother me being watched all the time at all. I was used to it after spending months and months on total supervision, so having no privacy wasn't a problem for me.

I did find claustrophobia a struggle in the first few days, though. At that time I was used to going out every single night, so being stuck in one place day and night for days on end was really tough.

But after the first week I became institutionalised all over again – and I didn't miss the outside world one bit.

Back at home things weren't so jolly. When Mum returned from Elstree Studios that first night, Natalie wouldn't even let her in the house because she was so mad she hadn't told her I was going on *Big Brother*.

And already, stretching all down the road, there was a line of cars full of reporters and photographers trying to find out any nugget of information about me. *Big Brother* had sent an advice pack to families about how to deal with press enquiries but it was still daunting for Mum, and Natalie even more, to find themselves thrust into the spotlight like that.

It took Natalie weeks to adjust to my being in the *Big Brother* house. For her it was bad history repeating itself. After years of working to gain her own identity she was back to being 'Nikki Grahame's sister'. Everywhere she went people only wanted to talk about me and she felt Mum was focusing all her attention on me again, dropping everything to make sure she was around on eviction nights and spending all her spare time glued to the live feeds on E4.

It nearly pushed Natalie over the edge and she went a bit off the rails until finally she got the sack from her job as a receptionist.

But I was unaware of any of that. Once you're in the *Big Brother* house you could be on the moon, you are so disconnected from the rest of the world.

I was certainly used to sitting around isolated from the rest of the world with nothing to do. I'd done that for years in different institutions. And I was used to living in communal groups, so I never felt bothered by the lack of privacy.

There was always someone to talk to in the house, or a conversation that you could join in with. The tasks were fun and every night was a party. I absolutely loved it.

On top of that there were none of the stresses of the outside world to deal with. They provided all the food, there were no bills and no job to turn up for every morning. It was like a holiday camp and I could have lived there for ever.

The only downside was how nasty and bitchy people could be to one another. I quickly realised it was a very false environment and that people could be acting as your friend one moment, then nominating you for eviction the next. I could always tell if someone had nominated me because they couldn't look me in the eye. But it was still tough to come to terms with. I'd struggled for years with low self-esteem and having people explain publicly what they thought was wrong with me was never easy.

Most of what they said, though, I only discovered after I came out of the house and saw some of the recorded clips. Perhaps it was for the best that I didn't know when I was in there.

At first I stuck with Leah, a model and mother figure, Richard, a gay Canadian, and Glynn, a slightly gormless kid from Wales. The four of us really clicked and would laugh at the silliest things for hours on end.

Then, about halfway through my first week, it hit me out of the blue – I'd fallen in love.

CHAPTER 22

THE MAGIC AND
THE MISERY

Pete Bennett was warm and gentle, with a spiritual side to him. I could tell he had been one of life's underdogs and outsiders because I had too. He suffered from Tourette's Syndrome – a disorder which meant he had uncontrollable tics and verbal outbursts – and I'd had anorexia. Because of this, of all the housemates in *Big Brother*, I could relate best to him. I felt close to him from the very beginning.

One day we were sitting in the house and Pete told me that he had seen his friend die when he was electrocuted on a railway line. It had clearly had a terrible impact on him and I thought, This guy is special, he really is. From then on we spent loads of time together and I totally fell for him.

Nothing ever happened between us before I was evicted from the house but it was clear to everyone that we really liked each other as we'd spend hours talking about our lives and thoughts.

I even told Pete a little about my anorexia, although I didn't mention it to anyone else in the house. My eating in there was fine so long as I was able to carry on exercising, which I did by pacing up and down on a step in the house.

But my OCD remained an issue. I had to wash my own plate and cutlery before eating and I wrote my name on a mug in nail varnish so no one else would use it.

'I'm just a bit funny about germs,' I explained to the other housemates one morning. I didn't want to tell them everything about my life but I needed them to be aware of my problems as we were all living together so closely.

My tantrums and histrionics, which Mum and Natalie had been subjected to week in week out at home, quickly became a national entertainment. I became the most talked-about contestant in *Big Brother* history.

My diary-room outbursts, shouting, crying and throwing my arms and body around in that huge, gold padded chair, were getting record viewing figures for the show. I was being discussed in newspapers and on radio shows even though I was only behaving the same as I always did.

We'd been in the house four weeks when a new arrival, Susie Verrico, nominated me for eviction. I was furious and went into the diary room to vent my anger. 'Who is she?' I kept yelling at the camera, flinging my arms around in outrage. 'Who is she?' Even now people come up to me in the street and say how funny it was.

Another time we had to do a task where we had to dance for as long as we possibly could wearing masks and mp3 players – except mine wouldn't work. I went mad about it and when they called me to the diary room I became hysterical because I thought I was being disqualified. People who watched it tell me it was hilarious – but that is really just the way I was when things are going wrong for me.

For another task we had to pretend to run a recruitment agency and I was the PA. I couldn't work out how to use the typewriter and that whole episode was pretty funny too.

People that I've spoken to since my time in the house have said that watching my outbursts on screen were hugely entertaining. They were able to see I had an anger and frustration inside me which could build up to such a pitch that I would be unable to control it and it would physically overtake my body.

One minute I could be acting like a petulant child and the next I was showing genuine feeling for Pete. And the next minute I'd be dancing and laughing my head off.

I think that is what the viewers found extraordinary about me – that I could change so much and there were such extremes of emotion which could spill out in such a violent fashion at the slightest provocation. The weird thing is that I'd never felt special in my whole life before *Big Brother*. I'd never felt I fitted in or belonged anywhere really until then. But finally I did.

I'm sure some people think I faked those tantrums and hysterical outbursts for the cameras, but that really was me. Mum and Natalie (who calmed down after a couple of weeks and agreed to watch it) say they could always see one of my fits of temper or crying coming on screen long before the other housemates had realised what was about to be unleashed. And although they found it entertaining on the good days, it was deeply distressing for them on the days when I was obviously low.

I was nominated for eviction five times and each time

was a huge blow to my confidence and took me longer and longer to bounce back from. It was just so hard knowing that people I had thought of as friends actually wanted me out of there.

When stories came out in the press about my anorexia there was criticism of Endemol, the production company, for selecting me and endangering my 'fragile mental state'. But it wasn't their fault – I'd lied to them about my past. Besides, I didn't feel mentally fragile at all – I was having the time of my life.

Mum also came under attack in the media for letting me go into the house, but there was never anything she could have done to stop me. From the moment I applied it was my dream to be selected and there is no way I would have let her stand in the way of that.

Being in the house was everything I had ever dreamed of – and more. There were parties and tasks and fun. And, of course, I loved being with Pete.

Then, around the seventh week, my ankle and foot became so swollen from doing my daily stepping exercise that I was walking around limping. I had to go to the diary room to see a doctor and he advised me I had to rest my foot. And as soon as I stopped exercising I rapidly felt I was losing control of the entire situation and began feeling very oppressed by the house. It got me down and I became preoccupied and withdrawn, unable to interact with the other housemates. I started eating less and less at mealtimes and could feel things sliding away from me.

After a few days I went into the diary room and begged them to let me have a cross-trainer so I could exercise. At first they wouldn't do it but by then I was crying and begging for any means to exercise. 'If I don't exercise, I'll leave,' I cried. 'I'll have to walk out.'

Then I told the *Big Brother* producers everything – all about my life and the anorexia and the obsessive need to exercise. I didn't know whether Endemol would go mad at me for not having told them earlier, but I was beyond caring. I just desperately needed to exercise.

They listened to everything I had to say and were really supportive and promised to sort things out for me. There wasn't a single word of reprimand for not having been honest with them. And they didn't televise that diary-room conversation either, which was a huge relief.

Each time I was up for eviction Mum would travel to the house and wait outside with all the thousands of fans. She was really missing me and although she wanted me to stay in there for as long as possible, she was desperate to see me again too. I missed Mum badly as well.

On Day 58, when I was nominated for eviction for the fifth time, I was finally voted out of the house with 37.2 per cent of the public vote.

'And the seventh housemate to be evicted,' Davina said in her most dramatic voice, 'is…' – and then there was a pause that seemed to last a lifetime – '…Nikki.'

At first I couldn't believe it. I'd known for weeks that it was a possibility but now my dream was over it came as a horrible shock. I desperately hadn't wanted it all to end. And the thought of leaving Pete was agony.

None of the other housemates could believe it either and they all gathered around me, hugging me and saying how shocked they were.

I changed into my eviction outfit – denim hotpants and a white blouse – and prepared to leave the house. Then, shortly before I had to walk out of the door, I suffered a panic attack, hyperventilating and crying uncontrollably. I'd heard the crowd booing when other housemates had been evicted before and I was terrified they would do that to me. What if they throw things at me? I thought. And what if Mum isn't there to meet me?

Again, just like at the point of leaving all those other institutions and hospitals I'd endured earlier in my life, suddenly the thought of facing the outside world was terrifying.

I kissed everyone goodbye, before a final hug with Pete which I never wanted to end. It was so sad leaving him there in the house and not knowing when I would see him again.

Finally I summoned up all my strength and climbed the stairs out of the house and waited for the double doors to shoot open to reveal the outside world once more. When they opened I was nearly knocked sideways by the noise. On my way into the house the screaming and shouting had been loud but this time it was utterly overwhelming.

I stood paralysed at the top of the stairs, initially unable to work out if they were booing or cheering me. Too scared to walk down the steps towards that throng of people, I just wanted to go back into the house, where I knew everyone and where I felt I belonged now.

But in front of me were thousands of people shouting, 'Nik-ki, Nik-ki,' and everywhere I looked they were waving and holding placards with my picture on them. I just couldn't understand what all these people were doing and why they were screaming for me.

Then I saw a banner which said, 'Nikki to win,' and I thought wow, in total amazement.

I started crying from all the extremes of emotion and really didn't know what to do. I put my hands over my face, wanting to hide myself from the madness in front of me.

In the end Davina had to come up the stairs and pull me out of the doorway and down the steps away from the house. All the way I was desperately scanning the crowd, searching for a glance of Mum, but I couldn't see her anywhere.

At the bottom of the steps we walked through the *Big Brother* fans and the photographers all trying to get a snap of me for the next morning's papers.

Then we reached the stage and I sat down opposite Davina to be interviewed about my time in the house. At the end of our chat they flashed up my 'best bits' on a huge screen behind me. I was overwhelmed as I saw myself in the house.

From the studios I was driven straight to Sopwell House, a beautiful hotel in St Albans, where I was told I'd meet my family, Carly and my other friend, Alana.

It was a warm, mid-July night and when I jumped out of the car and knocked on the door of our apartment in the grounds of the hotel, I felt invincible. As if things could never get any better than this.

Mum opened the door and for a second we just stood there grinning at each other. Then we hugged and it felt like we would never, ever let go.

'I'm so proud of you,' Mum said.

And that is all I had ever wanted to hear. I had finally achieved something Mum could be proud of. Yes, I thought. I've done it.

Inside the apartment, Mum, Dad, Natalie and I all hugged each other so tight. It was incredible, all of us together again like that. For a moment it was as if the past 16 years and all that bad stuff had never happened.

Even Natalie had got over all her concerns about *Big Brother* and was delighted for me. She knew it had been my dream to do something special, and I'd turned it into a reality.

We sat up all night, chatting, drinking champagne and eating cakes and crisps. I finally fell asleep at 6.40 in the morning. Then Mum woke me at seven, telling me there had been a phone call and I had to get back to London for a meeting with my new agent. Agent? Me? I certainly didn't expect it.

John Noel Management, a really well-respected agency which represents people like Dermot O'leary and Tess Daly, wanted to take me on.

When I turned up in their smart London offices a couple of hours later, they had a pile of interview requests from newspapers and magazines on the desk as well as offers of work and sponsorship opportunities.

A couple of hours later I was sitting in a trendy, bright photographic studio for a shoot and interview with the *Sun* newspaper. They treated me like royalty, with champagne and chocolate waiting for me when I arrived.

I did exactly what John had told me and explained to the reporter all about my past – the anorexia. It was a real relief to get all that stuff out in the open, because that way it could never hurt me in the future. And I loved the photo shoot – it was so exciting trying on all those lovely clothes and posing for the camera.

The next couple of days I spent doing back-to-back interviews and photographs with magazines, radio stations and televisions channels. I'd get up at 5am to do a radio interview, then the rest of the day it would be meetings about work projects or photo shoots.

The best shoot I did was for *Pop* magazine. A really high-fashion affair by candlelight at the Café Royal, it was amazing. No other *Big Brother* contestant had ever done that magazine before, so it was a great honour to be asked. I also did front covers for *New Woman* and *You* magazines, and they turned out wonderfully too.

In the evenings I was getting invited to functions with celebrities at nightclubs and posh restaurants. I went to the Cartier Polo tournament at Windsor Great Park and even the film premiere of *Miami Vice*.

I had gone from feeling I didn't belong anywhere on earth and was a totally unimportant object to people stopping me in the street to tell me they loved me. It was beyond incredible.

One day I had to do an autograph-signing event at Carphone Warehouse's head office. When I stepped out of the car I was mobbed by three thousand people all taking pictures of me and trying to get my autograph. I couldn't handle it and freaked out. I'm sure some people thought I was turning into some kind of prima donna, but at times I really did find the attention overwhelming. For so long I'd felt so shit about myself that it was very difficult to get my head around the idea that this was for real and all these people weren't playing some huge joke at my expense.

And my phone never stopped ringing. I had to change my number six times because all sorts of people I hadn't seen for years or barely met came out of the woodwork. All of a sudden everyone wanted to be my best friend. But I wasn't totally naive and I knew what they were after –

invitations to smart parties, new nightclubs and premieres. No, I knew who my real friends were.

I did 40 personal appearances in a row all over the country, from Scotland to Northern Ireland to Manchester and then on and on to other towns and cities. I lived in a car, going from one nightclub or shopping centre to the next. I'd be driven five and a half hours to somewhere like Aberystwyth, go to a hotel, fall asleep on the bed and then have to be woken up to go out to a nightclub where I'd have to do signings, have my picture taken with people and answer endless questions about *Big Brother*.

Any spare moments I had, I'd be glued to watching the live feed of *Big Brother* on E4. I was desperately missing Pete and seeing him on television was the only way I could feel close to him again.

One night he was shown on screen pining for me. Thinking that he might just feel about me the same way I'd felt about him made me love him even more.

I'd been out of the *Big Brother* house four weeks when I got a phone call out of the blue from Endemol. Would I be interested in returning? They'd had an idea to give the closing stages of the series a twist by allowing the public the chance to vote four evicted housemates back into the 'house next door', a smaller new house adjoining the existing one. Then, after a week, one of the four would be selected to return to the main house.

I didn't have to be asked twice. I'd loved my time in the house so much I was desperate to get back in there. I was also delighted at the thought that I could be there on final night and even still in with a chance of winning the £100,000 prize. And of course seeing Pete again.

I had just one day to get myself ready and ran round in a flurry of excitement, packing clothes and saying my goodbyes before the public vote.

Sixty-three per cent of the voting public voted me back into the 'house next door' and I was utterly delighted. But it proved hard living there as it was even more suffocating than the original house, smaller, with no windows and absolutely nothing to do all day.

At the end of the week the remaining housemates in the main house had to decide which of the four of us in the 'house next door' they would select to join them. They all knew how much Pete had been missing me and so they chose me so that we could be together again.

As I stepped back into the main house six weeks after leaving it, I was walking on air at being given this incredible opportunity all over again.

Pete came up to me, wrapped his arms around me and for the first time kissed me full on the lips. It was the first time I could be sure that he really liked me and I knew then we were going to be together. I was so happy.

Back in the house, I was blissfully ignorant of the fact that *Big Brother* had been inundated with viewers complaining because they had changed the rules to let evicted housemates back onto the show.

Pete and I spent that week lying on his bed, cuddling and talking. I knew I'd fallen for him deeply. Some people think the producers were so worried that I might win, causing a public outcry about rule changing, that they deliberately put me in situations that caused me to have tantrums in that last week to annoy voters.

The atmosphere was electric inside the house on the final night. And outside more than eight million people across

Britain were tuning in to watch what happened. When Davina called out my name I was really disappointed to be leaving again but at least this time I knew I'd be reunited with Pete within a couple of hours. When he did emerge – as winner of the show – I was delighted for him and so proud of him. The next few days were a whirlwind of interviews and public appearances for both of us.

Then, around that time, I started filming *Princess Nikki*, a series of programmes for Channel 4 in which I had to take on a string of really horrid jobs. The *Big Brother* producers had come up with the idea for the six-week series while I was still in the house. Apparently they'd been inspired by my working as a PA in the temping agency task in the house.

They knew from the way I reacted in there that I would find it really hard doing disgusting jobs and would inevitably throw tantrums when things got difficult. But that's what they wanted, as they knew it would make good TV.

Because of my OCD, *Princess Nikki* was very difficult for me. The jobs I had to do included working on a sewage works, cleaning out an abandoned council house which was infested with rats and maggots and back-flowing sewage in the bath, cleaning up shit at a dog kennel, mucking out at a zoo, being a dustman and mucking out pigs on a farm.

I can understand that they thought it would be funny for viewers to watch me have a screaming fit every time I had to do these awful jobs, but I hated it. I put my head down and got on with it, though, because the money was good and I was excited at the idea of working in television. The production team were really nice but I don't think any of them realised quite how hard I found filming in those places and how real my problems with germs and dirt were. Even at the wrap party the crew bought me a cake in the shape of a turd. It wasn't funny.

Then, just at the time I was struggling with the demands of *Princess Nikki*, things were going wrong between me and Pete.

When he first came out of the house I really believed we were going to be a proper couple and he could even be 'The One'. He and his mum came round to visit me and my mum and we all got on really well. But within days things were becoming strained. Inside the house Pete had been gentle and spiritual but outside he could be self-centred and I felt shut out of his life.

His friends didn't like me at all and he was really influenced by his Mum too. We spent a few nights together at the Covent Garden Hotel but everywhere we went she came too.

One morning I said to her, 'Can you please give us some time together tonight on our own? We really need it.'

Then Pete and I went out but when we returned that night his mum was fast asleep in our bed. So much for time on our own! In the end I had to get into bed next to her while Pete slept on the floor.

Things came to a horrible end two weeks after we left the house when we had an all-day photo shoot with *OK!* magazine, followed by an appearance on *Friday Night with Jonathan Ross*. You would think it would have been one of the best days of my life. But it became one of the most miserable. Pete ignored me throughout the photo shoot, preferring to talk to the photographer and the make-up girl instead.

So by the time we arrived at the television studios to film *Jonathan Ross*, things were already tense. It was OK at first and I was answering all Jonathan's questions but then Pete lay down on the sofa with his fingers in his ears like a child so he couldn't hear anything I was saying.

It was utterly humiliating. He was making a fool out of me and himself in front of millions of people on live television. That was the final straw. We returned to our hotel that night in silence.

The next morning I went home and that was pretty much it. I was devastated. I really had been madly in love with him. For me it was never a publicity stunt or to win votes in the house. I'd genuinely thought we could be together in the outside world.

All I wanted to do was lie down in a dark room. The newspapers were all reporting that we had split up and that I was heartbroken – and they were right. It was all so public and embarrassing.

It wasn't helped by reports in the papers about Pete discussing our sex life and saying that he'd found himself a new girlfriend within two days of our splitting up!

For two weeks I couldn't face leaving the house just at the time that all my offers of work were pouring in.

I was sacked from presenting *Celebrity Soup*, E! Entertainment's show based on reality-TV clips, with Ian Lee because I didn't turn up for work. And one day when I'd made it in to film *Princess Nikki*, I locked myself in a toilet and wouldn't come out. I was too upset.

Perhaps I'm oversensitive and feel pain terribly deeply when things go wrong. And maybe that's because of all the things I've been through in the past. But whatever the reason, it made that period, which should have been one of the best of my life, particularly hard.

The only good thing was that I managed to keep control of my eating, and although I was still thin, I'd gained far too much by then to throw it all away by starving myself again.

Then, at the beginning of October, came news which gave me a real boost. I'd been nominated for a National Television Award in the category of Most Popular TV Contender. This was a new category, so it was a real honour. But I was up against four other reality-TV contestants and didn't really believe I had much chance of winning. I thought Pete would get it. But it was exciting just to be nominated and invited to the ceremony at the Royal Albert Hall.

Mum and I spent ages wandering around London searching for the perfect dress until we finally spotted it hanging on a rail in the beautiful Betsey Johnson shop in Covent Garden. I'd never spent that much on an outfit before but this felt like such a special occasion that I had to go for it.

As soon as I stepped out of the limousine at the Albert Hall that evening, 31 October 2006, I knew it was going to be a very special night.

I was interviewed by Kelly and Jack Osbourne on the red carpet!

And inside, the hall was packed wall to wall with celebrities. Everywhere I turned, someone wanted to talk to me, and because so many people had been following me on *Big Brother* they all felt like they knew me personally.

Matt Lucas – I've always loved him and think he's so funny – came up to me. Hardly able to speak to him, I blurted out, 'I can't believe it's you.' He gave me a huge smile and replied, 'I feel like that about you! You're going to put me out of a job.'

Then we all took our seats and the awards ceremony started. When it came to our category, Michael Barrymore appeared on stage to present it.

He read out the award – Most Popular TV Contender – and then they showed a clip of me doing my 'Who is she?' rant on *Big Brother*. I remember Michael saying, 'And the winner is...' and then everything goes a bit blurry. He must have said my name, because I turned to my agent, who was sitting next to me, and asked, 'Has he made a mistake? Are you sure?'

I was so gobsmacked I practically stumbled up on to the stage. There I was handed the award and as I turned to look at all those people, all cheering and clapping, it felt unbelievable. And then a voice from the back of the hall shouted, 'You deserve it, Nikki.' I hadn't prepared a speech because I'd never thought I would win, so I just kept thanking everyone who had voted for me and then went to walk off the stage – but went completely the wrong way!

When I got back to my seat there was so much adrenalin running through my body that my hands and legs were visibly shaking.

Later on, *Big Brother* won an award for Most Popular Reality Show, so it was a magical night.

Afterwards we went to the show party with all the team from Endemol and then on to the Met Bar, drinking and dancing.

Mum was then working at the sorting office as a postlady in Pinner and started her shift at five in the morning. An hour later I was just returning from central London and I got the cab driver to drop me off there. It was a cold, sharp night and I was still just wearing my flimsy silk dress when I teetered up the ramp into the sorting office, holding my award behind my back.

I spotted Mum across the other side of the building in her uniform and I quietly tiptoed up behind her.

'Guess what's happened,' I laughed as she heard me and turned round. I whipped out the award from behind my back and watched as her face filled with delight.

Mum picked me up and spun me round and round, shouting at her colleagues, 'Everyone, look, she's won. My little girl has won.'

Now I keep that award – engraved with the words 'Most Popular TV Contender 2006 – Nikki Grahame' – on my coffee table at home. It's always there to remind me of that night and the most amazing time of my life on *Big Brother*.

According to a poll by Channel 4, I was the twelfth most written-about person in the newspapers in 2006. But I'm under no illusion that everyone loved me! I was also voted the Second Most Annoying Person of 2006 in a BBC3 poll. But the fact that I was appearing in TV polls at all was still pretty mind-blowing for me.

Towards the end of that year I finished filming *Princess Nikki* and after six months' non-stop activity and work, Mum and I finally escaped for a holiday to Dubai. The trip was a huge treat, but I'd been working so hard and earning good money and hadn't had a chance to enjoy any of it until then.

When we arrived in Dubai I turned off my mobile phone and slept on and off for days. I was so exhausted. In the evenings Mum and I would go for a cocktail at a bar overlooking the beach and talk about everything that had happened over the past year and how much my life had changed.

The *bad* part of my life had already ended well before I went into *Big Brother* and I'd been fit and well for several years. But *Big Brother* was still the defining point in my life. Entering the house was the moment when life became *good*.

CHAPTER 23

A LIFE WORTH LIVING

It's more than two years now since I stepped out of the *Big Brother* house and every day I'm grateful for the opportunities it has given me.

During the last two series of *Big Brother* I've been a roving reporter on *Big Brother's Little Brother*, the magazine show about the series which goes out on Channel 4 and E4. I've interviewed Dustin Hoffman on the red carpet, acted out comedy sketches and done background reports on housemates.

And I'm often a guest on all sorts of TV shows. I was on *8 Out Of 10 Cats*, *The Friday Night Project*, the quiz shows *The Weakest Link* and *Celebrity Juice*.

I've even starred in a TV ad for Domino's Pizza.

And, according to something I read recently, I'm the fifty-second most Googled woman in the world.

I'm grateful for my quiet life at home. It is as if getting that taste of stardom has made me appreciate more than ever the simple things, like walking my dogs in the fields near my flat, popping round for a coffee and a chat with Mum, or going for a quiet drink with a close friend.

Having a celebrity profile has also allowed me to help other people. I've worked with Macmillan Cancer Support and the Stroke Association and I was privileged to travel to Scotland to spend a day with a little girl who'd asked to meet me as a wish through the Rays of Sunshine Charity for kids with cystic fibrosis. We went shopping and had a McDonald's together but she died shortly afterwards, which was a shocking reminder of how precious and fragile life is.

Mum and I have been through so much together, both good and bad, that we are bound very tightly by it. Those experiences have made us stronger both individually and together. I don't know how I would cope without her around – she still looks after me a huge amount and is the rock on which my life is built.

Natalie and I still drive each other mad at times and still fight for Mum's attention, but we get on better now than we have ever done. Nat says ever since *Big Brother* she has found a respect for me that wasn't there before. She says seeing me pull myself up from the gutter, from having nothing when I came out of Rhodes Farm to winning a National Television Award, made her think about her life differently too.

After she was sacked from her receptionist's job while I was in *Big Brother* Natalie started thinking about what she really wanted to do, which was to become a scriptwriter. She'd loved writing stories since we were kids. So she enrolled on an MA course, which she has just completed, and now she is writing scripts for films and plays, hoping one of them will get commissioned.

I really respect her for following her dream too and I hope so much that she achieves it. I'm sure she will.

Dad lives a couple of minutes away and I see him about once a week. I still blame him a lot for my parents' divorce and ending my perfect childhood. But writing this book has made me see that things may not always have been easy for him either and perhaps he too was just someone muddling through life as best he could.

Now we get on pretty well and sometimes he'll pop around for a cup of tea with me and Natalie and we'll take the mickey out of him and he'll tease us like when we were kids. Just a few years ago I could never, ever have imagined that happening again. But it is because he's my dad and I love him. And I'll always love him.

I often think back to our house in Stanley Road where we all lived together before I was eight and everything seemed so good, so happy. Three times I've knocked on the door of that house and asked the people who live there now to show me around because I've felt so desperate to return there and to try to reclaim that life.

But I'm learning to accept that that life has gone for ever and isn't coming back. Instead I've got to focus my energy on this life, right now, and look to the future and all the opportunities it can bring.

At the moment I'm single and meeting Mr Right isn't easy. In fact I think becoming a recognised face from television has probably made finding a bloke harder than ever. Nowadays I tend to attract men who just like the idea of dating someone who has been on telly. I always fall for good-looking blokes with all the patter, but I've discovered they are generally not the ones to trust. I've been cheated on and mucked around by enough blokes to make me suspicious of their motives.

I'd love to settle down one day and have kids, but that is quite a lot for me to hope for. I'm 27 and I've still never had a natural period, which means I have virtually no chance of ever falling pregnant naturally. The prospect of never having children is probably the worst thing anorexia has left me with.

But another of its legacies is osteoporosis, a bone disease in which your bones become thinner and thinner, making them hugely susceptible to fractures. Osteoporosis can be caused by low oestrogen levels, which is a side effect of anorexia's preventing the body going through puberty.

Missing out on calcium in my food when I was younger has only made the problem worse. Women of my age can expect to have bone density of between 0 and –1. When it gets to –2.5 you're classed as having osteoporosis. A scan last year showed my spine is –2.9. My bone density is like that of a 68-year-old. There is little I can do to reverse the damage I've already done, but I take a calcium supplement and eat as much dairy food as I can to prevent it getting worse.

I've had two fractured ribs (one from just a strong hug), fractured toes (when a television fell on me in a nightclub) and a fractured elbow (from falling over). I'm constantly in danger of fracturing myself again, which means I have to be incredibly careful never to slip or hurt myself. The main concern is what it'll be like when I get older. In extreme cases of osteoporosis, even sneezing can cause a fracture and it can be incredibly painful.

My OCD remains with me too. I'm still obsessive about cleanliness and hygiene and I don't like other people touching things that I am about to eat or drink. Recently I was doing interviews at a radio station and a woman offered me a cup of tea. 'Thanks very much,' I said, 'but can I make it?'

She thought I was joking – but I was serious.

'No, you sit there, I'm making it,' I snapped at the poor woman when she still hadn't got the message after a couple of minutes.

And while I might let a friend make me a sandwich I still have to stand over them to supervise everything they do.

If I eat in a restaurant, as soon as the knife and fork are put on the table I wrap them in tissue so they can't get contaminated by anyone touching them or breathing on them. Minutes earlier the waiter or waitress may have had their hands all over them, but if I haven't seen it I can cope with. But if someone were to touch my cutlery in front of me, I'd freak out.

At home I still have just a couple of plates, knives, forks and spoons that I will use over and over again. And I love that pre-packed plastic cutlery they give away in shops. Even though logically I know it hasn't just magicked itself into that packet and someone, somewhere, has touched it, for me the thought of it being wrapped in cellophane makes it clean and safe.

My OCD is gradually getting better but it's still very tough if I'm feeling low or if I've been out all day and been unable to wash my hands.

And I have to work hard not to become compulsive about exercise too. I limit myself to three trips to the gym a week, one swimming session and have a very structured routine.

In my view you never fully get over anorexia but you

can learn to live with it. You can keep it in check and be aware of the danger signs if it is threatening to overcome you again. I still know the calories in virtually any food you can mention and it is hard for me to decide on what to eat for a meal without those numbers bouncing around my head. And I still weigh foods like pasta just to make sure that I don't have more than I feel comfortable with – 45 grams (1½ oz) and no more.

But I no longer feel those issues are putting my health in danger and I'm getting better all the time. Until fairly recently I was still mopping up grease on my food with a tissue but I've stopped that now. And this summer I ate a plate of chips when I was at a festival with my friends. It was the first time in ten years, since I was at Rhodes Farm.

I'm still reluctant to let my weight go above 40 kilos (6 stone 4 lb). To most people that will seem very thin but it is a weight I'm comfortable with.

So yes, there is still a lot of control in my relationship with food and my body. But so long as I can retain that control and exercise regularly I know I won't make myself sick again. The only danger is if for some reason I can't train as often as I want. It is then that I'll start to eat less and I have to be careful not to slip back into one of those dangerous cycles where I start enjoying the idea of not eating.

Last year I had a second boob job to correct some of the mistakes made during my first op when I was 18. After the surgery I couldn't exercise for a month and I did struggle with my food for a while and was becoming very conscious of how much I was eating every day. But once I was able to start exercising again it was fine.

I'll never return to the person I was before I was eight –

I'll never have that carefree attitude to life and my body and food. But I know I will never slip back into full-on anorexia again either. There is no way I'll ever starve myself to death now as I enjoy life too much. I've seen how much there is for me out here and I want to remain a part of it.

In the past couple of years I have met lots of young people – boys and girls – through B-eat, a charity which supports people with eating disorders.

I've also visited hospitals and gone to Rhodes Farm to speak to patients.

When I meet kids still fighting anorexia it is an in-your-face reminder of how far I have come. Because when I see girls with their twig-like legs and bones jutting out from their clothes I think, That's how I was – but probably worse. It makes me feel incredibly sad because I know they have a huge struggle ahead of them. But I also know the struggle is so worthwhile. And that is what I try to explain when I talk to them. All I can do is attempt to give them hope that they can get better and there is a life outside for them.

Every day I look at the scar across my stomach where my gastrostomy tube once was. It is a permanent reminder of the two-inch piece of plastic that stood between me and certain death.

Thinking back on those years to write this book has been at times excruciatingly painful and led to many nights of broken sleep and silent tears as I've relived those times.

I had some good times and made amazing friendships in the hospitals and units where I stayed, but in general the years from eight to 16 were marked by sadness, loneliness and anger. They were certainly not a childhood.

Sometimes I just can't believe it all happened – being pinned down by six nurses while a tube was shoved up my nose, being drugged up for weeks on end to stop me screaming and fighting like a demon, falling into a coma one Boxing Day night, crawling up stairs because I was too weak to walk, cramming paracetamol down my throat because I'd had enough of living, sleeping in a shop doorway.

The only reason I know it is all true is because when I do think over all that stuff, I can still feel the pain inside me. Because, despite all the good things that have happened since, that ball of hurt and sadness of a little girl so incredibly alone remains buried inside me. And I think it will probably always be there. It is part of who I am.

Dr Dee Dawson, who runs Rhodes Farm, told me recently that when she accepted me there she was told, 'Do what you can with her but it doesn't really matter – she is going to die anyway.'

It is stories like that that make me feel so incredibly lucky to be alive. And even more lucky to have had the opportunities and experiences that getting selected for *Big Brother* brought with it.

I have vowed I will never take this life for granted. It is all too much of a miracle.

For so long I cared about no one and nothing apart from starving myself. Anorexia was my best friend, my only friend. Thoughts of not eating dominated my every waking moment and gave me a superhuman strength to fight off anyone who tried to stop me pursuing my mission.

As for why I did it? I think maybe it was something I was born with and that I would have become anorexic at some point in my life, but my parents' divorce, Grandad's death and then my competitiveness at gymnastics were triggers when I was eight.

Add to that my ultra-competitive nature in general, which meant I didn't just want to be any old anorexic, I wanted to be the best.

And what was it that brought me back out of it? I believe it was purely my own decision that I wanted to live – I wanted to give the outside world a try after being away from it for so long.

I know I was very lucky to have stayed alive long enough to make that decision. Others were not so lucky. Sara, one of the 'hairdryer gang' at Rhodes Farm, died three years ago at 23 from heart failure brought on by anorexia. She was the same age as me.

But many others who I lived with at those clinics and specialist units have managed to go on to live amazing, fulfilled lives with great jobs, loving relationships and families of their own.

Because there is hope for anyone who has an eating disorder. And so there is hope for their parents, brothers, sisters, husbands and children. That's why I have written this book. Not to say, 'Hey, look at me and what a great time I had in *Big Brother*,' but to say to anyone who is now in the pit of despair that I once was in: There is a life out there for you. And it is worth living.

I guess it is pretty unlikely many other people with anorexia will end up getting selected for *Big Brother* and land their own TV show cleaning out pig shit! But there will be other things in their future that bring them the happiness and security that I know deep down they are desperately craving. Writing this has made me realise how much of my life I wasted before I got on with living and how much I want to prevent other girls making that same mistake.

So my advice to kids with anorexia now?

First, make the most of whatever help you are already receiving, because as you get older it gets harder and harder to get that specialist help and the places you will be sent will become more harsh and more uncaring.

Second, *you* have to make the decision that you want to get better. To do that, try thinking about how different your life could be if you weren't stuck in this battle to be thin. Because your life in the future will be better than what you are going through now, I promise.

And my advice to mums and dads worried that their kids are developing anorexia or an eating disorder? Get professional help as quickly as you can in the hope you can nip it in the bud, before it becomes more difficult to reverse patterns of thinking.

And please, please, don't be dissuaded by doctors or friends who think your child is 'being faddy' or 'just in a phase'. Trust your instincts and don't stop fighting until someone helps you. Because I know only too well that is what your child is screaming out for you to do, even if they are saying the total opposite.

But most of all never stop believing that things can get better. I am living proof of that. However much someone with anorexia might doubt it now, there is a fulfilling and happy life out there waiting for them, once they choose to live it.

I never, ever thought I would find such a special life and it took me almost 11 years of fighting to reach it, but now that I have, I know it has been worth every little bit of effort along the way. Because, as I have discovered, there is an amazing, special life out here for everyone.

It has been a horrible, long and painful journey, sodden with so many tears and bruised by so many knocks and setbacks. But I'm here – and it is good.

I've learned that the outside world doesn't have to be scary. Yes, it can be tough and there are pitfalls and people who want you to fail. But there are also people who will stand by you however bad everything gets. However much sadness and pain fill your life, they are still there beneath it all, next to you.

And those are the people who make your life worth living. So for them – Mum, Dad, Natalie and Carly – thanks for showing me my life *was* worth fighting for.

EPILOGUE

After my first stint in the *Big Brother* house, I was on top of the world. Finally, after years of dealing with painful feelings of rejection and loneliness, the public had shown me that I was accepted and loved, simply for being who I was. Offers of television work came flooding in and in between projects my life was an endless stream of glamorous parties and gigs. It certainly appeared as if I'd left the insecurities of my past behind, and I felt as though anything might be possible.

It would be misleading for me to claim that I ever let go of my eating disorder completely, but after *Big Brother* I felt more liberated from it than I ever had before. Whilst I was in the house I ate the same evening meal as the other contestants. I allowed myself to be cooked for by someone else (although I did insist on having my own cutlery and crockery). Anyone who has ever struggled with anorexia or OCD will know what a momentous leap forward that was for me, to relinquish even that tiny bit of control. I had a new life, full of new faces, new places and new possibilities. For the first time in as long as I could remember, health and happiness seemed to be within my grasp.

Unfortunately, it just wasn't that simple. Over the next five years, my illness continued to rear its ugly head on several occasions. Sometimes I'd be able to push the destructive voice of sickness to the back of my mind. Other times I'd lose the struggle: anorexia would completely dominate my thoughts and I'd be consumed by the desire to exercise compulsively and avoid food.

As I write this epilogue, I have voluntarily chosen to put myself into medical care again and I am attending the Inpatient Mental Health Unit at St Vincent's Square in the Chelsea and Westminster Hospital. Today, I weigh just 36 kilos. I know, logically, that I need to gain weight but despite the constant support of the wonderful staff here, I am struggling. The following pages document just what happened. How did the vibrant, confident young woman that I was when I left the *Big Brother* house deteriorate and once again succumb to her illness?

In May 2009, I published my first book (this one, in fact), which is the story of my life. I called it *Dying to be Thin*. I wanted to share my experiences to help young people battling an eating disorder and to allow others to really understand the illness. It was tough reliving my experiences and opening up old wounds, but eventually the book was finished. I'd had a huge hand in organising the launch and when I surveyed the celebrity guests who attended that night, I felt a massive sense of accomplishment. But there was one person in attendance who darkened my mood: Danny, my then boyfriend.

I'd met him a year beforehand and very quickly became

totally infatuated with him. He was a friend of a friend, and we'd met at a restaurant during an evening out. He made an instant beeline for me and I remember thinking I'd never met anyone quite like him before. He was the life and soul of the party, telling hilarious stories, buying everyone drinks, dancing on tables. His enthusiasm for life was infectious and I soon found myself under his spell.

Just days later, we had become inseparable. Our relationship grew extremely intense, very quickly – I even introduced him to my mum within the first week. He would always suggest where we should go, pick me up from my house in north-west London, chauffeur me from door to door and he paid for absolutely everything. In retrospect, I think there was a part of me that enjoyed not having to be responsible for any decision making; life had been a whirlwind since *Big Brother* and people were constantly making demands of me. Now, I never had to worry – everything was taken care of and Danny was totally in control. Or so it seemed.

Danny was always making extravagant gestures like meals in expensive restaurants and nights out in central London; he'd buy me clothes and jewellery. To many women he would have been the perfect fairytale fantasy but I quickly discovered there was a dark side to his apparent generosity and fun-loving spirit. He'd become angry and occasionally violent. He'd use dangerous measures to scare me or get my attention, like swerving his car across the road when I was in the passenger seat.

He was also incredibly possessive. I came to the horrible realisation that his initial desire to spend every minute with me wasn't because he couldn't bear to be parted – it was because he simply didn't trust me to be without him.

He would constantly want to know where I was and who I was with. Sometimes he'd follow me around London in his car. Other times, he'd ring me over and over again during a night out and if I didn't answer my phone, he'd resort to calling my friends, demanding that whoever I was with tell him exactly what I was doing at that moment. It was embarrassing.

The strange thing was that sometimes he would make me feel so safe and other times I was terrified of him. He'd shelter me from the world – but on the condition that I did everything he said and behave exactly as he wanted me to.

One incident with Danny will haunt me forever. We were driving to see my mum and granddad when suddenly he stopped the car in an isolated spot. It was dark, with no sign of civilisation for miles around; he knew I had nowhere to run. He said he had something to tell me, but first he snatched my phone from me and removed the battery. Then he told me, in graphic detail, how he had once killed someone. I was shaking uncontrollably, unable to speak or to react, I was so scared. The way he told the story, and the circumstances in which he chose to tell me, left me in no doubt that he wanted me to know just what he was capable of: it was a warning.

I was truly in over my head. Foolishly, I'd agreed to let him move into my flat quite early on in the relationship, when everything had seemed perfect. So, even though it was clear to me that we weren't working, it wasn't as simple as ending it and walking away – even if he hadn't bullied and frightened me into staying with him. The cash he had flashed when I first met him turned out to be technically not his. In reality, he was in debt and he began to rely on me for money. One by one, he managed to isolate me from my friends. He even caused a rift between my mum and me: she saw how he was treating me and, understandably, didn't approve.

My self-esteem suffered a catastrophic blow. In the early days of our relationship, I'd been reasonably happy with myself and my body. We went on holiday to Thailand at the start of 2009 and there, I ate as freely as I can ever remember doing. In the extravagant surroundings of our luxury hotel everything seemed surreal and this allowed me to relegate anorexia to a very small part of my mind. At the same time, though, Danny made it very clear that he wanted a thin, glamorous girlfriend. He'd look at gorgeous, curvaceous girls in magazines and on the television and say they were 'fat'. I feared if I gained too much weight, he'd start to look elsewhere.

By treating me like a princess one minute and screaming, threatening and bullying me the next, he chipped away at my self-confidence. He himself also had body image issues – I found a stash of illegal slimming tablets amongst his things, which brought the entire issue once more to the forefront of my mind. Looking back, I think this situation may have heralded my relapse – it was the first sign that the happiness I felt in the aftermath of *Big Brother* wasn't destined to last.

On Valentine's Day 2009, we argued during a night out. Whilst I can't remember what we were specifically rowing about (disagreements had become such a frequent thing between us), I do know it got very heated. I told him I was going home, hailed a taxi and was about to get in, when he grabbed me and herded me into the back of his friend's van, saying he would give us a lift. By this stage, I was too exhausted and drained to argue so I dutifully sat in the back as we sped through north London.

Suddenly, I blacked out. When I came to, blood was spraying at high velocity out of my head and streaming down my face. The van had crashed. Crying and bleeding, I stumbled out into Upper Street, Islington and eventually found my way to the Whittington Hospital, although I have absolutely no recollection of how I got there. When I woke up, bruised and bandaged in a hospital bed, Danny was there. I had been in the hospital overnight and he hadn't even called my mum or my sister Natalie – he'd put me in a dangerous situation and had been too self-absorbed to call the people I love. He even went as far as deleting my mum and Natalie's phone numbers off his phone, and then used the excuse that he didn't have their numbers to call them. It was at this point I knew for certain that I had to end things. A few weeks later, with the help of my family and friends, I told him to remove his things from my flat.

That relationship had left me shaken and lonely. After we split, I went off the rails to a certain extent. I went to countless festivals that summer, celebrating my freedom and when I wasn't doing that, I spent almost every evening in Harrow at the Trinity bar, out drinking with one of my best friends, Leon. Leon was dating a girl named Julie at the time and I instantly struck up a wonderful friendship with her, too. Although their relationship didn't last long, my friendship with Julie is still going strong to this day. She will be in my life a very long time and is like a mother figure to me. She has welcomed me into her family and she made me a Godparent to her son. It meant a lot to me that I could mean so much to Julie and her son, especially as I can't have children of my own. Around the same time that my friendship with Julie was forming another particular friendship started to develop.

I met a guy who was the lead singer and guitarist of a band I loved. Unfortunately, for legal reasons I haven't been able to name him. He had that rock-star look I adore in men – skinny jeans, slightly grubby-looking and incredibly skinny. Also, I associated music and going to gigs with the liberation I felt after leaving Danny. I looked at him and he epitomised all that: I wanted to be with him and I wanted to be like him. Once more, I began to fixate on losing weight.

Then he told me he was addicted to heroin. Rather than acting as a red flag, this made me like him even more: I wanted to save him, to mother him, to make him better. He became my 'project'. All summer long, I pursued him, convinced we were meant to be together. Eventually, he succumbed to my charms and we became a couple.

Our time was characterised by me putting myself out for him and him repaying this by ignoring me and depriving me of affection. After Danny, I can't explain why I immediately went for another man who didn't treat me particularly well – the only conclusion I can come to was that I didn't feel I deserved to be loved.

I took him to premieres and posh parties and introduced him to all my industry contacts. And I even arranged for his band to compete in a charity sports event. These were opportunities he could never have engineered on his own. In return, he'd take days to reply to my text messages, tell me he was 'too cool' to be dating a reality TV star contestant and frequently disappear without warning.

We broke up and reunited several times throughout

2010; he also lived with me for a while. During that time I witnessed his attempts to quit drugs cold turkey – he lay in bed, sweating, not talking and not eating. It was agony to watch. He finally kicked heroin in January 2011, when I took him to Champneys Spa Hotel in Henlow Grange for three days.

Although we remain friends to this day, I knew I couldn't stay with him long-term. Living with him drove me to the brink of insanity – my flat was constantly messy and when I asked him to clean up after himself, he'd scream at me, calling me a 'freak' with OCD. He'd also stay up late into the night watching television when I was trying to sleep and monopolise my laptop so that I couldn't use it myself. I've lived alone pretty much consistently for 10 years so it's hard enough attempting to share my space with another human being without the challenges of his habits, both drug and housework related, thrown into the mix.

We broke up for the last time in May 2011. I was on ITV's *This Morning* speaking out about my battle with anorexia in an interview with Phillip Schofield. For me, it was a momentous event, sharing private experiences with an audience of millions, but he couldn't even be bothered to watch the show. I knew then that he would never care for me the way I did him and so I asked him to leave my flat, where he was living rent-free. He begged me to let him stay, but I was resolute – things just weren't working.

By the time our relationship ended, the stress and the competitive dieting meant my BMI (Body Mass Index) had dropped to just 13 points (a healthy BMI is usually between 18 and 25 points). In sharp contrast to Danny, he used to beg me to put on weight, saying he would find me more attractive if I was a little curvier, but the words just didn't seem to sink in. Now I weighed around 36 kilos and I'd got used to my body as it was. I felt it was a body I knew, one I could deal with. In these turbulent times, I needed something familiar to cling onto; after years of being underweight, my malnourished body provided a much-needed touchstone.

After that final breakup, I felt a double whammy of devastation – it was as though the grief of both of the relationships hit me simultaneously. I was left feeling very vulnerable and incredibly low, emotionally.

There were some positive aspects during this time, however. In 2009, I became involved with Body Gossip, a charity campaign which allows the public to share their real body stories. I first heard about Body Gossip in my capacity as an ambassador for the Osteoporosis Society, one of the campaign's sponsors.

Body Gossip invites everyone in the UK to write something about their body and submit the piece to them via the website. They then have a selection of the pieces they receive performed by well known actors, musicians and television personalities like myself, either in live shows or short films, which they put on YouTube. The idea is that real people are given a powerful voice to shout about all things body-related. I immediately loved the concept and also knew that I wanted to help in any way that I could.

Although Body Gossip is not specifically an eating disorder campaign, a lot of the stories they receive from the public do fall into this category, as you'd expect. As part of the celebrity cast, I performed a piece written by a fellow sufferer of anorexia at the live stage show. As I read the young woman's story during the first performance (at the Hub, King's Cross, London), I broke down in tears. There was so much I could relate to in her experiences; it felt reassuring to know I wasn't alone in my body battles and also comforting to think perhaps my book was providing that reassurance for other people, too.

Body Gossip's live show was taken to the Edinburgh Fringe Festival in August 2009. I made fast friends with the rest of the celebrity cast, who included Shobna Gulati from *Coronation Street*, Anne Diamond and Cerrie Burnell from *CBeebies*. The best friend I made, however, was the actress Natalie Cassidy – we became incredibly close whilst performing in the show and remain great mates to this day. Natalie has been an incredible support to me throughout my various trials and tribulations; I like to think I fulfil the same role for her, too.

Donating my time to Body Gossip, to B-eat (the UK's largest eating disorder support charity) and to the Osteoporosis Society gave me a purpose. Part of the reason why I have written this book is because I am so motivated by the idea of helping other people and I went into 2010 feeling a little less worthless. During that year, Body Gossip made one of the stories they received into a short film, performed by some of their celebrity supporters including myself. Called *This One is For You*, it's an inspiring story of anorexia recovery written by a girl called Laura Nation. Within the first few months, it received tens of thousands of hits on YouTube. As a result of the film, and of my book, I received a lot of emails and messages of support from the public, which comforted me and made me feel significant and valued.

I'll always remember the summer of 2010 for three

reasons: my nephew Sunny was born, it was the summer I went to no less than 12 music festivals and it was the time when I entered *Ultimate Big Brother*.

Sunny came into the world on 17 July 2010 and as soon as I laid eyes on that child, I adored him unconditionally. I wanted to spend as much time with him as I could and was always offering to babysit and take him on walks. There was a part of me tinged with sadness, too, because anorexia has robbed me of the ability to have children of my own. I look at Natalie and the relationship she has with this little person she has created and I know I'll never experience that for myself, although I would like to adopt one day.

Despite all our previous differences, I admire my sister so much as a mother. I couldn't have imagined her in the role until I saw it with my own eyes but Natalie is an amazing mum. She and I now attend family therapy with our mum a couple of times a month. These sessions have shown me that my relationship with my sister has been destroyed, probably irreparably. It makes me so incredibly sad. We are united by the love we share for Sunny and he will always provide a reason for us to continue to try and work through our differences, though.

I loved going to the music festivals, it was my way of escaping the real world. At The Big Chill I almost fainted when I spotted Thom Yorke, lead singer of Radiohead. To say Radiohead are my favourite band would be a huge understatement; their lyrics resonate so much with me and often seem to express the things I am incapable of saying. I have some of their artwork from the album *OK Computer* and lyrics from their song 'The Bends' tattooed on my wrist. I'm not usually shy, but it took ages for Sarah, a friend of mine, to persuade me to go over and tell Thom how much his music has helped me over the years. Luckily for me, he seemed a little mesmerised by Sarah's astonishing beauty and, to my excitement, invited us both to watch the sun rise with him. In the end, though, we were all too tired to actually go through with the plan but the offer was enough. I'll treasure the memory of meeting Thom forever.

Glastonbury was a different experience entirely. For four days I hardly ate, instead surviving on vodka with diet mixers. I developed severe sunstroke and felt really unwell. On the Sunday I took two sleeping pills and slept for 12 hours in a baking hot tent. When I woke up, I had to wring what seemed like bucket-loads of sweat out of my top before being driven home.

Whether I consciously realised it or not, anorexia was gripping me more tightly at this stage. Perhaps I was too preoccupied by the events of that summer to notice. Whatever the truth, a psychologist pronounced me mentally stable enough to go into the *Ultimate Big Brother* house, which I did on 24 August 2010.

Ultimate Big Brother bore no comparison to my first time in the house. Instead I found the whole experience intensely difficult to cope with. I was apprehensive even before entering the show and hyper-aware of what had happened with the late Jade Goody, who'd been accused of racism and seen her popularity plummet after an altercation with Bollywood star Shilpa Shetty when she returned to the house. Naturally I was terrified of unintentionally saying or doing something that might have a similar effect. After *Big Brother*, the public had warmed to me – now I felt I'd placed myself at risk of losing the acceptance and love which was so important to me.

Soon I began to miss the people I'd become close to in the original *Big Brother* – I just didn't have the same affinity with my fellow *Ultimate Big Brother* housemates. For a start, because most of the housemates had seen footage of me in the original show, there was a preconception that I was going to be a nightmare to live with and that I'd constantly throw tantrums, which didn't particularly help any of us to bond. Then there were the sleeping arrangements: the bedroom in the house was like a barnyard, noisy and smelly. As a result, I began to suffer sleep deprivation, which put me even more on edge than I'd been to begin with. Just as when I'd tried to share my flat with past boyfriends, I found it difficult to share living quarters with the other contestants. I'm not sure why it was harder for me than first time around – perhaps it was simply that I was younger and more carefree back then.

The situation was further exacerbated by everyone's insistence on forming cliques, most of which I felt totally excluded from. These were formed either by people who had originally been in the house during the same year, or by those who liked to bitch about, or intimidate, other contestants. I found the American rapper Coolio the most difficult housemate to get along with. He bullied anyone in whom he could detect a sign of weakness. I was extremely vulnerable, both emotionally and physically during this time so of course his attentions were often focussed on me. Swedish presenter Ulrika Jonsson was also challenging – she seemed more interested in catching and maintaining the interest of the men in the house than actually forming a real bond with anyone. With her displays of jealous behaviour, she managed to isolate most of the female contestants.

During the programme, each housemate was given a message from home. Mine was from my mum and friend Carly, but I had nothing from Natalie. We'd quarrelled prior to me entering the house and I knew she must have been asked by the producers to participate and had refused. I have since found out that she religiously tuned into the show. She also made the dress I wore when I was evicted from the house – it's a 1960s-inspired design made of flowery, yellow fabric and remains a favourite. In spite of this the absence of a message from my sister definitely hurt. The incident didn't help my mindset or do anything to quell feelings of loneliness.

That isn't to suggest that I didn't make any friends at all. I became close to the broadcaster Vanessa Feltz for the short period she was in the house. She was kind and understanding, so I felt I could confide in her. I told her about my struggles with food and with my body. Vanessa empathised because she herself has battled with her own body image, albeit in another way. I also identified with Nadia, *Big Brother*'s only-ever transgender contestant. She, too, was a little different and knew what it was like to feel isolated and lonely. I appreciated Nadia's truthfulness and straightforwardness – I never felt as though I was competing with her or that our altercations were in any way superficial or false. With some of the other contestants, I felt as though they only ever spoke to me in order to gather ammunition for a future dispute. However, I share the same taste in music as Preston, which gave us an area of synergy; I also adored Brian.

Most of all, being in the *Ultimate Big Brother* house allowed me to see clearly just how much my eating and exercise habits had deteriorated. Whereas during my first time in the house I'd been relatively relaxed about sharing an evening meal, this time I insisted on cooking all my own food, separate from everyone else. Usually I'd have grilled chicken or fish with vegetables, a 'safe' option for me. I knew the foods I wanted would always be available to me since I'd made it a condition of my contract with *Big Brother* that we wouldn't be put on rations of any kind, as we had first time around. But I couldn't exercise in the way that I would ideally have liked whilst confined to the *Big Brother* house. There was no gym or pool in the house so I'd attempt to silence anorexia's constant nagging by running up and down the garden for 20 minutes each day. It helped to a degree but I was still incredibly frustrated. Even despite my strict portion control and attempts to exercise, I knew I was gaining weight. When I discovered I'd gained 3kg during the weeks I was in the *Big Brother* house, I was horrified. The papers were all saying how much better I looked a little curvier (I even made it into a few 'best dressed' columns, which is unusual for a *Big Brother* housemate), but this wasn't enough to curb my despair. All I was able to focus on was how alien my body felt to me, how I longed to be back to my former, more slender self.

Ultimate Big Brother was largely a negative experience for me. I suppose I'd had such a life-changing experience during the original *Big Brother*, the *Ultimate* version was never going to match up to my expectations. In the aftermath of the programme, I couldn't help feeling deflated. However, it did reassure me that the public were still behind me when I was voted the most popular female *Big Brother* contestant for the entire 11 years of the show. I'm still not sure what it is about me that the public relate to, but I'm very grateful and humbled they do.

After leaving *Ultimate Big Brother*, I focussed harder than ever on losing the weight I'd gained and my behaviour towards food and exercise became increasingly extreme. I found myself exercising harder than ever while restricting my calorie in take to 200 per meal. It was as though I'd boarded a train and it was hurtling towards a place where I'd be once more completely controlled by anorexia; I didn't know how I'd ever get off. I knew Mum was concerned about the amount of exercise I was doing and that I was sacrificing all the hard work I'd put in towards conquering my illness, so I decided to find myself a therapist. Soon I began seeing Kaumari, a counsellor at St Vincents – all the while mindful that I must combat the constant barrage of guilt and anger I was doing my best to vent through exercise, if I was ever going to get better again.

* * *

As I hurtled into 2011, I had no idea that the year would prove to be one of my most challenging yet. The obstacles to my happiness started in the very first month. On 12 January, I underwent an operation on my left foot to have my toe realigned. The damaged bone was cut and a section shaved off before a metal pin was put in its place to straighten it. As the doctors operated, a nerve in my foot became inflamed and had to be taken out. Knowing all these gruesome details played havoc with my already-squeamish mind. I was slung out of hospital at 1pm on the day of the procedure and Mum drove us directly to her house. At first I wasn't aware of the pain because I'd been put on such a high dosage of morphine but as the drugs wore off, it became so bad that I began to vomit uncontrollably.

Over the next few weeks I was utterly miserable – confined to the sofa, high on a cocktail of painkillers and the sleeping tablets I was taking to try and escape the whole situation. Around then, I became addicted to Co-codamol and Diazepam, requiring higher and higher doses as my body became used to their anaesthetising effects. I was unable to exercise at all, which was torture for a gym addict like me. Worse still, I'd reasoned since I couldn't exercise, I'd have to dramatically restrict my food portions. My mum quickly became aware that I was cutting down on my calorie intake and tried to talk me out of it, but there was no dissuading me: I was still terrified of putting on weight.

By the time I was up and walking (or rather hobbling about) in March, I was accustomed to surviving on hardly any food at all. Anorexia had firmly taken root – again. All that sitting around had left my mind idle and vulnerable to the disease's destructive voice. I began forcing my mum to drive me to the gym, where I'd use arm weights – the only thing my weakened physical state and the fact that I was still on crutches would allow me to do. The gym instructors and concerned friends would ask what on earth I was doing there, advising me in the strongest possible terms that I should be at home recuperating, but I wouldn't – or perhaps couldn't – listen to them. I believed I needed to put myself through the toughest workout I was capable of simply to justify my existence.

With the help of my counsellor, I came to the realisation that I use exercise to vent my emotions. The gym is my time and I ensure it's intensely private. Usually, I was delighted when I was recognised in the street or spoken to by fans but if anyone ever tried to talk to me whilst I was working out, they'd receive short shrift. This personal epiphany forced me to ask myself, what am I so angry about? Why do I need to punish my body in order to clear my mind? I still haven't reached a conclusion on this.

Despite still requiring a walking stick in order to move, I was determined to begin work and socialise again in March 2011. During those few months, all that resting had left me with cabin fever; I was also feeling isolated and very lonely. At certain times, I even considered getting back together with an ex. I'd lost about 6lb since the beginning of the year, a huge amount for my small and already slender frame. Now I was irrational and emotional, prone to tearful episodes and unable to think coherently.

I remember attending the International Endangered Species Summit as a representative for Body Gossip that March. It was a hugely prestigious event. Some of the world's leading experts in body image were attending and all I can recall is feeling insignificant and unworthy to be there. Even filming *Gok's Teens: The Naked Truth*, (a documentary about teenagers and body image, which aired in February 2012) as part of the Body Gossip cast, didn't help me to feel any more valued. Gok couldn't have been friendlier, and filming the documentary was a wonderful experience, but I knew I needed a break.

Ill-advised, I once more began going out and often got drunk. Now I was so weak, physically, that if a friend hugged me too tightly it could almost break my already-fragile bones. I suffer from severe osteoporosis as a result of my eating disorder, most acutely in my spine and hips. It has become so bad that I have the frame of an 85-year-old woman and can't even wash my hair by bending over the side of the bath. Technically speaking, the quickest and easiest solution would be to eat my way to a normal BMI, but for me that's the hardest challenge of all. On nights out, I have often broken my ribs from dancing around too much or being hugged, and I'm also prone to losing my phone, keys and purse. I knew I was becoming a liability to my friends but my mind was too clouded to see a way out of the situation.

In April 2011, I decided it might be a good idea to get away from it all and so I booked a trip to the Coachella Valley Music and Arts Annual Festival in the United States. With hindsight, I was trying to escape the one thing I could never run away from: myself. I travelled to LA, Las Vegas and then back to LA again over the course of a few weeks. At first, I felt an immense sense of liberty – I loved the anonymity as I'm usually recognised only by British people. My friend Nadia, who I'd met in her capacity as a journalist for the *Daily Mail* celebrity pages, took me shopping and on a trip to Universal Studios in a bid to cheer me up – we had a great time.

Soon, though, Nadia left and I was in the company of another friend with a tendency to get drunk and wander off, leaving me on my own in unfamiliar territory. My foot began to swell in the 100-degree heat and became painful again. Now I started to feel lost and frightened – all I could focus on was getting back. I changed my flight to three days earlier than planned and came home with a huge sense of relief.

On 28 April 2011, it was my 29th birthday. I'd booked Boogaloo, an indie music venue in Archway, north London, which I absolutely love. It should have been one of the best parties of my life (everyone had the next day off because of the Royal Wedding). I couldn't seem to dismiss a sense of foreboding, though: I was panicking at the prospect of this being the last year of my twenties. Even the arrival of Alex Zane, my friend and ultimate celebrity crush, couldn't quell this sense of unease.

Work kept me busy throughout the summer and for a while I thought perhaps everything would be OK. I filmed *Celebrity Coach Trip* in June, taking my fellow *Big Brother* contestant Ashlene as my partner. We toured Italy, Slovenia and Croatia with celebrity passengers Edwina Curry and her husband John, as well as Paul Burrell and his wife Jeanie and Cannon & Ball.

Anyone who has watched the show will be only too aware of the difficulties I faced in trying to be understood by my fellow passengers. Although everyone involved had been alerted to the fact that I suffer OCD and anorexia and they were asked to be as accommodating and tolerant as possible, that didn't stop them accusing me of being 'difficult' and 'disruptive'. Every mealtime was an ordeal – the crew refused to tell us where and when we were having dinner. It meant I couldn't plan my day's calorie consumption or have any sense of the routine I so desperately need to feel a sense of calm. My mum had packed healthy snacks such as snack bars, crisp breads and tins of tuna in an attempt to try and help me achieve some regularity and routine in my eating habits.

Every morning we were woken up at 6.30am and given just half an hour to hastily consume our breakfasts. After that, when and where we would eat was anyone's guess. Often, we'd have our evening meal as late as 10pm after filming. This not only played havoc with my fragile mindset but really set me back in doing the things I knew I must do in order to stop myself from slipping further into my anorexia: eating little and often. Jeanie made it clear that she had an issue with what she perceived to be my 'peculiar' eating habits. But Edwina took her distaste for my condition (and me) a step further, shouting that she thought I 'had issues' and 'they weren't carers'. I knew my fellow passengers thought I was attention seeking and deliberately being difficult, which made me feel resentful and misunderstood in turn. Things were strained between us.

Ultimately, I lasted three days on *Celebrity Coach Trip* before walking out of the show. I was distressed by the idea that my eating disorder had now permeated every element of my life. Friendships were hanging on by a thread, there was no new love interest on the horizon and my food obsession was starting to affect my ability to work.

On 24 July 2011, the world was shocked and shaken by the news that the immensely talented musician and north London treasure Amy Winehouse had died aged just 27 years old. I was deeply affected by it. Although I never got to know Amy personally, we had many friends in common and people had told me that she was aware of me and liked to watch me on TV. Amy always seemed to me to be an outsider – although adored by millions, she appeared fragile and unsure of herself. I could totally relate to those feelings. For Amy, the struggle was over and she was at peace now and, as guilty as it made me feel, I realised there was a part of me that envied her for that. It was the first time I remember being consciously aware that the suicidal thoughts which have plagued me throughout my lengthy illness were back.

Either way, I was at one of my lowest ebbs when in August 2011, my mum had a mental breakdown.

Throughout my life, she has been my rock – solid, dependable, always there to catch me when I fall. Just as I felt my world was tumbling down around me, the very thing that constantly made me feel secure was taken away. Without Mum, I was utterly adrift.

My mum tells me her breakdown had been brewing for a long time. She was often tearful in the months preceding the actual event and felt she wasn't coping. My sister and I knew she was going through the menopause and that this can be a difficult phase for any middle-aged woman but she later told us there were many other contributing factors.

For a start, Mum's first relationship in six years had abruptly come to an end. Although she and the man concerned were friends before they got together, when their relationship ended, things soon turned hostile. I tried to protect her and stick up for her during this turbulent time, telling her ex exactly what I thought of his behaviour. Mum had also been struggling with some legal issues relating to a property she was buying in Dorset. There were endless delays and obstacles, only adding to the stress and strain. On top of all this, the man we called Granddad (a very close family friend) was suffering dementia and had to be put into a home after being assessed as a danger to himself. This also hit Mum hard.

Inevitably, an argument between my sister and me in the summer of 2011 proved to be the straw that finally broke the camel's back. We'd all arranged to travel to Richmond together to take her son Sunny to a theatrical performance of *In the Night Garden*, one of his favourite TV shows. Natalie was driving us there and as I was sitting in the back seat of the car, I asked her if she could close the car windows because the breeze was blowing my hair all over the place. In response to this, she opened the windows even wider. We began to squabble, trading more and more violent insults back and forth. I started to cry. Suddenly, Mum snapped. 'Turn the car around!' she demanded. As we had only set off a few minutes previously, Natalie duly obliged.

When we reached Mum's house, she got out of the car and headed straight for her own without saying a word. Then she sped down the street, leaving my sister and me open-mouthed. For days after that, Mum left her phone switched off. Natalie and I were frantic, calling her all the time and speculating as to where she might have gone. Eventually, Mum let us know that she was at a family friend's house in Dorset.

Later, I found out that Mum had had what she described as a 'mini-breakdown' whilst away in Dorset. The combined pressure of her legal worries, the breakdown of her relationship and the emotional strain of caring for me whilst acting as referee during frequent feuds between Natalie and me had finally taken its toll. Mum has always been there for me throughout all my ups and downs but I knew that this was a time when she had to focus on herself and get better. For the first time ever, I was forced to contemplate a life without her continued support.

I realised that Mum needed her own life and freedom from the constant worry of what my illness was doing to me but the thought of her lack of proximity, either emotional or physically, completely terrified me. At this stage there was no denying anorexia had me firmly back in its grips and the situation with Mum, both worrying about her and what I would do without her, pushed me further down that dangerous path. Once again I'd hit self-destruct mode and what happened over the next few months proved pivotal.

On 16 October 2011, I visited Barfly in Camden on a night out with some friends to watch Carl Barat perform live. Due to my vulnerability, I was constantly losing things and this made me feel like a liability. Although my friends were concerned for me, I can't have been much fun to hang out with at that point in my life. On this particular night out, after losing another phone, it was more evident than ever that I was putting a downer on the social occasion. In my mind, I interpreted this as meaning my mates thought they were doing me a favour by spending time with me.

A comment made by my friend Rachel at the Reading Festival some months back was still haunting me and it was playing on my mind that night, and has done so ever since. 'It's not always about you, Nikki,' she said pointedly. In many ways that innocent remark, playing over and over in my mind that night, contributed to the way I was feeling and amplified my feelings of unworthiness, depression and despair.

In an effort to block out all the painful feelings I was experiencing, I drank heavily. Of course at such a low weight, my body found it hard to deal with any amount of alcohol. Very quickly I became drunk.

I decided it would be better if I left. Darren, who is a good friend of mine, made contact with me via another friend at the venue. He told me to get in a cab and go to his flat straight away, and offered me a place to stay. I agreed – too drunk to argue and bereft of a phone to make other plans anyway. When we reached Darren's house, another friend locked me in a room with a couple of the people I'd fallen out with during the summer, including Zoe and Julie. I'm sure he believed he was doing us a favour and we'd resolve our differences. In reality, we'd all drunk far too much alcohol to have a sensible conversation. I was deeply uncomfortable and remember thinking this was the cherry on the cake of a truly awful night out.

To my great relief, the door was eventually unlocked. Darren could see the events of the past few months, as well as that horrendous night had left me in a dark place and advised a good night's sleep. He went to bed, leaving me on the sofa. I waited until all signs of movement had subsided, then raided his flat in search of a blade. At that stage, I just needed to somehow express all the hurt I was feeling; I wasn't even sure what I was going to do when I found it. Eventually, I discovered an old razor blade and began hacking away, ineffectually, at my arms. Still the emotional pain was there and whatever physical hurt I managed to inflict on myself with the blade, it didn't seem like enough.

It was then that the thought assailed me brutally from nowhere: I didn't want to feel this way anymore and so I must put an end to my misery. With absolute clarity, I knew what I had to do. So I got a rope from a dressing gown that was hanging in Darren's bathroom. I blacked out.

I must have made a noise because the next thing I was aware of was being sat between Darren and his friend on his bed. As I regained consciousness so the enormity of what I had just done dawned on me: I had tried to take my own life, I could have died. Shocked, I began hyper-ventilating. Darren simply cuddled me until my breathing returned to normal. That night I slept in his bed, terrified to the core of being left alone with my own thoughts and what I now knew I was capable of.

When it comes down to it, having anorexia is an extremely long, drawn-out suicide attempt. If you starve yourself, there is always the risk that you will die but somehow the reality never quite seems to hit home. What happened at Darren's house that night was more immediate and tangible than anything previously experienced. With an urgency I'd never felt before, I realised how precious my life was; I did not want to die and I needed to get help.

My first instinct was to be with my mum. When I thought of everything I had to live for, she was the first person to spring to my mind. I went to Dorset with her, thinking it might be beneficial to get out of London for a few weeks. The first day was a disaster. As I sped down the motorway on my way to our family retreat, I realised I'd forgotten to bring my electronic scales. I'm rarely without them and the more preoccupied I am with my illness, the more important they become. At this point in time it seemed vital for me to know (and to as an accurate degree as possible) exactly how much I was eating.

I knew it was too late to turn back and fetch the scales yet I really wasn't sure how I'd survive without them. At this point, I began to cry hysterically. I was panicked, unable to deal with the enormity of the situation. Now I know my reaction might seem ridiculous to some people but to them I say, imagine everything you know is crumbling around you and amidst all this uncertainty, the only thing you can ever be sure of is exactly how many calories you will consume in any given day. Imagine even this small grain of surety is snatched away from you and you're entirely at sea, swimming in your own despair. Now you have an idea of how I felt.

Arriving in Dorset, I called everyone I could think of to ask if they had any scales they could lend me. When all my efforts proved fruitless, I spent the first night wide-awake. The constant nagging worry circling in my mind meant that sleep eluded me. Breakfast the next morning was an ordeal, as I attempted to guess the weight of cereal. In my frustration, I kicked the wall of the house with my bad foot, setting back recovery by weeks.

Eventually, Mum and I located some scales and after that, I began to relax. I spent my entire time in Dorset in a tracksuit. Mum and me would spend our days talking and walking the dogs. The break became the retreat I had intended it to be.

When I returned from Dorset, I booked myself into St Vincent's Square as a day patient. I'd been seeing Kumari, my counsellor (who I continue to see), for almost a year and we both agreed this was the right thing to do. My diary entry for that day read: *On the train on the way there, I had all these mixed emotions running through me. Fear, feelings of failure, panic, sadness and even guilt?*

I weighed just 35 kilos, a whopping 11 kilos less than when I left Rhodes Farm, aged 16. It was a relief to have a sense of routine again and the burden of thinking about what I would eat and when it should be eaten was now removed. At St Vincent's we ate three meals and two snacks a day at designated times and were constantly monitored. After all my former years spent in institutions, St Vincent's felt like coming home. It was also nice to be around other young women who understood just what I was going through.

Between the hours of 11am and noon, we'd have group sessions after our morning snack on topics such as relapse prevention or body awareness. After lunch (between 1pm and 1.45pm), there was a community meeting, followed by activities such as art psychotherapy or self-esteem counselling. Some days the food I consumed would feel 'safe', but on others I'd feel uncomfortably full and desperate as a result.

Unlike other eating disorder clinics I'd experienced, St Vincent's didn't 'watch over us' in between activities. We were given short periods of complete freedom and much more responsibility for ourselves. This gave me the time and space I needed to really take control of my eating habits; this time I had the reins. After all, I'd be on my own again after I left. It was time for me to take charge of my own health and path to recovery.

I kept a food/emotions diary every day to record how various meals affected me psychologically. My first day on the 'full diet' was 31 October, meaning what I ate was completely out of my hands. For breakfast we were fed a large bowl of cereal, a crumpet, half a banana and a cup of tea. The morning snack was Horlicks made with full-fat milk, followed by lunch consisting of fish in cheese sauce, carrots and two scoops of mashed potato. Afterwards there was apricot and apple pie with custard. My afternoon snack was a Lion Bar. On that day I wrote: *By the end of all this I was feeling pretty suicidal and completely violated by food. I questioned if this treatment program was actually making me worse??? To feel this full up is the most scary and out of control I have felt in 10 years.*

I'm pleased to tell you that I've made some progress since that first horrible day. Other days at St Vincent's

Square were certainly better, although I still found it hard to sit down after meals and recorded in one diary entry that I telephoned a friend after I'd eaten to try and take my mind off the constant nagging need to exercise. When I first entered the clinic I had to compile a list of my 'food fears' and 'safe foods'. What I ate during a typical day tended to be a mixture of the two so I'd have things from my 'safe' list like vegetables, fish and baked potatoes but also others that made me feel deeply uncomfortable to eat, like full-fat milk and sauces.

St Vincent's Square has been wonderful and the best treatment I have experienced. I've made so much progress since that first awful day back in October and have put on two kilos. My stay has helped me to take control of a physical need to starve myself, but I still struggle emotionally. Denying myself food and exercising excessively were coping mechanisms for whenever it became uncomfortable to be in my own head. Now, if I want to keep myself healthy and alive, I no longer have the option to go without food. With the help of Kumari, I am trying to find a more productive and healthy outlet for my feelings of worthlessness and despair.

Some days, I still find it hard to justify my existence. I have realised that a huge key to recovery is surrounding myself with the right sort of people and I treasure those friends who have been there for me when things really got tough. Darren, who saved me during that terrible night when I tried to kill myself, is incredibly special to me and always will be. Even now, when I am battling with my emotions, invariably the phone will ring and it will be him – it's as if he knows I need someone to lean on. I feel that we are spiritually in tune. I'm still very close to Nadia, who missed a day of work to come back and get me when I was delirious with heat stroke in that tent at Glastonbury. Also, Carly who, despite battling her own food and body demons, has now met a lovely man and is going to get married. Seeing her reborn and creating a new and exciting life has given me hope for my own future. I also feel that my friendship with Rachel will last a long time, as we have both been through many highs and lows together.

One thing about which I feel more strongly than ever is that I want to use my experiences to help other people, which is why I've updated this book. I want to tell the world that sometimes people with eating disorders do relapse but it's OK for them to ask for help. In 2011, I was used as a psychologist on the Channel 5 programme *Big Brother's Bit On The Side* (ironically, if you think about it). I really enjoyed the experience. Tough as it's been, I realised that suffering mental health issues myself has allowed me to empathise with others and given me a greater understanding of people and how they tick.

In December 2011, I left Chelsea and Westminster Hospital to do Panto in Wrexham, north Wales. On the one hand, I didn't want to leave my newfound and oh-so-welcome safety net, but they promised me that I could return if ever I felt the need and I knew it was important to keep on working and maintain some kind of grasp on the former life I'd worked so hard to accomplish. I played the Fairy Godmother in *Cinderella*, working alongside Welsh pop star Andy Scott-Lee (who played Prince Charming) and singer and performer Alison Crawford (who played Cinderella).

Although I formed a good bond with my fellow cast

mates, especially Alison, it was unsettling for me to return to the 'real' world after the safety of St Vincent's Square. For me, those few weeks were an emotional rollercoaster. We worked incredibly hard and I was exhausted a lot of the time. I craved my own familiar surroundings back home. It must have been hard for those I was working with – I'd be euphoric one minute, crying the next.

Then, and to this day, I still occasionally battle with suicidal thoughts and more frequent feelings of inadequacy, failure, terror and uncertainty but for the first time in a long while, I believe I possess the necessary reserves of strength to conquer my demons.

It would be remiss of me to suggest I've entirely recovered now – there is still a huge mountain to climb. However, my experiences over the past few years have taught me one thing: I'm a fighter. Even in my darkest hour, I chose life. Now I know that I have a loving family, many supportive friends and a lot of fans out there. I cannot express how grateful I am to them for making me realise my life is worth battling for. Today, I look forward to a future where anorexia's voice will be silenced, where I can simply be Nikki Grahame and not be defined or controlled by my illness. In the meantime, I'll do everything I can to ensure anyone else who is struggling with this terrible affliction knows they are not alone.

Fragile represents the battle of thousands of men and women, girls and boys throughout the UK and millions worldwide. To those people, I say: Never give up hope.

FURTHER READING AND RESOURCES

Anorexia and Bulimia: A Parent's Guide to Recognising Eating Disorders and Taking Control by Dee Dawson. Vermilion (2001)

Eating Disorders: A Parents' Guide by Rachel Bryant-Waugh and Dr Brian Lask. Routledge (2004)

Eating Disorders: The Path to Recovery by Dr Kate Middleton. Lion Hudson plc (2007)

Coping with Eating Disorders and Body Image (overcoming common problems) by Christine Craggs-Hinton. Sheldon Press (2006)

- B-eat – leading UK charity for people with eating disorders www.b-eat.co.uk
- Body Gossip – A campaign to promote body confidence www.bodygossip.org
- National Osteoporosis Society – www.nos.org.uk

Another day of tears and pain
Lying here I'm going insane,
Fighting hard not to be fed,
Trapped in my body lost in my head

Feeling fat and looking thin
Rejecting life my gravest sin,
Leave me upon my bed,
Trapped in my body lost in my head.

I want to be free and seal my fate
Why is my life all about weight?
Hope is gone though it's never said,
Trapped in my body lost in my head.

Nikki Grahame